Natural Language Processing Fundamentals

Build intelligent applications that can interpret the human language to deliver impactful results

Sohom Ghosh and Dwight Gunning

Natural Language Processing Fundamentals

Authors: Sohom Ghosh and Dwight Gunning

Reviewer: Ankit Malik

Managing Editor: Bhavesh Bangera

Acquisitions Editor: Koushik Sen

Production Editor: Shantanu Zagade

Editorial Board: David Barnes, Ewan Buckingham, Simon Cox, Shivangi Chatterji, Manasa Kumar, Alex Mazonowicz, Douglas Paterson, Dominic Pereira, Shiny Poojary, Saman Siddiqui, Erol Staveley, Ankita Thakur, Mohita Vyas, and Jonathan Wray

First Published: March 2019

Production Reference: 2150120

Published by Packt Publishing Ltd.

Livery Place, 35 Livery Street

Birmingham B3 2PB, UK

ISBN: 978-1-78995-404-3

Table of Contents

Preface   i

Chapter 1: Introduction to Natural Language Processing   1

Introduction 2

History of NLP 2

Text Analytics and NLP 3

   Exercise 1: Basic Text Analytics 4

Various Steps in NLP 6

   Tokenization 7

   Exercise 2: Tokenization of a Simple Sentence 7

   PoS Tagging 8

   Exercise 3: PoS Tagging 9

   Stop Word Removal 10

   Exercise 4: Stop Word Removal 10

   Text Normalization 12

   Exercise 5: Text Normalization 12

   Spelling Correction 13

   Exercise 6: Spelling Correction of a Word and a Sentence 13

   Stemming 15

   Exercise 7: Stemming 15

   Lemmatization 17

   Exercise 8: Extracting the base word using Lemmatization 17

   NER 18

   Exercise 9: Treating Named Entities 18

   Word Sense Disambiguation 19

Exercise 10: Word Sense Disambiguation 20

Sentence Boundary Detection 21

Exercise 11: Sentence Boundary Detection 21

Activity 1: Preprocessing of Raw Text 22

Kick Starting an NLP Project 23

Data Collection 23

Data Preprocessing 23

Feature Extraction 24

Model Development 24

Model Assessment 24

Model Deployment 24

Summary 24

Chapter 2: Basic Feature Extraction Methods   27

Introduction 28

Types of Data 28

Categorizing Data Based on Structure 28

Categorization of Data Based on Content 30

Cleaning Text Data 31

Tokenization 31

Exercise 12: Text Cleaning and Tokenization 31

Exercise 13: Extracting n-grams 33

Exercise 14: Tokenizing Texts with Different Packages – Keras
and TextBlob 36

Types of Tokenizers 38

Exercise 15: Tokenizing Text Using Various Tokenizers 38

Issues with Tokenization 45

Stemming 45

RegexpStemmer 45

Exercise 16: Converting words in gerund form
into base words using RegexpStemmer 45

The Porter Stemmer 46

Exercise 17: The Porter Stemmer 46

Lemmatization 47

Exercise 18: Lemmatization 47

Exercise 19: Singularizing and Pluralizing Words 48

Language Translation 49

Exercise 20: Language Translation 49

Stop-Word Removal 49

Exercise 21: Stop-Word Removal 49

Feature Extraction from Texts 50

Extracting General Features from Raw Text 50

Exercise 22: Extracting General Features from Raw Text 51

Activity 2: Extracting General Features from Text 54

Bag of Words 55

Exercise 23: Creating a BoW 56

Zipf's Law 57

Exercise 24: Zipf's Law 58

TF-IDF 62

Exercise 25: TF-IDF Representation 62

Activity 3: Extracting Specific Features from Texts 65

Feature Engineering 65

Exercise 26: Feature Engineering (Text Similarity) 66

Word Clouds 69

Exercise 27: Word Clouds 69

Other Visualizations 70

Exercise 28: Other Visualizations (Dependency Parse Trees
and Named Entities) 71

Activity 4: Text Visualization 72

Summary 73

Chapter 3: Developing a Text classifier 75

Introduction 76

Machine Learning 76

Unsupervised Learning 76

Hierarchical Clustering 77

Exercise 29: Hierarchical Clustering 78

K-Means Clustering 84

Exercise 30: K-Means Clustering 84

Supervised Learning 88

Classification 89

Logistic Regression 89

Naive Bayes Classifiers 89

K-Nearest Neighbors 90

Exercise 31: Text Classification (Logistic regression,
Naive Bayes, and KNN) 90

Regression 95

Linear Regression 95

Exercise 32: Regression Analysis Using Textual Data 96

Tree Methods 100

Random Forest 101

GBM and XGBoost 101

Exercise 33: Tree-Based Methods (Decision Tree,
Random Forest, GBM, and XGBoost) 102

Sampling 111

Exercise 34: Sampling (Simple Random, Stratified, Multi-Stage) 112

Developing a Text Classifier 114

Feature Extraction 114

Feature Engineering 115

Removing Correlated Features 115

Exercise 35: Removing Highly Correlated Features (Tokens) 115

Dimensionality Reduction 120

Exercise 36: Dimensionality Reduction (PCA) 120

Deciding on a Model Type 124

Evaluating the Performance of a Model 124

Exercise 37: Calculate the RMSE and MAPE 126

Activity 5: Developing End-to-End Text Classifiers 127

Building Pipelines for NLP Projects 128

Exercise 38: Building Pipelines for NLP Projects 128

Saving and Loading Models 129

Exercise 39: Saving and Loading Models 130

Summary 132

Chapter 4: Collecting Text Data from the Web   135

Introduction 136

Collecting Data by Scraping Web Pages 136

Exercise 40: Extraction of Tag-Based Information from HTML Files 137

Requesting Content from Web Pages 139

Exercise 41: Collecting Online Text Data 139

Exercise 42: Analyzing the Content of Jupyter
Notebooks (in HTML Format) 141

Activity 6: Extracting Information from an Online HTML Page 144

Activity 7: Extracting and Analyzing Data Using Regular Expressions 144

Dealing with Semi-Structured Data 145

JSON 145

Exercise 43: Dealing with JSON Files 146

Activity 8: Dealing with Online JSON Files 148

XML 148

Exercise 44: Dealing with a Local XML File 150

Using APIs to Retrieve Real-Time Data 152

Exercise 45: Collecting Data Using APIs 152

API Creation 153

Activity 9: Extracting Data from Twitter 154

Extracting Data from Local Files 154

Exercise 46: Extracting Data from Local Files 155

Exercise 47: Performing Various Operations on Local Files 157

Summary 158

Chapter 5: Topic Modeling 161

Introduction 162

Topic Discovery 162

Discovering Themes 163

Exploratory Data Analysis 163

Document Clustering 164

Dimensionality Reduction 164

Historical Analysis 164

Bag of Words 165

Topic Modeling Algorithms 165

Latent Semantic Analysis 166

LSA – How It Works 166

Exercise 48: Analyzing Reuters News Articles
with Latent Semantic Analysis 168

Latent Dirichlet Allocation 174

LDA – How It Works 174

Exercise 49: Topics in Airline Tweets 176

Topic Fingerprinting 182

Exercise 50: Visualizing Documents Using Topic Vectors 183

Activity 10: Topic Modelling Jeopardy Questions 190

Summary 191

Chapter 6: Text Summarization and Text Generation   193

Introduction 194

What is Automated Text Summarization? 194

Benefits of Automated Text Summarization 195

High-Level View of Text Summarization 196

Purpose 196

Input 197

Output 197

Extractive Text Summarization 197

Abstractive Text Summarization 198

Sequence to Sequence 199

Encoder Decoder 199

TextRank 199

Exercise 51: TextRank from Scratch 200

Summarizing Text Using Gensim 207

Activity 11: Summarizing a Downloaded Page
Using the Gensim Text Summarizer 208

Summarizing Text Using Word Frequency 208

Exercise 52: Word Frequency Text Summarization 209

Generating Text with Markov Chains 212

Markov Chains 213

Exercise 53: Generating Text Using Markov Chains 213

Summary 217

Introduction 220

Vector Definition 220

Why Vector Representations? 222

Encoding 222

Character-Level Encoding 222

Exercise 54: Character Encoding Using ASCII Values 223

Exercise 55: Character Encoding with the Help of NumPy Arrays 224

Positional Character-Level Encoding 226

Exercise 56: Character-Level Encoding Using Positions 227

One-Hot Encoding 228

Key Steps in One-Hot Encoding 229

Exercise 57: Character One-Hot Encoding – Manual 230

Exercise 58: Character-Level One-Hot Encoding with Keras 231

Word-Level One-Hot Encoding 238

Exercise 59: Word-Level One-Hot Encoding 238

Word Embeddings 244

Word2Vec 246

Exercise 60: Training Word Vectors 246

Using Pre-Trained Word Vectors 252

Exercise 61: Loading Pre-Trained Word Vectors 252

Document Vectors 259

Uses of Document Vectors 259

Exercise 62: From Movie Dialogue to Document Vectors 259

Activity 12: Finding Similar Movie Lines Using Document Vectors 265

Summary 266

Chapter 8: Sentiment Analysis 269

Introduction 270

Why is Sentiment Analysis Required? 270

Growth of Sentiment Analysis 270

    Monetization of Emotion 271

    Types of Sentiments 271

    Key Ideas and Terms 272

    Applications of Sentiment Analysis 273

Tools Used for Sentiment Analysis 274

    NLP Services from Major Cloud Providers 274

    Online Marketplaces 275

    Python NLP Libraries 276

    Deep Learning Libraries 276

TextBlob 277

    Exercise 63: Basic Sentiment Analysis Using the TextBlob Library 277

    Activity 13: Tweet Sentiment Analysis Using the TextBlob library 278

Understanding Data for Sentiment Analysis 280

    Exercise 64: Loading Data for Sentiment Analysis 280

Training Sentiment Models 284

    Exercise 65: Training a Sentiment Model
    Using TFIDF and Logistic Regression 285

Summary 289

Appendix 291

Index 349

Preface

About

This section briefly introduces the authors, the coverage of this book, the technical skills you'll need to get started, and the hardware and software requirements required to complete all of the included activities and exercises.

About the Book

If Natural Language Processing (NLP) isn't really your forte, *Natural Language Processing Fundamentals* will make sure you get off to a steady start in the realm of NLP. This comprehensive guide will show you how to effectively use Python libraries and NLP concepts to solve various problems.

You'll be introduced to NLP and its applications through examples and exercises. This will be followed by an introduction to the initial stages of solving a problem, which includes problem definition, getting text data, and preparing text data for modeling. With exposure to concepts such as advanced NLP algorithms and visualization techniques, you'll learn how to create applications that can extract information from unstructured data and present it as impactful visuals. Although you will continue to learn NLP-based techniques, the focus will gradually shift to developing useful applications. In those sections, you'll gain an understanding of how to apply NLP techniques to answer questions, as can be used for chatbots.

By the end of this book, you'll be able to accomplish a varied range of assignments, ranging from identifying the most suitable type of NLP task for solving a problem, to using a tool such as spaCy or Gensim to perform sentiment analysis. The book will equip you with the knowledge you need to build applications that interpret human language.

About the Authors

Sohom Ghosh is a passionate data detective with expertise in Natural Language Processing. He has publications in several international conferences and journals.

Dwight Gunning is a data scientist at FINRA, a financial services regulator in the US. He has extensive experience in Python-based machine learning and hands-on experience with the most popular NLP tools, such as NLTK, Gensim, and spaCy.

Learning Objectives

By the end of this book, you will be able to:

- Obtain, verify, and clean data before transforming it into a correct format for use
- Perform data analysis and machine learning tasks using Python
- Gain an understanding of the basics of computational linguistics
- Build models for general NLP tasks
- Evaluate the performance of a model with the right metrics
- Visualize, quantify, and perform exploratory analysis from any text data

Audience

Natural Language Processing Fundamentals is designed for novice and mid-level data scientists and machine learning developers who want to gather and analyze text data to build an NLP-powered product. It'll help you to have prior experience of coding in Python using data types, writing functions, and importing libraries. Some experience with linguistics and probability is useful but not necessary.

Approach

This book starts with the very basics of reading text into Python code and progresses through the required pipeline of cleaning, stemming, and tokenizing text into a form suitable for NLP. The book then proceeds on to the fundamentals of NLP statistical methods, vector representation, and building models – using the most commonly used NLP libraries. Finally, the book gives students actual practice in using NLP models and code in applications.

Hardware Requirements

For the optimal student experience, we recommend the following hardware configuration:

- Any entry-level PC/Mac with Windows, Linux, or macOS is sufficient
- Processor: Dual core or equivalent
- Memory: 4 GB RAM
- Storage: 10 GB available space

Software Requirements

You'll also need the following software installed in advance:

- Operating system: Windows 7 SP1 32/64-bit, Windows 8.1 32/64-bit or Windows 10 32/64-bit, Ubuntu 14.04 or later, or macOS Sierra or later
- Browser: Google Chrome or Mozilla Firefox
- Anaconda
- Jupyter Notebook
- Python 3.x

Conventions

Code words in the text, database table names, folder names, filenames, file extensions, pathnames, dummy URLs, user input, and Twitter handles are shown as follows: "Find out the **index** value of the word **fox** using the following code."

A block of code is set as follows:

```
words = sentence.split()
first_word = words[0]
last_word = words[len(words)-1]
concat_word = first_word + last_word
print(concat_word)
```

New terms and important words are shown in bold. Words that you see on the screen, for example, in menus or dialog boxes, appear in the text like this: "Stemming leads to inappropriate results such as "battling" getting transformed into **battl**, which has no meaning."

Installation and Setup

Before you start this book, we'll install Python 3.6, pip, scikit-learn, and the other libraries used in this book. You will find the steps to install these here:

Installing Python

Install Python 3.6 by following the instructions in this link: https://realpython.com/installing-python/.

Installing pip

1. To install pip, go to this link and download the **get-pip.py** file: https://pip.pypa.io/en/stable/installing/.

2. Then, use the following command to install it:

   ```
   python get-pip.py
   ```

   You might need to use the **python3 get-pip.py** command, due to previous versions of Python on your computer that already use the **python** command.

Installing libraries
Using the pip command, install the following libraries:

```
python -m pip install --user numpy scipy matplotlib pandas scikit-learn nltk
```

Working with the Jupyter Notebook

You'll be working on different exercises and activities in a Jupyter notebook. These exercises and activities can be downloaded from the associated GitHub repository:

1. Download the repository from here: https://github.com/TrainingByPackt/Natural-Language-Processing-Fundamentals.

    You can either download it using GitHub or as a zipped folder by clicking on the green **Clone or download** button on the upper-right side.

2. In order to open Jupyter notebooks, you have to traverse into the directory with your terminal. To do that, type:

    ```
    cd Natural-Language-Processing-Fundamentals/<your current lesson>.
    ```

    For example:

    ```
    cd Natural-Language-Processing-Fundamentals/Lesson_01/
    ```

3. To reach each activity and exercise, you have to use **cd** once more to go into each folder, like so:

    ```
    cd Activity01
    ```

4. Once you are in the folder of your choice, simply call **jupyter notebook**.

Importing Python Libraries

Every exercise and activity in this book will make use of various libraries. Importing libraries into Python is very simple and here's how we do it:

1. To import libraries such as NumPy and pandas, we have to run the following code. This will import the whole **numpy** library into our current file.

    ```
    import numpy# import numpy
    ```

2. In the first cells of the exercises and activities of this book ware, you will see the following code. We can use **np** instead of **numpy** in our code to call methods from **numpy**:

    ```
    import numpy as np# import numpy and assign alias np
    ```

3. In later chapters, partial imports will be present, as shown in the following code. This only loads the **mean** method from the library:

    ```
    from numpy import mean# only import the mean method of numpy
    ```

Installing the Code Bundle

Copy the code bundle for the class to the `C:/Code` folder.

Additional Resources

The code bundle for this book is also hosted on GitHub at https://github.com/TrainingByPackt/Natural-Language-Processing-Fundamentals.

The high-quality color images used in book can be found at: https://github.com/TrainingByPackt/Natural-Language-Processing-Fundamentals/tree/master/Graphics.

We also have other code bundles from our rich catalog of books and videos available at https://github.com/PacktPublishing/. Check them out!

1

Introduction to Natural Language Processing

Learning Objectives

By the end of this chapter, you will be able to:

- Describe what natural language processing (NLP) is all about
- Describe the history of NLP
- Differentiate between NLP and Text Analytics
- Implement various preprocessing tasks
- Describe the various phases of an NLP project

In this chapter, you will learn about the basics of natural language processing and various preprocessing steps that are required to clean and analyze the data.

Introduction

To start with looking at NLP, let's understand what natural language is. In simple terms, it's the language we use to express ourselves. It's a basic means of communication. To define more specifically, language is a mutually agreed set of protocols involving words/ sounds we use to communicate with each other.

In this era of digitization and computation, we tend to comprehend language scientifically. This is because we are constantly trying to make inanimate objects understand us. Thus, it has become essential to develop mechanisms by which language can be fed to inanimate objects such as computers. NLP helps us do this.

Let's look at an example. You must have some emails in your mailbox that have been automatically labeled as spam. This is done with the help of NLP. Here, an inanimate object – the email service – analyzes the content of the emails, comprehends it, and then further decides whether these emails need to be marked as spam or not.

History of NLP

NLP is an area that overlaps with others. It has emerged from fields such as artificial intelligence, linguistics, formal languages, and compilers. With the advancement of computing technologies and the increased availability of data, the way natural language is being processed has changed. Previously, a traditional rule-based system was used for computations. Today, computations on natural language are being done using machine learning and deep learning techniques.

The major work on machine learning-based NLP started during the 1980s. During the 1980s, developments across various disciplines such as artificial intelligence, linguistics, formal languages, and computations led to the emergence of an interdisciplinary subject called NLP. In the next section, we'll look at text analytics and how it differs from NLP.

Text Analytics and NLP

Text analytics is the method of extracting meaningful insights and answering questions from text data. This text data need not be a human language. Let's understand this with an example. Suppose you have a text file that contains your outgoing phone calls and SMS log data in the following format:

Field 1	Field 2	Field 3	Field 4	Field 5
Date	Time	Voice call or sms	Phone number and name of the person contacted. If the number is not in the contact list, then the name tag is left blank.	Duration of call in seconds. In case of sms it's the text message.

Figure 1.1: Format of call data

In the preceding figure, the first two fields represent the **date** and **time** at which the call was made or the SMS was sent. The third field represents the type of data. If the data is of the call type, then the value for this field will be set as **voice_call**. If the type of data is **sms**, the value of this field will be set to **sms**. The fourth field is for the phone number and name of the contact. If the number of the person is not in the contact list, then the **name** value will be left blank. The last field is for the duration of the call or text message. If the type of the data is **voice_call**, then the value in this field will be the **duration** of that call. If the type of data is **sms,** then the value in this field will be the text message.

The following figure shows records of call data stored in a text file:

```
2019-01-01 10:00:53 voice_call <phno>033 21345661</phno><name>Shyam</name> 138s

2019-01-01 11:07:24 sms <phno>9441235645</phno><name>Jagat</name> "Hi Jagat!
Happy New Year. Can we meet?"

2019-01-01 14:08:25 sms <phno>9111335687</phno><name>Neil</name> "Hi Neil!
Greetings of the New Year. How are you doing?"

2019-01-02 13:09:01 voice_call <phno>8900134981</phno> 68s
```

Figure 1.2: Call records in a text file

Now, the data shown in the preceding figure is not exactly a human language. But it contains various information that can be extracted by analyzing it. A couple of questions that can be answered by looking at this data are as follows:

- How many New Year greetings were sent by SMS on 1st January?

- How many people were contacted whose name is not in the contact list?

The art of extracting useful insights from any given text data can be referred to as text analytics. NLP, on the other hand, is not just restricted to text data. Voice (speech) recognition and analysis also come under the domain of NLP. NLP can be broadly categorized into two types: Natural Language Understanding (NLU) and Natural Language Generation (NLG). A proper explanation of these terms is provided as follows:

- **NLU**: NLU refers to a process by which an inanimate object with computing power is able to comprehend spoken language.

- **NLG**: NLG refers to a process by which an inanimate object with computing power is able to manifest its thoughts in a language that humans are able to understand.

For example, when a human speaks to a machine, the machine interprets the human language with the help of the NLU process. Also, by using the NLG process, the machine generates an appropriate response and shares that with the human, thus making it easier for humans to understand. These tasks, which are part of NLP, are not part of text analytics. Now we will look at an exercise that will give us a better understanding of text analytics.

Exercise 1: Basic Text Analytics

In this exercise, we will perform some basic text analytics on the given text data. Follow these steps to implement this exercise:

1. Open a Jupyter notebook.

2. Insert a new cell. Assign a **sentence** variable with 'The quick brown fox jumps over the lazy dog'. Insert a new cell and add the following code to implement this:

```
sentence = 'The quick brown fox jumps over the lazy dog'
```

3. Check whether the word 'quick' belongs to that text using the following code:

```
'quick' in sentence
```

The preceding code will return the output '**True**'.

4. Find out the **index** value of the word **'fox'** using the following code:

```
sentence.index('fox')
```

The code will return the output **16**.

5. To find out the rank of the word **'lazy'**, use the following code:

```
sentence.split().index('lazy')
```

The code generates the output **7**.

6. For printing the third word of the given text, use the following code:

```
sentence.split()[2]
```

This will return the output **'brown'**.

7. To print the third word of the given sentence in reverse order, use the following code:

```
sentence.split()[2][::-1]
```

This will return the output **'nworb'**.

8. To concatenate the first and last words of the given sentence, use the following code:

```
words = sentence.split()
first_word = words[0]
last_word = words[len(words)-1]
concat_word = first_word + last_word
print(concat_word)
```

The code will generate the output **'Thedog'**.

9. For printing words at even positions, use the following code:

```
[words[i] for i in range(len(words)) if i%2 == 0]
```

The code generates the following output:

```
['The', 'brown', 'jumps', 'the', 'dog']
```

Figure 1.3: List of words at even positions

10. To print the last three letters of the text, use the following code:

```
sentence[-3:]
```

This will generate the output '**dog**'.

11. To print the text in reverse order, use the following code:

```
sentence[::-1]
```

The code generates the following output:

```
'god yzal eht revo spmuj xof nworb kciuq ehT'
```

Figure 1.4: Text in reverse order

12. To print each word of the given text in reverse order, maintaining their sequence, use the following code:

```
print(' '.join([word[::-1] for word in words]))
```

The code generates the following output:

```
ehT kciuq nworb xof spmuj revo eht yzal god
```

Figure 1.5: Printing the text in reverse order while preserving word sequence

We are now well acquainted with NLP. In the next section, let's dive deeper into the various steps involved in it.

Various Steps in NLP

Earlier, we talked about the types of computations that are done on natural language. There are various standard NLP tasks. Apart from these tasks, you have the ability to design your own tasks as per your requirements. In the coming sections, we will be discussing various preprocessing tasks in detail and demonstrating them with an exercise.

Tokenization

Tokenization refers to the procedure of splitting a sentence into its constituent words. For example, consider this sentence: "I am reading a book." Here, our task is to extract words/tokens from this sentence. After passing this sentence to a tokenization program, the extracted words/tokens would be "I", "am", "reading", "a", "book", and ".". This example extracts one token at a time. Such tokens are called **unigrams**. However, we can also extract two or three tokens at a time. We need to extract tokens because, for the sake of convenience, we tend to analyze natural language word by word. If we extract two tokens at a time, it is called **bigrams**. If three tokens, it is called **trigrams**. Based on the requirements, n-grams can be extracted (where "n" is a natural number).

> **Note**
>
> **n-gram** refers to a sequence of n items from a given text.

Let's now try extracting trigrams from the following sentence: "The sky is blue." Here, the first trigram would be "The sky is". The second would be "sky is blue". This might sound easy. However, tokenization can be difficult at times. For instance, consider this sentence: "I would love to visit the United States". The tokens generated are "I", "would", "love", "to", "visit", "the", and "United States". Here, "United States" has to be treated as a single entity. Individual words such as "United" and "States" do not make any sense here.

To get a better understanding of tokenization, let's solve an exercise based on it in the next section.

Exercise 2: Tokenization of a Simple Sentence

In this exercise, we will tokenize the words in a given sentence with the help of the **NLTK** library. Follow these steps to implement this exercise:

1. Open a Jupyter notebook.

2. Insert a new cell and add a following code to import the necessary libraries:

```
import nltk
from nltk import word_tokenize
```

3. The **word_tokenize()** method is used to split the sentence into words/tokens. We need to add a sentence as input to the **word_tokenize()** method, so that it performs its job. The result obtained would be a list, which we will store in a **word** variable. To implement this, insert a new cell and add the following code:

    ```
    words = word_tokenize("I am reading NLP Fundamentals")
    ```

4. In order to view the list of tokens generated, we need to view it using the **print()** function. Insert a new cell and add the following code to implement this:

    ```
    print(words)
    ```

    The code generates the following output:

    ```
    ['I', 'am', 'reading', 'NLP', 'Fundamentals']
    ```

    Figure 1.6: List of tokens

Thus we can see the list of tokens generated with the help of the **word_tokenize()** method. In the next section, we will see another pre-processing step: **Parts-of-Speech (PoS) tagging**.

PoS Tagging

PoS refers to parts of speech. PoS tagging refers to the process of tagging words within sentences into their respective parts of speech and then finally labeling them. We extract Part of Speech of tokens constituting a sentence, so that we can filter out the PoS that are of interest and analyze them. For example, if we look at the sentence, "The sky is blue," we get four tokens – "The," "sky," "is," and "blue" – with the help of tokenization. Now, using **PoS tagger**, we tag parts of speech to each word/token. This will look as follows:

[('The', 'DT'), ('sky', 'NN'), ('is', 'VBZ'), ('blue', 'JJ')]

DT = *determiner*

NN = *noun, common, singular or mass*

VBZ = *verb, present tense, 3rd person singular*

JJ = *Adjective*

An exercise in the next section will definitely give a better understanding of this concept.

Exercise 3: PoS Tagging

In this exercise, we will find out the PoS for each word in the sentence, "**I am reading NLP Fundamentals**". We first make use of tokenization in order to get the tokens. Later, we use a PoS tagger, which will help us find PoS for each word/token. Follow these steps to implement this exercise:

1. Open a Jupyter notebook.

2. Insert a new cell and add the following code to import the necessary libraries:

    ```
    import nltk
    from nltk import word_tokenize
    ```

3. For finding the tokens in the sentence, we make use of the **word_tokenize()** method. Insert a new cell and add the following code to implement this:

    ```
    words = word_tokenize("I am reading NLP Fundamentals")
    ```

4. Print the tokens with the help of the **print()** function. To implement this, add a new cell and write the following code:

    ```
    print(words)
    ```

    The code generates the following output:

    ```
    ['I', 'am', 'reading', 'NLP', 'Fundamentals']
    ```

    Figure 1.7: List of tokens

5. In order to find the PoS for each word, we make use of the **pos_tag()** method of the **nltk** library. Insert a new cell and add the following code to implement this:

    ```
    nltk.pos_tag(words)
    ```

    The code generates the following output:

    ```
    [('I', 'PRP'),
     ('am', 'VBP'),
     ('reading', 'VBG'),
     ('NLP', 'NNP'),
     ('Fundamentals', 'NNS')]
    ```

    Figure 1.8: PoS tag of words

6. In the preceding output, we can see that for each token, a PoS has been allotted. Here, **PRP** stands for **personal pronoun**, **VBP** stands for **verb present**, **VGB** stands for **verb gerund**, **NNP** stands for **proper noun singular**, and **NNS** stands for **noun plural**.

We have learned about labeling appropriate PoS to tokens in a sentence. In the next section, we will learn about **stop words** in sentences and ways to deal with them.

Stop Word Removal

Stop words are common words that are just used to support the construction of sentences. We remove stop words from our analysis as they do not impact the meaning of sentences they are present in. Examples of stop words include a, am, and the. Since they occur very frequently and their presence doesn't have much impact on the sense of the sentence, they need to be removed.

In the next section, we will look at the practical implementation of removing stop words from a given sentence.

Exercise 4: Stop Word Removal

In this exercise, we will check the list of stopwords provided by the **nltk** library. Based on this list, we will filter out the stopwords included in our text. Follow these steps to implement this exercise:

1. Open a Jupyter notebook.

2. Insert a new cell and add the following code to import the necessary libraries:

```
import nltk
nltk.download('stopwords')
from nltk import word_tokenize
from nltk.corpus import stopwords
```

3. In order to check the list of stopwords provided for the **English** language, we pass it as a parameter to the **words()** function. Insert a new cell and add the following code to implement this:

```
stop_words = stopwords.words('English')
```

4. In the code, the list of stopwords provided by the **English** language is stored in the **stop_words** variable. In order to view the list, we make use of the **print()** function. Insert a new cell and add the following code to view the list:

```
print(stop_words)
```

The code generates the following output:

```
['i', 'me', 'my', 'myself', 'we', 'our', 'ours', 'ourselves', 'you', "you're", "you've", "you'll", "you'd", 'your', 'yours', 'y
ourself', 'yourselves', 'he', 'him', 'his', 'himself', 'she', "she's", 'her', 'hers', 'herself', 'it', "it's", 'its', 'itself',
'they', 'them', 'their', 'theirs', 'themselves', 'what', 'which', 'who', 'whom', 'this', 'that', "that'll", 'these', 'those',
'am', 'is', 'are', 'was', 'were', 'be', 'been', 'being', 'have', 'has', 'had', 'having', 'do', 'does', 'did', 'doing', 'a', 'a
n', 'the', 'and', 'but', 'if', 'or', 'because', 'as', 'until', 'while', 'of', 'at', 'by', 'for', 'with', 'about', 'against', 'b
etween', 'into', 'through', 'during', 'before', 'after', 'above', 'below', 'to', 'from', 'up', 'down', 'in', 'out', 'on', 'of
f', 'over', 'under', 'again', 'further', 'then', 'once', 'here', 'there', 'when', 'where', 'why', 'how', 'all', 'any', 'both',
'each', 'few', 'more', 'most', 'other', 'some', 'such', 'no', 'nor', 'not', 'only', 'own', 'same', 'so', 'than', 'too', 'very',
's', 't', 'can', 'will', 'just', 'don', "don't", 'should', "should've", 'now', 'd', 'll', 'm', 'o', 're', 've', 'y', 'ain', 'ar
en', "aren't", 'couldn', "couldn't", 'didn', "didn't", 'doesn', "doesn't", 'hadn', "hadn't", 'hasn', "hasn't", 'haven', "have
n't", 'isn', "isn't", 'ma', 'mightn', "mightn't", 'mustn', "mustn't", 'needn', "needn't", 'shan', "shan't", 'shouldn', "should
n't", 'wasn', "wasn't", 'weren', "weren't", 'won', "won't", 'wouldn', "wouldn't"]
```

Figure 1.9: List of stopwords provided by the English language

5. To remove the stop words from a sentence, we first assign a string to the **sentence** variable and tokenize it into words using the **word_tokenize()** method. Insert a new cell and add the following code to implement this:

    ```
    sentence = "I am learning Python. It is one of the most popular
    programming languages"
    sentence_words = word_tokenize(sentence)
    ```

6. To print the list of tokens, insert a new cell and add the following code:

    ```
    print(sentence_words)
    ```

    The code generates the following output:

```
['I', 'am', 'learning', 'Python', '.', 'It', 'is', 'one', 'of', 'the', 'most', 'popular', 'programming', 'languages']
```

Figure 1.10: List of tokens in the sentence_words variable

7. To remove the stopwords, first we need to loop through each word in the sentence, check whether there are any stop words, and then finally combine them to form a complete sentence. To implement this, insert a new cell and add the following code:

    ```
    sentence_no_stops = ' '.join([word for word in sentence_words if word not
    in stop_words])
    ```

8. To check whether the stopwords are filtered out from our sentence, we print the **sentence_no_stops** variable. Insert a new cell and add the following code to print:

    ```
    print(sentence_no_stops)
    ```

The code generates the following output:

```
I learning Python . It one popular programming languages
```

Figure 1.11: Text without stopwords

As you can see in the preceding figure, stopwords such as **"am," "is,"** **"of,"** **"the,"** and **"most"** are being filtered out and text without stop words is produced as output.

We have learned how to remove stop words from given text. In the next section, we will focus on normalizing text.

Text Normalization

There are some words that are spelt, pronounced, and represented differently, for example, words such as Mumbai and Bombay, and US and United States. Although they are different, they mean the same thing. There are also different forms words that need to be converted into base forms. For example, words such as "does" and "doing," when converted to their base form, become "do". Along these lines, **text normalization** is a process wherein different variations of text get converted into a standard form. We need to perform text normalization as there are some words that can mean the same thing as each other. There are various ways of normalizing text, such as spelling correction, stemming, and lemmatization, which will be covered later.

For a better understanding of this topic, we will look into practical implementation in the next section.

Exercise 5: Text Normalization

In this exercise, we will normalize a given text. Basically, we will be trying to replace selected words with new words, using the **replace()** function, and finally produce the normalized text. Follow these steps to implement this exercise:

1. Open a Jupyter notebook.

2. Insert a new cell and add the following code to assign a string to the **sentence** variable:

```
sentence = "I visited US from UK on 22-10-18"
```

3. We want to replace "**US**" with "**United States**", "**UK**" with "**United Kingdom**", and "**18**" with "**2018**". To do so, we make use of the **replace()** function and store the updated output in the "**normalized_sentence**" variable. Insert a new cell and add the following code to implement this:

```
normalized_sentence = sentence.replace("US", "United States").
replace("UK", "United Kingdom").replace("-18", "-2018")
```

4. Now, in order to check whether the text has been normalized, we insert a new cell and add the following code to print it:

```
print(normalized_sentence)
```

The code generates the following output:

```
I visited United States from United Kingdom on 22-10-2018
```

Figure 1.12: Normalized text

In the preceding figure, we can see that our text has been normalized.

Now that we have learned the basics of text normalization, in the next section, we explore various other ways that text can be normalized.

Spelling Correction

Spelling correction is one of the most important tasks in any NLP project. It can be time consuming, but without it there are high chances of losing out on required information. We make use of the "**autocorrect**" Python library to correct spellings. Let's look at the following exercise to get a better understanding of this.

Exercise 6: Spelling Correction of a Word and a Sentence

In this exercise, we will perform spelling correction on a word and a sentence, with the help of the '**autocorrect**' library of Python. Follow these steps in order to implement this exercise:

1. Open a Jupyter notebook.

2. Insert a new cell and add the following code to import the necessary libraries:

```
import nltk
from nltk import word_tokenize
from autocorrect import spell
```

3. In order to correct the spelling of a word, pass a wrongly spelled word as a parameter to the **spell()** function. Insert a new cell and add the following code to implement this:

```
spell('Natureal')
```

The code generates the following output:

'Natural'

Figure 1.13: Corrected word

4. In order to correct the spelling of a sentence, we first need to tokenize it into words. After that, we loop through each word in **sentence**, autocorrect them, and finally combine them. Insert a new cell and add the following code to implement this:

```
sentence = word_tokenize("Ntural Luanguage Processin deals with the art of extracting insightes from Natural Languaes")
```

5. We make use of the **print()** function to print all tokens. Insert a new cell and add the following code to print tokens:

```
print(sentence)
```

The code generates the following output:

```
['Ntural', 'Luanguage', 'Processin', 'deals', 'with', 'the', 'art', 'of', 'extracting', 'insightes', 'from', 'Natural', 'Languaes']
```

Figure 1.14: Tokens in sentences

6. Now that we have got the tokens, we loop through each token in **sentence**, correct them, and assign them to new variable. Insert a new cell and add the following code to implement this:

```
sentence_corrected = ' '.join([spell(word) for word in sentence])
```

7. To print the correct sentence, we insert a new cell and add the following code:

```
print(sentence_corrected)
```

The code generates the following output:

```
Natural Language Procession deals with the art of extracting insights from Natural Languages
```

Figure 1.15: Corrected sentence

8. In the preceding figure, we can see that most of the wrongly spelled words have been corrected. But the word "**Processin**" was wrongly converted into "**Procession**". It should have been "**Processing**". It happened because to change "Processin" to "Procession" or "Processing," an equal number of edits is required. To rectify this, we need to use other kinds of spelling correctors that are aware of context.

In the next section, we will look at **stemming**, which is another form of text normalization.

Stemming

In languages such as English, words get transformed into various forms when being used in a sentence. For example, the word "product" might get transformed into "production" when referring to the process of making something or transformed into "products" in plural form. It is necessary to convert these words into their base forms, as they carry the same meaning. Stemming is a process that helps us in doing so. If we look at the following figure, we get a perfect idea about how words get transformed into their base forms:

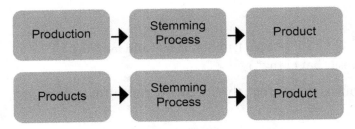

Figure 1.16: Stemming of the word product

To get a better understanding about stemming, we shall look into an exercise in the next section.

Exercise 7: Stemming

In this exercise, we will pass a few words through the stemming process such that they get converted into their base forms. Follow these steps to implement this exercise:

1. Open a Jupyter notebook.

2. Insert a new cell and add the following code to import the necessary libraries:

```
import nltk
stemmer = nltk.stem.PorterStemmer()
```

3. Now pass the following words as parameters to the **stem()** method. To implement this, insert a new cell and add the following code:

```
stemmer.stem("production")
```

When the input is "**production**", the following output is generated:

```
'product'
```

Figure 1.17: Stemmed word for production

```
stemmer.stem("coming")
```

When the input is "**coming**", the following output is generated:

```
'come'
```

Figure 1.18: Stemmed word for coming

```
stemmer.stem("firing")
```

When the input is "**firing**", the following output is generated:

```
'fire'
```

Figure 1.19: Stemmed word for firing

```
stemmer.stem("battling")
```

When the input is "**battling**", the following output is generated:

```
'battl'
```

Figure 1.20: Stemmed word for battling

4. From the preceding figures, we can see that the entered words are converted into their base forms.

In the next section, we will focus on **lemmatization**, which is another form of text normalization.

Lemmatization

Sometimes, the stemming process leads to inappropriate results. For example, in the last exercise, the word "battling" got transformed to "battl," which has no meaning. To overcome these problems with stemming, we make use of lemmatization. In this process, an additional check is being made, by looking through the dictionary to extract the base form of a word. However, this additional check slows down the process. To get a better understanding about lemmatization, we will look at an exercise in the next section.

Exercise 8: Extracting the base word using Lemmatization

In this exercise, we use the lemmatization process to produce the proper form of a given word. Follow these steps to implement this exercise:

1. Open a Jupyter notebook.

2. Insert a new cell and add the following code to import the necessary libraries:

```
import nltk
nltk.download('wordnet')
from nltk.stem.wordnet import WordNetLemmatizer
```

3. Create object of the **WordNetLemmatizer** class. Insert a new cell and add the following code to implement this:

```
lemmatizer = WordNetLemmatizer()
```

4. Bring the word to its proper form by using the **lemmatize()** method of the **WordNetLemmatizer** class. Insert a new cell and add the following code to implement this:

```
lemmatizer.lemmatize('products')
```

With the input "**products**", the following output is generated:

```
'product'
```

Figure 1.21: Lemmatized word

```
lemmatizer.lemmatize('production')
```

With the input "**production**", the following output is generated:

```
'production'
```

Figure 1.22: Lemmatized word

```
lemmatizer.lemmatize('coming')
```

With the input "**coming**", the following output is generated:

'coming'

Figure 1.23: Lemmatized word

```
lemmatizer.lemmatize('battle')
```

With the input "**battle**", the following output is generated:

'battle'

Figure 1.24: Lemmatized word

We have learned how to use the lemmatization process to transform a given word into its base form.

In the next section, we will look at another preprocessing step in NLP: **named entity recognition (NER)**.

NER

Named entities are usually not present in dictionaries. So, we need to treat them separately. The main objective of this process is to identify the named entities (such as proper nouns) and map them to the categories that are already defined. For example, the categories might include names of persons, places, and so on. To get a better understanding of this process, we'll look at an exercise.

Exercise 9: Treating Named Entities

In this exercise, we will find out the named entities in a sentence. Follow these steps to implement this exercise:

1. Open a Jupyter notebook.

2. Insert a new cell and add the following code to import the necessary libraries:

```
import nltk
from nltk import word_tokenize
nltk.download('maxent_ne_chunker')
nltk.download('words')
```

3. Declare the **sentence** variable and assign it a string. Insert a new cell and add the following code to implement this:

```
sentence = "We are reading a book published by Packt which is based out of Birmingham."
```

4. To find the named entities from the preceding text, insert a new cell and the following code:

```
i = nltk.ne_chunk(nltk.pos_tag(word_tokenize(sentence)), binary=True)
[a for a in i if len(a)==1]
```

The code generates the following output:

```
[Tree('NE', [('Packt', 'NNP')]), Tree('NE', [('Birmingham', 'NNP')])]
```

Figure 1.25: Named entity

In the preceding figure, we can see that the code identifies the named entities **"Packt"** and **"Birmingham"** and maps them to an already-defined category such as **"NNP"**.

In the next section, we will focus on <u>**word sense disambiguation**</u>, which helps us identify the right sense of any word.

Word Sense Disambiguation

There's a popular saying, "A man is known by the company he keeps". Similarly, a word's meaning depends on its association with other words in the sentence. This means two or more words with the same spelling may have different meanings in different contexts. This often leads to ambiguity. Word sense disambiguation is the process of mapping a word to the correct sense it carries. We need to disambiguate words based on the sense they carry so that they can be treated as different entities when being analyzed. The following figure displays a perfect example of how ambiguity is caused due to the usage of the same word in different sentences:

Figure 1.26: Word sense disambiguition

To get a better understanding about this process, let's look at an exercise in the next section.

Exercise 10: Word Sense Disambiguation

In this exercise, we will find the sense of the word "bank" in two different sentences. Follow these steps to implement this exercise:

1. Open a Jupyter notebook.

2. Insert a new cell and add the following code to import the necessary libraries:

    ```
    import nltk
    from nltk.wsd import lesk
    from nltk import word_tokenize
    ```

3. Declare two variables, **sentence1** and **sentence2**, and assign them with appropriate strings. Insert a new cell and the following code to implement this:

    ```
    sentence1 = "Keep your savings in the bank"
    sentence2 = "It's so risky to drive over the banks of the road"
    ```

4. In order to find the sense of the word "bank" in the preceding two sentences, we make use of the **lesk** algorithm provided by the **nltk.wsd** library. Insert a new cell and add the following code to implement this:

    ```
    print(lesk(word_tokenize(sentence1), 'bank'))
    ```

    The code generates the following output:

    ```
    Synset('savings_bank.n.02')
    ```

    Figure 1.27: Sense carried by the word "bank" in sentence1

Here, **savings_bank.n.02** refers to a container for keeping money safely at home. To check the other sense of the word bank, write the following code:

```
print(lesk(word_tokenize(sentence2), 'bank'))
```

The code generates the following output:

```
Synset('bank.v.07')
```

Figure 1.28: Sense carried by the word "bank" in sentence2

Here, **bank.v.07** refers to a slope in the turn of a road.

Thus, with the help of the **lesk** algorithm, we are able to identify the sense of a word in whatever context. In the next section, we will focus on **sentence boundary detection**, which helps detect the start and end points of sentences.

Sentence Boundary Detection

Sentence boundary detection is the method of detecting where one sentence ends and where another sentence begins. If you are thinking that it is pretty easy, as a full stop (.) denotes the end of any sentence and the beginning of another sentence, then you are wrong. This is because there can be instances wherein abbreviations are separated by full stops. Various analyses need to be performed at a sentence level, so detecting boundaries of sentences is essential. An exercise in the next section will provide a better understanding of this process.

Exercise 11: Sentence Boundary Detection

In this exercise, we will extract sentences from a paragraph. Follow these steps to implement this exercise:

1. Open a Jupyter notebook.

2. Insert a new cell and add the following code to import the necessary libraries:

    ```
    import nltk
    from nltk.tokenize import sent_tokenize
    ```

3. We make use of the **sent_tokenize()** method to detect sentences in a given text. Insert a new cell and add the following code to implement this:

    ```
    sent_tokenize("We are reading a book. Do you know who is the publisher? It
    is Packt. Packt is based out of Birmingham.")
    ```

    The code generates the following output:

    ```
    ['We are reading a book.',
     'Do you know who is the publisher?',
     'It is Packt.',
     'Packt is based out of Birmingham.']
    ```

    Figure 1.29: List of sentences

    As you can see in the figure, we are able to separate out the sentences from given text.

We have covered all the preprocessing steps that are involved in NLP. Now, based on the knowledge we've gained, we will complete an activity in the next section.

Activity 1: Preprocessing of Raw Text

We have a text corpus that is in an improper format. In this activity, we will perform all the pre-processing steps that were discussed earlier to get some meaning out of the text.

> **Note**
>
> The **file.txt** file can be found at this location: https://bit.ly/2V3ROAa.

Follow these steps to implement this activity:

1. Import the necessary libraries.

2. Load the text corpus to a variable.

3. Apply the tokenization process to the text corpus and print the first 20 tokens.

4. Apply spelling correction on each token and print the initial 20 corrected tokens as well as the corrected text corpus.

5. Apply PoS tags to each corrected token and print them.

6. Remove stop words from the corrected token list and print the initial 20 tokens.

7. Apply stemming and lemmatization to the corrected token list and the print initial 20 tokens.

8. Detect the sentence boundaries in the given text corpus and print the total number of sentences.

> **Note**
>
> The solution for this activity can be found on page 254.

By now, you should be familiar with what NLP is and what basic pre-processing steps are needed to carry out any NLP project. In the next section, we will focus on different phases that are included in an NLP project.

Kick Starting an NLP Project

We can divide an NLP project into several sub-projects or phases. These phases are followed sequentially. This tends to increase the overall efficiency of the process as each phase is generally carried out by specialized resources. An NLP project has to go through six major phases, which are outlined in the following figure:

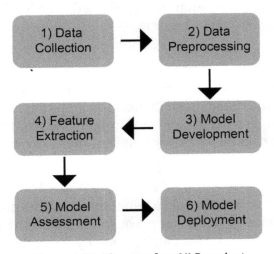

Figure 1.30: Phases of an NLP project

Suppose you are working on a project in which you need to collect tweets and analyze their sentiments. We will explain how this is carried out by discussing each phase in the coming section.

Data Collection

This is the initial phase of any NLP project. Our sole purpose is to collect data as per our requirements. For this, we may either use existing data, collect data from various online repositories, or create our own dataset by crawling the web. In our case, we will collect tweets.

Data Preprocessing

Once the data is collected, we need to clean it. For the process of cleaning, we make use of the different pre-processing steps that we have used in this chapter. It is necessary to clean the collected data, as dirty data tends to reduce effectiveness and accuracy. In our case, we will remove the unnecessary URLs, words, and more from the collected tweets.

Feature Extraction

Computers understand only binary digits: 0 and 1. Thus, every instruction we feed into a computer gets transformed into binary digits. Similarly, machine learning models tend to understand only numeric data. As such, it becomes necessary to convert the text data into its equivalent numerical form. In our case, we represent the cleaned tweets using different kinds of matrices, such as bag of words and TF-IDF. We will be learning more about these matrices in later chapters.

Model Development

Once the feature set is ready, we need to develop a suitable model that can be trained to gain knowledge from the data. These models are generally statistical, machine learning-based, deep learning-based, or reinforcement learning-based. In our case, we will build a model that is capable of extracting sentiments from numeric matrices.

Model Assessment

After developing a model, it is essential to benchmark it. This process of benchmarking is known as model assessment. In this step, we will evaluate the performance of our model by comparing it to others. This can be done by using different parameters or metrics. These parameters include F1, precision, recall, and accuracy. In our case, we will evaluate the newly created model by checking how well it performs when extracting the sentiments of the tweets.

Model Deployment

This is the final stage for most industrial NLP projects. In this stage, the models are put into production. They are either integrated into an existing system or new products are created by keeping this model as a base. In our case, we will deploy our model to production, such that it can extract sentiments from tweets in real time.

Summary

In this chapter, we learned how NLP is different from text analytics. We also covered the various pre-processing steps that are included in NLP. We looked at the different phases an NLP project has to pass through. In the next chapter, you will learn about the different methods required for extracting features from unstructured texts, such as TF-IDF and bag of words. You will also learn about NLP tasks such as tokenization, lemmatization, and stemming in more detail. Furthermore, text visualization techniques such as word clouds will be introduced.

2

Basic Feature Extraction Methods

Learning Objectives

By the end of this chapter, you will be able to:

- Categorize data based on content and structure
- Describe pre-processing steps in detail and implement them to clean text data
- Describe feature engineering
- Calculate the similarity between texts
- Visualize text using word clouds and other visualization techniques

In this chapter, you will learn about basic feature extraction methods in detail and also visualize text with the help of word clouds and other visualization techniques.

Introduction

In the previous chapter, we learned about the concepts of Natural Language Processing (NLP) and text analytics. We also looked at various pre-processing steps in brief. In this chapter, we will learn how to deal with text data whose formats are mostly unstructured. Unstructured data cannot be represented in a tabular format. Therefore, it is essential to convert it into numeric features because most machine learning algorithms are capable of dealing only with numbers. More emphasis will be put on steps such as tokenization, stemming, lemmatization, and stop-word removal. You will also learn about two popular methods for feature extraction: bag of words and Term Frequency-Inverse Document Frequency, as well as various methods for creating new features from existing features. Finally, you will become familiar with how text data can be visualized.

Types of Data

To deal with data effectively, we need to understand the various forms in which it exists. Let's first understand the types of data that exist. There are two main ways to categorize data, by structure and by content, as explained in the upcoming sections.

Categorizing Data Based on Structure

On the basis of structure, data can be divided into three categories, namely structured, semi-structured, and unstructured, as shown in the following diagram:

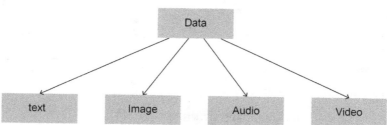

Figure 2.1: Categorization based on content

These three categories are explained in detail here:

- **Structured Data:** This is the most organized form of data. It is represented in tabular formats such as Excel files and Comma-Separated Value (CSV) files. The following figure shows what structured data usually looks like:

Name	Age	Location
Ram	25	Delhi
Shyam	28	Banglore
Jon	35	Kolkata
Madhu	28	Mumbai
Hari	56	Chennai

Figure 2.2: Structured data

- **Semi-Structured Data:** This type of data is not presented in a tabular structure, but it can be represented in a tabular format after transformation. Here, information is usually stored between tags following a definite pattern. XML and HTML files can be referred to as semi-structured data. The following figure shows how semi-structured data can appear:

Figure 2.3: Semi-structured data

- **Unstructured Data:** This type of data is the most difficult to deal with. Machine learning algorithms would find it difficult to comprehend unstructured data without any loss of information. Text corpora and images are examples of unstructured data. The following figure shows how unstructured data looks like:

> Hello! Welcome to the second chapter of the book. In this chapter you will learn how to convert unstructured raw texts to structured numeric features. Unstructured data means that kind of data which cannot be represented in row-column format. It is

Figure 2.4: Unstructured data

Categorization of Data Based on Content

On the basis of content, data can be divided into four categories, as shown in the following figure:

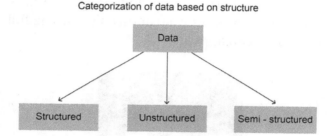

Figure 2.5: Categorization of data based on structure

Let's look at each category here:

- **Text Data:** This refers to text corpora consisting of written sentences. This type of data can only be read. An example would be the text corpus of a book.

- **Image Data:** This refers to pictures that are used to communicate messages. This type of data can only be seen.

- **Audio Data:** This refers to recordings of someone's voice, music, and so on. This type of data can only be heard.

- **Video Data:** A continuous series of images coupled with audio forms a video. This type of data can be seen as well as heard.

We have learned about the different types of data as well their categorization on the basis of structure and content. When dealing with unstructured data, it is necessary to clean it first. In the coming section, we will look into some pre-processing steps for cleaning data.

Cleaning Text Data

Most of the time, text data cannot be used as it is. This is because the presence of various unknown symbols or links makes it dirty or unfit for use. **Data cleaning** is the art of extracting meaningful portions from data by eliminating unnecessary details. Consider the sentence, *He tweeted, 'Live coverage of General Elections available at this. tv/show/ge2019. _/_ Please tune in :) '.*

Various symbols, such as "_/_" and ":)," are present in the sentence. They do not contribute much to its meaning. We need to remove such unwanted details. This is done not only to focus more on the actual content but also to reduce computations. To achieve this, methods such as **tokenization** and **stemming** are used. We will learn about them one by one in the upcoming sections.

Tokenization

Tokenization and word tokenizers were briefly described in *Chapter 1, Introduction to Natural Language Processing*. Tokenization is the process of splitting sentences into their constituents; that is, words. In this chapter, we will see how tokenization is done using various packages.

The cleaning of text data is essential before tokenization. **Regular expressions** are widely used for cleaning. A regular expression is a set of characters in a given order that represents a pattern. This pattern is searched for in the texts. In Python, the **re** package is used to develop regular expressions. To get a better understanding of this, we will carry out the exercise in the next section.

Exercise 12: Text Cleaning and Tokenization

In this exercise, we will clean a text and extract the tokens from it. Follow these steps to implement this exercise:

1. Open a Jupyter notebook.

2. Import the **re** package:

   ```
   import re
   ```

3. Store the text to be cleaned in a **sentence** variable:

   ```
   sentence = 'Sunil tweeted, "Witnessing 70th Republic Day of India from
   Rajpath, \
   New Delhi. Mesmerizing performance by Indian Army! Awesome airshow! @
   india_official \
   @indian_army #India #70thRepublic_Day. For more photos ping me sunil@
   photoking.com :)"'
   ```

4. Delete all characters other than digits, alphabetical characters, and whitespaces from the text. Use the **split()** function to split the strings into parts. Add the following code to implement this:

```
re.sub(r'([^\s\w]|_)+', ' ', sentence).split()
```

This command fragments the string wherever any blank space is present. The output should be as follows:

```
['Sunil',
 'tweeted',
 'Witnessing',
 '70th',
 'Republic',
 'Day',
 'of',
 'India',
 'from',
 'Rajpath',
 'New',
 'Delhi',
 'Mesmerizing',
 'performance',
 'by',
 'Indian',
 'Army',
 'Awesome',
 'airshow',
 'india',
 'official',
 'indian',
 'army',
 'India',
 '70thRepublic',
 'Day',
 'For',
 'more',
 'photos',
 'ping',
 'me',
 'sunil',
 'photoking',
 'com']
```

Figure 2.6: Fragmented string

We have learned about how to extract the tokens from a text. Often, extracting each token separately does not help. For instance, consider the sentence, "I don't hate you, but your behavior." Here, if we process each of the tokens, such as "hate" and "behavior," separately, then the true meaning of the sentence would not be comprehended. In this case, the context in which these tokens are present becomes essential. Thus, we consider n consecutive tokens at a time. **n-grams** refers to the grouping of n consecutive tokens together. In the next section, we will look at an exercise where n-grams can be extracted from a given text.

Exercise 13: Extracting n-grams

In this exercise, we will extract n-grams using three different methods; namely, via custom-defined functions, via **nltk**, and via **TextBlob**. Follow these steps to implement this exercise:

1. Open a Jupyter notebook.

2. Import the **re** package and define a custom-defined function, which we can use to extract n-grams. Add the following code to do this:

```
import re
def n_gram_extractor(sentence, n):
    tokens = re.sub(r'([^\s\w]|_)+', ' ', sentence).split()
    for i in range(len(tokens)-n+1):
        print(tokens[i:i+n])
```

3. To check the bi-grams, we pass the function with text and n. Add the following code to do this:

```
n_gram_extractor('The cute little boy is playing with the kitten.', 2)
```

The code generates the following output:

```
['The', 'cute']
['cute', 'little']
['little', 'boy']
['boy', 'is']
['is', 'playing']
['playing', 'with']
['with', 'the']
['the', 'kitten']
```

Figure 2.7: Bi-grams

4. To check the tri-grams, we pass the function with the text and n. Add the following code to do this:

```
n_gram_extractor('The cute little boy is playing with the kitten.', 3)
```

The code generates the following output:

```
['The', 'cute', 'little']
['cute', 'little', 'boy']
['little', 'boy', 'is']
['boy', 'is', 'playing']
['is', 'playing', 'with']
['playing', 'with', 'the']
['with', 'the', 'kitten']
```

Figure 2.8: Tri-grams

5. To check the bi-grams using the **nltk** library, add the following code:

```
from nltk import ngrams
list(ngrams('The cute little boy is playing with the kitten.'.split(), 2))
```

The code generates the following output:

```
[('The', 'cute'),
 ('cute', 'little'),
 ('little', 'boy'),
 ('boy', 'is'),
 ('is', 'playing'),
 ('playing', 'with'),
 ('with', 'the'),
 ('the', 'kitten.')]
```

Figure 2.9: Bi-grams

6. To check the tri-grams using the **nltk** library, add the following code:

```
list(ngrams('The cute little boy is playing with the kitten.'.split(), 2))
```

```
[('The', 'cute', 'little'),
 ('cute', 'little', 'boy'),
 ('little', 'boy', 'is'),
 ('boy', 'is', 'playing'),
 ('is', 'playing', 'with'),
 ('playing', 'with', 'the'),
 ('with', 'the', 'kitten.')]
```

Figure 2.10: Tri-grams

7. To check the bi-grams using the **TextBlob** library, add the following code:

```
from textblob import TextBlob
blob = TextBlob("The cute little boy is playing with the kitten.")
blob.ngrams(n=2)
```

The code generates the following output:

```
[WordList(['The', 'cute']),
 WordList(['cute', 'little']),
 WordList(['little', 'boy']),
 WordList(['boy', 'is']),
 WordList(['is', 'playing']),
 WordList(['playing', 'with']),
 WordList(['with', 'the']),
 WordList(['the', 'kitten'])]
```

Figure 2.11: Bi-grams

8. To check the tri-grams using the TextBlob library, add the following code:

```
blob.ngrams(n=3)
```

The code generates the following output:

```
[WordList(['The', 'cute', 'little']),
 WordList(['cute', 'little', 'boy']),
 WordList(['little', 'boy', 'is']),
 WordList(['boy', 'is', 'playing']),
 WordList(['is', 'playing', 'with']),
 WordList(['playing', 'with', 'the']),
 WordList(['with', 'the', 'kitten'])]
```

Figure 2.12: Tri-grams

Keras and **TextBlob** are two of the most popular Python libraries used for performing various NLP tasks. TextBlob provides a simple and easy-to-use interface to do so. Keras is used mainly for performing deep learning-based NLP tasks. In the next section, we will carry out an exercise where we use the Keras and TextBlob libraries to tokenize texts.

Exercise 14: Tokenizing Texts with Different Packages – Keras and TextBlob

In this exercise, we will make use of Keras and TextBlob to tokenize texts. Follow these steps to implement this exercise:

1. Open a Jupyter notebook, insert a new cell, and declare a variable **sentence**:

```
sentence = 'Sunil tweeted, "Witnessing 70th Republic Day of India from
Rajpath, \
New Delhi. Mesmerizing performance by Indian Army! Awesome airshow! @
india_official \
@indian_army #India #70thRepublic_Day. For more photos ping me sunil@
photoking.com :)"'
```

2. Import the **keras** and **textblob** libraries:

```
from keras.preprocessing.text import text_to_word_sequence
from textblob import TextBlob
```

3. To tokenize using the **keras** library, add the following code:

```
text_to_word_sequence(sentence)
```

The code generates the following output:

```
['Sunil',
 'tweeted',
 'witnessing',
 '70th',
 'republic',
 'day',
 'of',
 'india',
 'from',
 'rajpath',
 'new',
 'delhi',
 'mesmerizing',
 'performance',
 'by',
 'indian',
 'army',
 'awesome',
 'airshow',
 'india',
 'official',
 'indian',
 'army',
 'india',
 '70threpublic',
 'day',
 'for',
 'more',
 'photos',
 'ping',
 'me',
 'sunil',
 'photoking,'
 'com']
```

Figure 2.13: Tokenization using Keras

4. To tokenize using the **TextBlob** library, add the following code:

```
blob = TextBlob(sentence)
blob.words
```

The code generates the following output:

```
WordList(['Sunil', 'tweeted', 'witnessing', '70th', 'Republic', 'Day', 'of', 'India', 'from', 'Rajpath',
'New', 'Delhi', 'Mesmerizing', 'performance', 'by', 'Indian', 'Army', 'Awesome', 'airshow', 'india_official',
'indian_army', 'India', '70thRepublic_Day', 'For', 'more', 'photos', 'ping', 'me', 'sunil', 'photoking.com'])
```

Figure 2.14: Tokenization using TextBlob

We have learned how to tokenize texts using the Keras and TextBlob libraries. In the next section, we will discuss different types of tokenizers.

Types of Tokenizers

There are different types of tokenizers that come in handy for specific tasks. Let's look at them one by one:

- **Tweet tokenizer:** This is specifically designed for tokenizing tweets. It is capable of dealing with emotions and expressions of sentiment, which are used widely on Twitter.

- **MWE tokenizer:** MWE stands for **Multi-Word Expression**. Here, certain groups of multiple words are treated as one entity during tokenization, such as "United States of America," "People's Republic of China," "not only," and "but also."

- **Regular expression tokenizer:** These tokenizers are developed using regular expressions. Sentences are split based on the occurrence of a particular pattern.

- **Whitespace tokenizer:** This tokenizer splits a string whenever a space, tab, or newline character is present.

- **Word Punkt tokenizer** : This splits a text into a list of alphabetical characters, digits, and non-alphabetical characters.

Now that we have learned about the different types of tokenizers, in the next section, we will carry out an exercise to get a better understanding of them.

Exercise 15: Tokenizing Text Using Various Tokenizers

In this exercise, we will use make use of different tokenizers to tokenize text. Follow these steps to implement this exercise:

1. Open a Jupyter notebook.

2. Insert a new cell and the following code to declare a variable sentence:

```
sentence = 'Sunil tweeted, "Witnessing 70th Republic Day of India from Rajpath, \
New Delhi. Mesmerizing performance by Indian Army! Awesome airshow! @india_official \
@indian_army #India #70thRepublic_Day. For more photos ping me sunil@photoking.com :)"'
```

3. To tokenize the text using **TweetTokenizer**, add the following code:

```
from nltk.tokenize import TweetTokenizer
tweet_tokenizer = TweetTokenizer()
tweet_tokenizer.tokenize(sentence)
```

The code generates the following output:

```
['sunil',
 'tweeted',
 ',',
 '"',
 'witnessing',
 '70th',
 'Republic',
 'Day',
 'of',
 'India',
 'from',
 'Rajpath',
 ',',
 'New',
 'Delhi',
 '.',
 'Mesmerizing',
 'performance',
 'by',
 'Indian',
 'Army',
 '!',
 'Awesome',
 'airshow',
 '!',
 '@india_official',
 '@indian_army',
 '#India',
 '#70thRepublic_Day',
 '.',
 'For',
 'more',
 'photos',
 'ping',
 'me',
 'sunil@photoking.com',
 ':)',
 '"']
```

Figure 2.15: Tokenization using TweetTokenizer

4. To tokenize the text using the MWE tokenizer, add the following code:

```
from nltk.tokenize import MWETokenizer
mwe_tokenizer = MWETokenizer([('Republic', 'Day')])
mwe_tokenizer.add_mwe(('Indian', 'Army'))
mwe_tokenizer.tokenize(sentence.split())
```

The code generates the following output:

```
['Sunil',
 'tweeted,',
 '"Witnessing',
 '70th',
 'Republic_Day',
 'of',
 'India',
 'from',
 'Rajpath,',
 'New',
 'Delhi.',
 'Mesmerizing',
 'performance',
 'by',
 'Indian',
 'Army!',
 'Awesome',
 'airshow!',
 '@india_official',
 '@indian_army',
 '#India',
 '#70thRepublic_Day.',
 'For',
 'more',
 'photos',
 'ping',
 'me',
 'sunil@photoking.com',
 ':)"']
```

Figure 2.16: Tokenization using the MWE tokenizer

5. In the preceding figure, the words "Indian" and "Army!" were supposed to be treated as a single identity, but they got separated. This is because "Army!" (not "Army") is treated as a token. Let's see how this can be fixed in the next step.

6. Add the following code to fix the issues in the previous step:

```
mwe_tokenizer.tokenize(sentence.replace('!','').split())
```

The code generates the following output:

```
['Sunil',
 'tweeted,',
 '"Witnessing',
 '70th',
 'Republic_Day',
 'of',
 'India',
 'from',
 'Rajpath,',
 'New',
 'Delhi.',
 'Mesmerizing',
 'performance',
 'by',
 'Indian_Army',
 'Awesome',
 'airshow',
 '@india_official',
 '@indian_army',
 '#India',
 '#70thRepublic_Day.',
 'For',
 'more',
 'photos',
 'ping',
 'me',
 'sunil@photoking.com',
 ':)"']
```

Figure 2.17: Tokenization using the MWE tokenizer after removing the "!" sign

7. To tokenize the text using the regular expression tokenizer, add the following code:

```
from nltk.tokenize import RegexpTokenizer
reg_tokenizer = RegexpTokenizer('\w+|\$[\d\.]+|\S+')
reg_tokenizer.tokenize(sentence)
```

The code generates the following output:

```
['Sunil',
 'tweeted',
 ',',
 '"witnessing',
 '70th',
 'Republic',
 'Day',
 'of',
 'India',
 'from',
 'Rajpath',
 ',',
 'New',
 'Delhi',
 '.',
 'Mesmerizing',
 'performance',
 'by',
 'Indian',
 'Army',
 '!',
 'Awesome',
 'airshow',
 '!',
 '@india_official',
 '@indian_army',
 '#India',
 '#70thRepublic_Day.',
 'For',
 'more',
 'photos',
 'ping',
 'me',
 'sunil',
 '@photoking.com',
 ':)"']
```

Figure 2.18: Tokenization using the regular expression tokenizer

8. To tokenize the text using the whitespace tokenizer, add the following code:

```
from nltk.tokenize import WhitespaceTokenizer
wh_tokenizer = WhitespaceTokenizer()
wh_tokenizer.tokenize(sentence)
```

The code generates the following output:

```
['sunil',
 'tweeted,',
 '"witnessing',
 '70th',
 'Republic',
 'Day',
 'of',
 'India',
 'from',
 'Rajpath,',
 'New',
 'Delhi.',
 'Mesmerizing',
 'performance',
 'by',
 'Indian',
 'Army!',
 'Awesome',
 'airshow!',
 '@india_official',
 '@indian_army',
 '#India',
 '#70thRepublic_Day.',
 'For',
 'more',
 'photos',
 'ping',
 'me',
 'sunil@photoking.com',
 ':)"']
```

Figure 2.19: Tokenization using the whitespace tokenizer

9. To tokenize the text using the Word Punkt tokenizer, add the following code:

```
from nltk.tokenize import WordPunctTokenizer
wp_tokenizer = WordPunctTokenizer()
wp_tokenizer.tokenize(sentence)
```

The code generates the following output:

```
['sunil',
 'tweeted',
 ',',
 '"',
 'witnessing',
 '70th',
 'Republic',
 'Day',
 'of',
 'India',
 'from',
 'Rajpath',
 ',',
 'New',
 'Delhi',
 '.',
 'Mesmerizing',
 'performance',
 'by',
 'Indian',
 'Army',
 '!',
 'Awesome',
 'airshow',
 '!',
 '@',
 'india_official',
 '@',
 'indian_army',
 '#',
 'India',
 '#',
 '70thRepublic_Day',
 '.',
 'For',
 'more',
 'photos',
 'ping',
 'me',
 'sunil',
 '@',
 'photoking',
 '.',
 'com',
 ':)"']
```

Figure 2.20: Tokenization using the Word Punkt tokenizer

We have learned how to tokenize text using different tokenizers.

Issues with Tokenization

Although tokenization appears to be an easy task, in reality, it is not so. This is primarily because of ambiguities that arise due to the presence of whitespaces and hyphens. Moreover, sentences in certain languages, such as Chinese and Japanese, do not have words separated by whitespaces, thus making it difficult to tokenize them. In the next section, we will discuss another pre-processing step: stemming.

Stemming

In languages such as English, the original forms of words get changed when used in sentences. The process of restoring the original form of a word is known as **stemming**. It is essential to restore words back to their base form, because without this, compilers and computing machines would treat two or more different forms of the same word as different entities, despite them having the same meaning. **RegexpStemmer** and the **Porter stemmer** are the most widely used stemmers. Let's learn about them one by one.

RegexpStemmer

RegexpStemmer uses regular expressions to check whether morphological or structural prefixes or suffixes are present. For instance, in many cases, the gerund form of a verb (so, the form ending with "ing") can be restored back to the base form simply by removing "ing" from the end; for example, "playing" -> "play".

Let's do the following exercise to get some hands-on experience of using RegexpStemmer.

Exercise 16: Converting words in gerund form into base words using RegexpStemmer

In this exercise, we will use RegexpStemmer on text to transform words ending with "ing" into their base form. Follow these steps to implement this exercise:

1. Open a Jupyter notebook.

2. Insert a new cell and add the following code to declare a **sentence** variable:

    ```
    sentence = "I love playing football"
    ```

3. Now we'll make use of **regex_stemmer** to stem each word of the **sentence** variable. Add the following code to do this:

    ```
    from nltk.stem import RegexpStemmer
    regex_stemmer = RegexpStemmer('ing$', min=4)
    ' '.join([regex_stemmer.stem(wd) for wd in sentence.split()])
    ```

The code generates the following output:

```
'I love play football'
```

Figure 2.21: Stemming using RegexpStemmer

In the next section, we will discuss the Porter stemmer.

The Porter Stemmer

The Porter stemmer is the most common stemmer for dealing with English words. It removes various morphological and inflectional endings (such as suffixes and prefixes) from English words. In doing so, it helps us to extract the base form of a word from its variations. To get a better understanding of this, we will carry out an exercise in the next section.

Exercise 17: The Porter Stemmer

In this exercise, we will apply the Porter stemmer to some text. Follow these steps to implement this exercise:

1. Open a Jupyter notebook.

2. Import **nltk** and related packages, and declare a **sentence** variable. Add the following code to do this:

```
sentence = "Before eating, it would be nice to sanitize your hands with a sanitizer"
from nltk.stem.porter import *
```

3. Now we'll make use of the Porter stemmer to stem each word of the **sentence** variable:

```
ps_stemmer = PorterStemmer()
' '.join([ps_stemmer.stem(wd) for wd in sentence.split()])
```

The code generates the following output:

```
'before eating, it would be nice to sanit your hand with a sanit'
```

Figure 2.22: Stemming using the Porter stemmer

In the next section, we will learn about another pre-processing step: lemmatization.

Lemmatization

A problem that occurs while stemming is that, often, stemmed words do not carry any meaning. For instance, if we use the Porter stemmer on the word "independence," we get "independ." Now, the word "independ" is not present in the English dictionary; it does not carry any meaning. Lemmatization deals with such cases by using a vocabulary and analyzing the words' morphologies. It returns the base forms of words that can actually be found in dictionaries. To get a better understanding of this, let's look at an exercise in the next section.

Exercise 18: Lemmatization

In this exercise, we will make use of lemmatization to lemmatize a given text. Follow these steps to implement this exercise:

1. Open a Jupyter notebook.

2. Import **nltk** and related packages, then declare a **sentence** variable. Add the following code to implement this:

```
import nltk
from nltk.stem import WordNetLemmatizer
from nltk import word_tokenize
nltk.download('wordnet')
lemmatizer = WordNetLemmatizer()
sentence = "The products produced by the process today are far better than
what it produces generally."
```

3. To lemmatize the tokens extracted from the sentence, add the following code:

```
' '.join([lemmatizer.lemmatize(word) for word in word_tokenize(sentence)])
```

The code generates the following output:

```
'The product produced by the process today are far better than what it produce generally.'
```

Figure 2.23: Lemmatization using the WordNet lemmatizer

In the next section, we will deal with other kinds of word variations, looking at singularizing and pluralizing words. TextBlob provides a nice function to singularize and pluralize words. Let's see how this is done in the next section.

Exercise 19: Singularizing and Pluralizing Words

In this exercise, we will make use of the TextBlob library to singularize and pluralize the words in a given text. Follow these steps to implement this exercise:

1. Open a Jupyter notebook.

2. Import TextBlob and declare a sentence variable. Add the following code to implement this:

```
from textblob import TextBlob
sentence = TextBlob('She sells seashells on the seashore')
```

To check the list of words in sentence, type the following code:

```
sentence.words
```

The code generates the following output:

```
WordList(['She', 'sells', 'seashells', 'on', 'the', 'seashore'])
```

Figure 2.24: Extracting words from a sentence using TextBlob

3. To singluarize the second word in the given sentence, type the following code:

```
sentence.words[2].singularize()
```

The code generates the following output:

```
'seashell'
```

Figure 2.25: Singularizing a word using TextBlob

4. To pluralize the fifth word in the given sentence, type the following code:

```
sentence.words[5].pluralize()
```

The code generates the following output:

```
'seashores'
```

Figure 2.26: Pluralizing a word using TextBlob

In the next section, we will learn about another pre-processing task: language translation.

Language Translation

Different languages are often used together to convey something. In such cases, translating the entire text into a single language becomes an essential pre-processing task for analyzing it. Let's look at an exercise in the next section.

Exercise 20: Language Translation

In this exercise, we will make use of the TextBlob library to translate a sentence from Spanish to English. Follow these steps to implement this exercise:

1. Open a Jupyter notebook.

2. Import the TextBlob library:

   ```
   from textblob import TextBlob
   ```

3. Make use of the **translate** function of TextBlob to translate the input text from Spanish to English. Add the following code to do this:

   ```
   en_blob = TextBlob(u'muy bien')
   en_blob.translate(from_lang='es', to='en')
   ```

   The code generates the following output:

   ```
   TextBlob("very well")
   ```

   Figure 2.27: Language translation using TextBlob

In the next section, we will look at another pre-processing task: stop-word removal.

Stop-Word Removal

Stop words, such as "am," "the," and "are," support words and sentences. They help us to construct sentences. But they do not affect the meaning of the sentence in which they are present. Thus, we can safely ignore their presence. To get a better understanding of this, let's look at an exercise in the next section.

Exercise 21: Stop-Word Removal

In this exercise, we will remove the stop words from a given text. Follow these steps to implement this exercise:

1. Open a Jupyter notebook.

2. Import **nltk** and declare a **sentence** variable with the text in question:

   ```
   from nltk import word_tokenize
   sentence = "She sells seashells on the seashore"
   ```

3. Define a custom list of stop words and execute the following lines of code:

```
custom_stop_word_list = ['she', 'on', 'the', 'am', 'is', 'not']
' '.join([word for word in word_tokenize(sentence) if word.lower() not in custom_stop_word_list])
```

The code generates the following output:

```
'sells seashells seashore'
```

Figure 2.28: Removing a custom set of stop words

We have learned how to remove the stop words from a given sentence. In the next section, we will explore the concept of extracting features from texts.

Feature Extraction from Texts

Let's understand feature extraction with real-life examples. Features represent the characteristics of a person or a thing. These characteristics may or may not uniquely represent a person or a thing. For instance, the general characteristics that a person possesses, such as the number of ears, hands, and legs, are generally not enough to identify that person uniquely. But characteristics such as fingerprints and DNA sequences can be used to recognize that person distinctly. Similarly, in feature extraction, we try to extract attributes from texts that represent those texts uniquely. These attributes are called features. Machine learning algorithms take only numeric features as input. So, it is of utmost importance to represent texts as numeric features. When dealing with texts, we extract both general and specific features. Sometimes, individual words constituting texts do not affect some features directly, such as the language of the text and the total number of words. These features can be referred to as general features. Specific features include bag of words, and TF-IDF representations of texts. Let's understand these in the coming sections.

Extracting General Features from Raw Text

General features refer to those that are not directly dependent on the individual tokens constituting a text corpus, such as the number of words, the number of occurrences of each part of speech, and the number of uppercase and lowercase words.

Let's consider two sentences: "The sky is blue." and "The pillar is yellow.". Here, both sentences have the same number of words (a general feature), that is, four. But the individual constituent tokens are different. Let's complete an exercise to understand this better.

Exercise 22: Extracting General Features from Raw Text

In this exercise, we will extract general features from input text. These general features include detecting the number of words, the presence of "wh-" words (words beginning with "wh"), the polarity, the subjectivity, and the language in which the text is written. Follow these steps to implement this exercise:

1. Open a Jupyter notebook.

2. Import the **pandas** library and create a **DataFrame** with four sentences. Add the following code to implement this:

```
import pandas as pd
df = pd.DataFrame([['The interim budget for 2019 will be announced on 1st
February.'], ['Do you know how much expectation the middle-class working
population is having from this budget?'], ['February is the shortest month
in a year.'], ['This financial year will end on 31st March.']])
df.columns = ['text']
df
```

The code generates the following output:

	text
0	The interim budget for 2019 will be announced...
1	Do you know how much expectation the middle-cl...
2	February is the shortest month in a year.
3	This financial year will end on 31st March

Figure 2.29: DataFrame consisting of four sentences

3. Use the **apply** function to iterate through each row of the column text, convert them to TextBlob objects, and extract words from them. Add the following code to implement this:

```
from textblob import TextBlob
df['number_of_words'] = df['text'].apply(lambda x : len(TextBlob(str(x)).
words))
df['number_of_words']
```

The code generates the following output:

```
0    11
1    15
2     8
3     8
Name: number_of_words, dtype: int64
```

Figure 2.30: Number of words in a sentence

4. Now, again, we make use of the **apply** function to iterate through each row of the column text, convert them to TextBlob objects, and extract the words from them to check whether any of the words belong to the list of *wh* words that has been declared:

```
wh_words = set(['why', 'who', 'which', 'what', 'where', 'when', 'how'])
df['is_wh_words_present'] = df['text'].apply(lambda x : True if \
                                    len(set(TextBlob(str(x)).
words).intersection(wh_words))>0 else False)
df['is_wh_words_present']
```

The code generates the following output:

```
0    False
1     True
2    False
3    False
Name: is_wh_words_present, dtype: bool
```

Figure 2.31: Checking the presence of wh words

5. Use the **apply** function to iterate through each row of the column text, convert them to TextBlob objects, and extract their sentiment scores:

```
df['polarity'] = df['text'].apply(lambda x : TextBlob(str(x)).sentiment.
polarity)
df['polarity']
```

The code generates the following output:

```
0       0.000
1       0.200
2       0.000
3.      0.000
Name: polarity, dtype: float64
```

Figure 2.32: Polarity of each sentence

6. Use the **apply** function to iterate through each row of the column text, convert them to TextBlob objects, and extract their subjectivity scores:

```
df['subjectivity'] = df['text'].apply(lambda x : TextBlob(str(x)).
sentiment.subjectivity)
df['subjectivity']
```

The code generates the following output:

```
0       0.000
1       0.200
2       0.000
3.      0.000
Name: subjectivity, dtype: float64
```

Figure 2.33: Subjectivity of each sentence

Note

Sentiment scores such as subjectivity and polarity will be explained in detail in *Chapter 8, Sentiment Analysis.*

7. Use the apply function to iterate through each row of the column text, convert them to TextBlob objects, and detect their languages:

```
df['language'] = df['text'].apply(lambda x : TextBlob(str(x)).detect_
language())
df['language']
```

The code generates the following output:

```
0        en
1        en
2        en
3        en
Name: language, dtype: object
```

Figure 2.34: Language of each sentence

We have learned how to extract general features from a given text. In the next section, we will solve an activity to get a better understanding of this.

Activity 2: Extracting General Features from Text

In this activity, we will extract various general features from documents. The dataset that we are using consists of random statements. Our objective is to find various general features such as punctuation, uppercase and lowercase words, letter characters, digits, words, and whitespaces.

> **Note**
>
> The **data.csv** dataset used in this activity can be found at this link: https://bit. ly/2CIkCa4.

Follow these steps to implement this activity:

1. Open a Jupyter notebook.

2. Import **pandas**, **nltk**, and the other necessary libraries.

3. Load **data.csv** using pandas' **read_csv** function.

4. Find the number of occurrences of each part of speech (PoS). You can see the PoS that nltk provides by loading it from **help/tagsets/upenn_tagset.pickle**.

5. Find the amount of punctuation marks.

6. Find the amount of uppercase and lowercase words.

7. Find the number of letters.

8. Find the number of digits.

9. Find the amount of words.

10. Find the amount of whitespaces for each sentence.

> **Note**
>
> The solution for this activity can be found on page 259.

We have learned how to extract general features from a given text. In the next section, we will explore special features that can be extracted from a given text.

Bag of Words

The Bag-of-Words (BoW) model is one of the most popular methods for extracting features from raw texts. The output of this model for a set of text documents is a matrix. Each column of the matrix represents a word from the vocabulary and each row corresponds to one of these text documents. Here, "vocabulary" refers to a unique set of words present in a document. Let's understand this with an example. Suppose you have two text documents:

Document 1: *I like detective Byomkesh Bakshi.*

Document 2: *Byomkesh Bakshi is not a detective, he is a truth seeker.*

The corresponding BoW representation would be as follows:

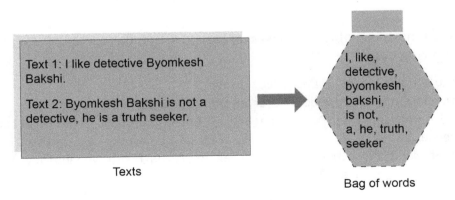

Figure 2.35: Diagram of the BoW model

The tabular representation of the BoW model would be as follows:

	i	like	detective	byomkesh	bakshi	is	not	a	he	truth	seeker
Text-1	1	1	1	1	1	0	0	0	0	0	0
Text-2	0	0	1	1	1	2	1	2	1	1	1

Figure 2.36: Tabular representation of the BoW model

Let's see how BoW can be implemented using Python.

Exercise 23: Creating a BoW

In this exercise, we will create a BoW representation for all the terms in a document and ascertain the 10 most frequent terms. Follow these steps to implement this exercise:

1. Open a Jupyter notebook.

2. Import the necessary libraries and declare a list corpus. Add the following code to implement this:

```
import pandas as pd

from sklearn.feature_extraction.text import CountVectorizer
corpus = [
'Data Science is an overlap between Arts and Science',
'Generally, Arts graduates are right-brained and Science graduates are
left-brained',
'Excelling in both Arts and Science at a time becomes difficult',
'Natural Language Processing is a part of Data Science'
]
```

3. Now we'll make use of the **CountVectorizer** function to create the BoW model. Add the following code to do this:

```
bag_of_words_model = CountVectorizer()
print(bag_of_words_model.fit_transform(corpus).todense())
bag_of_word_df = pd.DataFrame(bag_of_words_model.fit_transform(corpus).
todense())
bag_of_word_df.columns = sorted(bag_of_words_model.vocabulary_)
bag_of_word_df.head()
```

The code generates the following output:

	an	and	are	arts	at	becomes	between	both	brained	data	...	language	left	natural	of	overlap	part	processing	right	science	time
0	1	1	0	1	0	0	1	0	0	1	...	0	0	0	0	1	0	0	0	2	0
1	0	1	2	1	0	0	0	0	2	0	...	0	1	0	0	0	0	0	1	1	0
2	0	1	0	1	1	1	0	1	0	0	...	0	0	0	0	0	0	0	0	1	1
3	0	0	0	0	0	0	0	0	0	1	...	1	0	1	1	0	1	1	0	1	0

Figure 2.37: DataFrame of the output of the BoW model

4. Now we create a BoW model for the 10 most frequent terms. Add the following code to implement this:

```
bag_of_words_model_small = CountVectorizer(max_features=10)
bag_of_word_df_small = pd.DataFrame(bag_of_words_model_small.fit_
transform(corpus).todense())
bag_of_word_df_small.columns = sorted(bag_of_words_model_small.
vocabulary_)
bag_of_word_df_small.head()
```

The code generates the following output:

	an	and	are	arts	brained	data	graduates	is	right	science
0	1	1	0	1	0	1	0	1	0	2
1	0	1	2	1	2	0	2	0	1	1
2	0	1	0	1	0	0	0	0	0	1
3	0	0	0	0	0	1	0	1	0	1

Figure 2.38: DataFrame of the output of the BoW model for the 10 most frequent terms

Zipf's Law

According to Zipf's law, "for a given corpus of natural language utterances, the frequency of any word is inversely proportional to its rank in the frequency table." In simple terms, if the words in a corpus are arranged in descending order of their frequency of occurrence, then the frequency of the word at ith rank will be proportional to $1/i$. To get a better understanding of this, let's look at an exercise in the next section.

Exercise 24: Zipf's Law

In this exercise, we will plot the actual ranks and frequencies of tokens, along with the expected ranks and frequencies, with the help of Zipf's law. We will be using the 20newsgroups dataset provided by the **sklearn** library, which is a collection of newsgroup documents. Follow these steps to implement this exercise:

1. Open a Jupyter notebook.

2. Import the necessary libraries, declare a **newsgroups_data_sample** variable, and fetch the dataset provided by **sklearn**, that is, **fetch_20newsgroups**. Add the following code to do this:

```
from pylab import *
import nltk
nltk.download('stopwords')
from sklearn.datasets import fetch_20newsgroups
from nltk import word_tokenize
from nltk.corpus import stopwords
import matplotlib.pyplot as plt
%matplotlib inline
import re
import string
from collections import Counter
newsgroups_data_sample = fetch_20newsgroups(subset='train')
```

3. Now we'll add individual printable characters to get a list of stop words. Add the following code to implement this:

```
stop_words = stopwords.words('english')
stop_words = stop_words + list(string.printable)
```

4. To tokenize the corpus, add the following code:

```
tokenized_corpus = [word.lower() for sentence in newsgroups_data_
sample['data'] \
                    for word in word_tokenize(re.sub(r'([^\s\w]|_)+', ' ',
sentence)) \
                    if word.lower() not in stop_words]
```

5. Add the following code to calculate the frequency of each token:

```
token_count_di = Counter(tokenized_corpus)
token_count_di.most_common(50)
```

The code generates the following output:

```
[('ax', 62412),
 ('edu', 21321),
 ('subject', 12265),
 ('com', 12134),
 ('lines', 11835),
 ('organization', 11233),
 ('one', 9017),
 ('would', 8910),
 ('writes', 7844),
 ('article', 7438),
 ('people', 5977),
 ('like', 5868),
 ('university', 5589),
 ('posting', 5507),
 ('know', 5134),
 ('get', 4998),
 ('host', 4996),
 ('nntp', 4814),
 ('max', 4776),
 ('think', 4583),
 ('also', 4308),
 ('use', 4187),
 ('time', 4102),
 ('new', 3986),
 ('good', 3759),
 ('ca', 3546),
 ('could', 3511),
 ('well', 3480),
 ('us', 3364),
 ('may', 3313),
 ('even', 3280),
 ('see', 3065),
 ('cs', 3041),
```

Figure 2.39: The 50 most frequent words of the corpus

6. Now, to plot the actual ranks and frequencies of the tokens along with the expected ranks and frequencies as per Zipf's law, we add the following code:

```
frequencies = [b for (a,b) in token_count_di.most_common(10000)]

tokens = [a for (a,b) in token_count_di.most_common(10000)]
ranks = range(1, len(frequencies)+1)


plt.figure(figsize=(8,8))
plt.ylim(1,10**4)
plt.xlim(1,10**4)

#Actual ranks and frequencies
obtained_line, = loglog(ranks, frequencies, marker=".", label="Line
obtained from the Text Corpus")
obtained_legend = plt.legend(handles=[obtained_line], loc=1)
ax = plt.gca().add_artist(obtained_legend)

#Expected ranks and frequencies as per Zipf's law
expected_line, = plt.
plot([1,frequencies[0]],[frequencies[0],1],color='r',label="Line expected
as per Zipf's Law")
plt.legend(handles=[expected_line], loc=4)

title("Plot stating Zipf law's in log-log scale")
xlabel("Rank of token in descending order of frequency of occurrence")
ylabel("Frequency of ocurrence of token")
grid(True)
```

The code generates the following output:

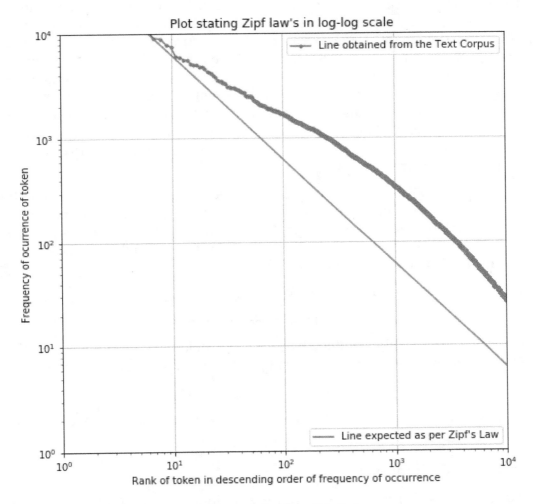

Figure 2.40: Illustration of Zipf's law

TF-IDF

Previously, we looked at the BoW model. That model has a severe drawback. The frequency of occurrence of a token does not fully represent how much information it carries about a document. This is because a term occurring multiple times in many documents does not convey much information. Rare terms can carry much more information about the documents they are present in. TF–IDF, or Term Frequency-Inverse Document Frequency, is a method of representing text data in a matrix format (row-column/table format) using numbers that quantify how much information these terms carry in the given documents. Just like the BoW model, each row, i, represents a text document from the given set of text documents. Each column, j, corresponds to a word from the vocabulary.

The Term Frequency (TF) for a given term, j, in a document, i, is equal to the number of times term j occurs in document i. Rarely occurring terms are more informative than frequently occurring general terms. To account for this, we need to multiply another factor by T. This factor denotes how specific a term is to a given document. This is called the Inverse Document Frequency (IDF).

The IDF for a given term is given by the following formula:

$$\text{term } j \ (idf_j) = \log_{10} (N/df_j)$$

Here, dfj refers to the number of documents with term j. N is the total number of documents. Thus, the TF-IDF score for term j in document i will be as follows:

$$a_{ij} = tf\text{-}idf_{ij} = tf_{ij} \times idf_j = tf_{ij} \times \log_{10} (N/df_j)$$

Let's do an exercise in the next section and learn how TF–IDF can be implemented in Python.

Exercise 25: TF-IDF Representation

In this exercise, we will create a TF–IDF representation of the input texts for all the terms in a given corpus and identify the 10 most frequent terms. Follow these steps to implement this exercise:

1. Open a Jupyter notebook.

2. Import all the necessary libraries and create a DataFrame consisting of the sentences. Add the following code to implement this:

```
import pandas as pd

from sklearn.feature_extraction.text import TfidfVectorizer
corpus = [
'Data Science is an overlap between Arts and Science',
```

```
'Generally, Arts graduates are right-brained and Science graduates are
left-brained',
'Excelling in both Arts and Science at a time becomes difficult',
'Natural Language Processing is a part of Data Science'
]
```

3. Now, to create a TF-IDF model, we write the following code:

```
tfidf_model = TfidfVectorizer()
print(tfidf_model.fit_transform(corpus).todense())
```

The code generates the following output:

```
[[0.40332811  0.25743911  0.          0.25743911  0.          0.
  0.40332811  0.          0.          0.31798852  0.          0.
  0.          0.          0.          0.31798852  0.          0.
  0.          0.          0.40332811  0.          0.          0.
  0.42094668  0.          ]
 [0.          0.159139    0.49864399  0.159139    0.          0.
  0.          0.          0.49864399  0.          0.          0.
  0.24932199  0.49864399  0.          0.          0.          0.24932199
  0.          0.          0.          0.          0.          0.24932199
  0.13010656  0.          ]
 [0.          0.22444946  0.          0.22444946  0.35164346  0.35164346
  0.          0.35164346  0.          0.          0.35164346  0.35164346
  0.          0.          0.35164346  0.          0.          0.
  0.          0.          0.          0.          0.          0.
  0.18350214  0.35164346  ]
 [0.          0.          0.          0.          0.          0.
  0.          0.          0.          0.30887228  0.          0.
  0.          0.          0.          0.30887228  0.39176533  0.
  0.39176533  0.39176533  0.          0.39176533  0.39176533  0.
  0.2044394   0.          ]]
```

Figure 2.41: TF-IDF representation of the corpus in matrix form

4. Now, to create a DataFrame from the generated **tf-idf** matrix, we write the following code:

```
tfidf_df = pd.DataFrame(tfidf_model.fit_transform(corpus).todense())
tfidf_df.columns = sorted(tfidf_model.vocabulary_)
tfidf_df.head()
```

The code generates the following output:

an	and	are	arts	at	becomes	between	both	brained	data	...	language	left	natural	of	overlap	part
0.403328	0.257439	0.000000	0.257439	0.000000	0.000000	0.403328	0.000000	0.000000	0.317989	...	0.000000	0.000000	0.000000	0.000000	0.403328	0.000000
0.000000	0.159139	0.498644	0.159139	0.000000	0.000000	0.000000	0.000000	0.498644	0.000000	...	0.000000	0.249322	0.000000	0.000000	0.000000	0.000000
0.000000	0.224449	0.000000	0.224449	0.351643	0.351643	0.000000	0.351643	0.000000	0.000000	...	0.000000	0.000000	0.000000	0.000000	0.000000	0.000000
0.000000	0.000000	0.000000	0.000000	0.000000	0.000000	0.000000	0.000000	0.000000	0.308872	...	0.391765	0.000000	0.391765	0.391765	0.000000	0.391765

Figure 2.42: TF-IDF representation of a corpus in DataFrame form

5. Now we'll create a DataFrame from the **tf-idf** matrix for the 10 most frequent terms. Add the following code to implement this:

```
tfidf_model_small = TfidfVectorizer(max_features=10)
tfidf_df_small = pd.DataFrame(tfidf_model_small.fit_transform(corpus).todense())
tfidf_df_small.columns = sorted(tfidf_model_small.vocabulary_)
tfidf_df_small.head()
```

The code generates the following output:

	an	and	are	arts	brained	data	graduates	is	right	science
0	0.491042	0.313426	0.000000	0.313426	0.000000	0.387143	0.000000	0.387143	0.000000	0.512492
1	0.000000	0.170061	0.532867	0.170061	0.532867	0.000000	0.532867	0.000000	0.266433	0.139036
2	0.000000	0.612172	0.000000	0.612172	0.000000	0.000000	0.000000	0.000000	0.000000	0.500491
3	0.000000	0.000000	0.000000	0.000000	0.000000	0.640434	0.000000	0.640434	0.000000	0.423897

Figure 2.43: TF-IDF representation of the 10 most frequent terms

In the next section, we will solve an activity to extract specific features from texts.

Activity 3: Extracting Specific Features from Texts

In this activity, we will extract specific features from the texts present in a dataset. The dataset that we will be using here is `fetch_20newsgroups`, provided by the sklearn library. Follow these steps to implement this activity:

1. Import the necessary packages.

2. Fetch the dataset provided by sklearn, `fetch_20newsgroup`, and store the data in a DataFrame.

3. Clean the data in the DataFrame.

4. Create a BoW model.

5. Create a TF-IDF model.

6. Compare both models on the basis of the 20 most frequently occurring words.

> **Note**
>
> The solution for this activity can be found on page 263.

We have learned how to compare the BoW and TF-IDF models. In the next section, we will learn more about feature engineering.

Feature Engineering

Feature engineering is a method for extracting new features from existing features. These new features are extracted as they tend to effectively explain variability in data. One application of feature engineering could be to calculate how similar different pieces of text are. There are various ways of calculating the similarity between two texts. The most popular methods are cosine similarity and Jaccard similarity. Let's learn about each of them:

- **Cosine similarity**: The cosine similarity between two texts is the cosine of the angle between their vector representations. BoW and TF-IDF matrices can be regarded as vector representations of texts.

- **Jaccard similarity**: This is the ratio of the number of terms common between two text documents to the total number of unique terms present in those texts.

  Let's understand this with the help of an example. Suppose there are two texts:

  Text 1: I like detective Byomkesh Bakshi.

  Text 2: Byomkesh Bakshi is not a detective, he is a truth seeker.

  The common terms are "Byomkesh," "Bakshi," and "detective."

  The number of common terms in the texts is three.

  The unique terms present in the texts are "I," "like," "is," "not," "a," "he," "is," "truth," "seeker."

  The number of unique terms is nine.

  Therefore, the Jaccard similarity is 3/9 = 0.3.

To get a better understanding of text similarity, we will solve an exercise in the next section.

Exercise 26: Feature Engineering (Text Similarity)

In this exercise, we will calculate the Jaccard and cosine similarity for a given pair of texts. Follow these steps to implement this exercise:

1. Open a Jupyter notebook.

2. Insert a new cell and add the following code to import the necessary packages:

    ```
    from nltk import word_tokenize
    from nltk.stem import WordNetLemmatizer
    from sklearn.feature_extraction.text import TfidfVectorizer
    from sklearn.metrics.pairwise import cosine_similarity
    lemmatizer = WordNetLemmatizer()
    ```

3. Now we declare the **pair1**, **pair2**, and **pair3** variables, as follows:

    ```
    pair1 = ["What you do defines you","Your deeds define you"]
    pair2 = ["Once upon a time there lived a king.", "Who is your queen?"]
    pair3 = ["He is desperate", "Is he not desperate?"]
    ```

4. We will create a function to extract the Jaccard similarity between a pair of sentences. Add the following code to do this:

```
def extract_text_similarity_jaccard (text1, text2):
    words_text1 = [lemmatizer.lemmatize(word.lower()) for word in word_
tokenize(text1)]
    words_text2 = [lemmatizer.lemmatize(word.lower()) for word in word_
tokenize(text2)]
    nr = len(set(words_text1).intersection(set(words_text2)))
    dr = len(set(words_text1).union(set(words_text2)))
    jaccard_sim = nr/dr
    return jaccard_sim
```

5. To check the Jaccard similarity between statements in **pair1**, write the following code:

```
extract_text_similarity_jaccard(pair1[0],pair1[1])
```

The code generates the following output:

0.14285714285714285

Figure 2.44: Jaccard similarity coefficient

6. To check the Jaccard similarity between statements in **pair2**, write the following code:

```
extract_text_similarity_jaccard(pair2[0],pair2[1])
```

The code generates the following output:

0.0

Figure 2.45: Jaccard similarity coefficient

7. To check the Jaccard similarity between statements in **pair3**, write the following code:

```
extract_text_similarity_jaccard(pair3[0],pair3[1])
```

The code generates the following output:

0.6

Figure 2.46: Jaccard similarity coefficient

8. To check the cosine similarity, we first create a corpus that will have texts of **pair1**, **pair2**, and **pair3**. Add the following code to do this:

```
tfidf_model = TfidfVectorizer()
corpus = [pair1[0], pair1[1], pair2[0], pair2[1], pair3[0], pair3[1]]
```

9. Now we store the **tf-idf** representations of the texts of pair1, pair2, and pair3 in a **tfidf_results** variable. Add the following code to do this:

```
tfidf_results = tfidf_model.fit_transform(corpus).todense()
```

10. To check the cosine similarity between the initial two texts, we write the following code:

```
cosine_similarity(tfidf_results[0],tfidf_results[1])
```

The code generates the following output:

```
array([[0.3082764]])
```

Figure 2.47: Cosine similarity

11. To check the cosine similarity between the third and fourth texts, we write the following code:

```
cosine_similarity(tfidf_results[2],tfidf_results[3])
```

The code generates the following output:

```
array([[0.]])
```

Figure 2.48: Cosine similarity

12. To check the cosine similarity between the fifth and sixth texts, we write the following code:

```
cosine_similarity(tfidf_results[4],tfidf_results[5])
```

The code generates the following output:

```
array([[0.80368547]])
```

Figure 2.49: Cosine similarity

Word Clouds

Unlike numeric data, there are very few ways in which text data can be represented visually. The most popular way of visualizing text data is using word clouds. A word cloud is a visualization of a text corpus in which the sizes of the tokens (words) represent the number of times they have occurred. Let's go through an exercise to understand this better.

Exercise 27: Word Clouds

In this exercise, we will visualize the first 10 articles from sklearn's fetch_20newsgroups text dataset using a word cloud. Follow these steps to implement this exercise:

1. Open a Jupyter notebook.

2. Import the necessary libraries and dataset. Add the following code to do this:

```
import matplotlib.pyplot as plt
from sklearn.datasets import fetch_20newsgroups
newsgroups_data_sample = fetch_20newsgroups(subset='train')
```

3. To check the data has been fetched, type the following code:

```
newsgroups_data_sample['data'][:10]
```

The code generates the following output:

```
["From: lerxst@wam.umd.edu (where's my thing)\nSubject: WHAT car is this!?\nNntp-Posting-Host: rac3.wam.umd.edu\nOrganizatio
n: University of Maryland, College Park\nLines: 15\n\n I was wondering if anyone out there could enlighten me on this car I s
aw\nthe other day. It was a 2-door sports car, looked to be from the late 60s/\nearly 70s. It was called a Bricklin. The door
s were really small. In addition,\nthe front bumper was separate from the rest of the body. This is \nall I know. If anyone c
an tellme a model name, engine specs, years\nof production, where this car is made, history, or whatever info you\nhave on th
is funky looking car, please e-mail.\n\nThanks,\n- IL\n    ---- brought to you by your neighborhood Lerxst ----\n\n\n\n\n",
 "From: guykuo@carson.u.washington.edu (Guy Kuo)\nSubject: SI Clock Poll - Final Call\nSummary: Final call for SI clock repor
ts\nKeywords: SI,acceleration,clock,upgrade\nArticle-I.D.: shelley.1qvfo9INNc3s\nOrganization: University of Washington\nLine
s: 11\nNNTP-Posting-Host: carson.u.washington.edu\n\nA fair number of brave souls who upgraded their SI clock oscillator have
\nshared their experiences for this poll. Please send a brief message detailing\nyour experiences with the procedure. Top spe
ed attained, CPU rated speed,\nadd on cards and adapters, heat sinks, hour of usage per day, floppy disk\nfunctionality with
800 and 1.4 m floppies are especially requested.\n\nI will be summarizing in the next two days, so please add to the network
\nknowledge base if you have done the clock upgrade and haven't answered this\npoll. Thanks.\n\nGuy Kuo <guykuo@u.washington.
edu>\n",
```

Figure 2.50: Sample from the sklearn dataset

4. Now add the following lines of code to create a word cloud:

```
other_stopwords_to_remove = ['\\n', 'n', '\\', '>', 'nLines', 'nI',"n'"]
STOPWORDS = STOPWORDS.union(set(other_stopwords_to_remove))
stopwords = set(STOPWORDS)
text = str(newsgroups_data_sample['data'][:10])
wordcloud = WordCloud(width = 800, height = 800,
            background_color ='white',
            max_words=200,
```

```
            stopwords = stopwords,
            min_font_size = 10).generate(text)
plt.imshow(wordcloud, interpolation='bilinear')
plt.axis("off")
plt.show()
```

The code generates the following output:

Figure 2.51: Word cloud representation of the first 10 articles

In the next section, we will explore other visualizations, such as dependency parse trees and named entities.

Other Visualizations

Apart from word clouds, there are various other ways of visualizing texts. Some of the most popular ways are listed here:

- **Visualizing sentences using a dependency parse tree:** Generally, the phrases constituting a sentence depend on each other. We depict these dependencies by using a tree structure known as a dependency parse tree. For instance, the word "*helps*" in the sentence "God helps those who help themselves" depends on two other words. These words are "*God*" (the one who helps) and "*those*" (the ones who are helped).

- **Visualizing named entities in a text corpus:** In this case, we extract the named entities from texts and highlight them by using different colors.

Let's go through the following exercise to understand this better.

Exercise 28: Other Visualizations (Dependency Parse Trees and Named Entities)

In this exercise, we will look at other visualization methods, such as dependency parse trees and using named entities. Follow these steps to implement this exercise:

1. Open a Jupyter notebook.

2. Insert a new cell and add the following code to import the necessary libraries:

```
import spacy
from spacy import displacy
import en_core_web_sm
nlp = en_core_web_sm.load()
```

3. Now we'll depict the sentence "God helps those who help themselves" using a dependency parse tree. Add the following code to implement this:

```
doc = nlp('God helps those who help themselves.')
displacy.render(doc, style='dep', jupyter=True)
```

The code generates the following output:

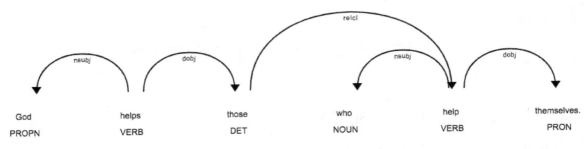

Figure 2.52: Dependency parse tree

4. Now we will visualize the named entities of the text corpus. Add the following code to implement this:

```
text = 'Once upon a time there lived a saint named Ramakrishna
Paramahansa. \
        His chief disciple Narendranath Dutta also known as Swami
Vivekananda \
        is the founder of Ramakrishna Mission and Ramakrishna Math.'
doc2 = nlp(text)
displacy.render(doc2, style='ent', jupyter=True)
```

The code generates the following output:

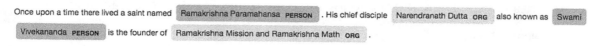

Figure 2.53: Named entities

Now that you have learned about visualizations, in the next section, we will solve an activity based on them to gain an even better understanding.

Activity 4: Text Visualization

In this activity, we will create a word cloud for the 50 most frequent words in a dataset. The dataset we will use consists of random sentences that are not clean. First, we need to clean them and create a unique set of frequently occurring words.

> **Note**
>
> The text_corpus.txt dataset used in this activity can found at this location: https://bit.ly/2HQ2luS.

Follow these steps to implement this activity:

1. Import the necessary libraries.

2. Fetch the dataset.

3. Perform the pre-processing steps, such as text cleaning, tokenization, stop-word removal, lemmatization, and stemming, on the fetched data.

4. Create a set of unique words along with their frequencies for the 50 most frequently occurring words.

5. Create a word cloud for these top 50 words.

6. Justify the word cloud by comparing it with the word frequency calculated.

> **Note**
>
> The solution for this activity can be found on page 266.

Summary

In this chapter, you have learned about various types of data and ways to deal with unstructured text data. Text data is usually untidy and needs to be cleaned and pre-processed. Pre-processing steps mainly consist of tokenization, stemming, lemmatization, and stop-word removal. After pre-processing, features are extracted from texts using various methods, such as BoW and TF-IDF. This step converts unstructured text data into structured numeric data. New features are created from existing features using a technique called feature engineering. In the last part of the chapter, we explored various ways of visualizing text data, such as word clouds.

In the next chapter, you will learn how to develop machine learning models to classify texts using the features you have learned to extract in this chapter. Moreover, different sampling techniques and model evaluation parameters will be introduced.

3

Developing a Text classifier

Learning Objectives

By the end of this chapter, you will be able to:

- Describe the different types of machine learning algorithms
- Differentiate between unsupervised and supervised learning methodologies
- Distinguish between classification and regression problems
- Describe various sampling techniques
- Develop end-to-end text classifiers
- Evaluate models using metrics such as accuracy, precision, and recall
- Build pipelines for streamlining NLP projects
- Save and load models

In this chapter, you will learn about the various types of machine learning algorithms and develop classifiers with their help.

Introduction

In the previous chapter, you learned about various extraction methods, such as tokenization, stemming, lemmatization, and stop-word removal, which are used to extract features from unstructured text. We also discussed Bag-of-Words and Term Frequency-Inverse Document Frequency (TF-IDF).

In this chapter, you will learn how to use these extracted features to develop machine learning models. These models are capable of solving real-world problems such as detecting whether sentiments carried by texts are positive or negative, predicting whether emails are spam or not, and so on. We will also cover concepts such as supervised and unsupervised learning, classifications and regressions, the sampling and splitting of data, along with evaluating the performance of a model in depth. This chapter also discusses how to load and save these models for future use.

Machine Learning

Machine learning refers to the process of comprehending the patterns present in a dataset. It helps machines to learn from any given data and produce appropriate results, without being programmed explicitly. Basically, machine learning algorithms are fed with large amounts of data that they can work on and build a model. This model is later used by businesses to generate solutions that help them with analysis and building strategies for the future.

Machine learning is further categorized into **unsupervised** and **supervised** learning. Let's understand these in detail in the next section.

Unsupervised Learning

Unsupervised learning is the method by which algorithms tend to learn patterns within data that is not labeled. Since labels (supervisors) are absent, it is referred to as unsupervised learning. In unsupervised learning, you provide the algorithm with the feature data and it learns patterns from the data on its own.

Unsupervised learning is further classified into clustering and association:

- **Clustering**

  The data that is used for unsupervised learning is not labeled. For example, if there are 50 students who need to be categorized based on their attributes, we do not use any specific attribute(s) to create segments. Rather, we try to learn the hidden patterns that exist in their attributes and categorize them accordingly. This process is known as cluster analysis or clustering (one of the most popular types of unsupervised learning). When handed a set of text documents, we can divide them into groups that are similar with the help of clustering. A real-world example of clustering could be when you search for something in a search engine like Google, similar pages or links are recommended. These recommendations are powered by document clustering.

- **Association**

  Another type of unsupervised learning is association rule mining. We use association rule mining to obtain groups of items that occur together frequently. The most common use case of association rule mining is to identify customers' buying patterns. For example, in a particular supermarket, customers who tend to buy milk and bread, generally tend to buy cheese. This information can then be used to design supermarket layouts. The detailed theoretical explanations of these algorithms are beyond the scope of this chapter.

Now that you understand what unsupervised learning is and its types, in the next section, you will learn about different types of clustering.

Hierarchical Clustering

In this algorithm, we can vary the number of clusters as per our requirement. First, we construct a matrix consisting of distances between each pair of instances (data points). After that, we follow either of two approaches: **Agglomerative** (bottom-up) or **Divisive** (top-down) to construct a **dendrogram**. A dendrogram is a representation of clusters in the form of a tree based on the distances between them. We truncate the tree at a location corresponding to the number of clusters we need.

For example, if you have 10 documents, want to group them into a number of categories based on their attributes (the number of words they contain, the number of paragraphs, punctuation, and so on), and don't have any fixed number of categories in mind, it is a use case of hierarchical clustering. Firstly, the distances between each pair of documents from the set of 10 documents are calculated. Distance can be referred to as the inverse of similarity between documents. After that, we use either agglomerative (bottom-up) or divisive (top-down) to construct a dendrogram. Finally, we truncate the dendrogram at different places to get a suitable number of clusters.

In the next section, we will solve an exercise to get a better understanding of **hierarchical clustering**.

Exercise 29: Hierarchical Clustering

In this exercise, we will create four clusters from text documents of sklearn's "fetch_20 newsgroups" dataset. We will make use of hierarchical clustering. Once the clusters are created, we will compare them with their actual categories. Follow these steps to implement this exercise:

1. Open a Jupyter notebook.

2. Insert a new cell and add the following code to import the necessary libraries:

```
from sklearn.datasets import fetch_20newsgroups
from scipy.cluster.hierarchy import ward, dendrogram
import matplotlib as mpl
from scipy.cluster.hierarchy import fcluster
from sklearn.metrics.pairwise import cosine_similarity
import pandas as pd
import numpy as np
import matplotlib.pyplot as plt
%matplotlib inline
import re
import string
from nltk import word_tokenize
from nltk.corpus import stopwords
from nltk.stem import WordNetLemmatizer
from sklearn.feature_extraction.text import TfidfVectorizer
from collections import Counter
from pylab import *
import nltk
import warnings
warnings.filterwarnings('ignore')
```

3. Now, we will download a list of stop words and the **Wordnet** corpus from **nltk**. Insert a new cell and add the following code to implement this:

```
nltk.download('stopwords')
stop_words=stopwords.words('english')
stop_words=stop_words+list(string.printable)
nltk.download('wordnet')
lemmatizer=WordNetLemmatizer()
```

4. Now, we'll specify the categories of news articles we want to fetch by. Add the following code to do this:

```
categories= ['misc.forsale', 'sci.electronics', 'talk.religion.misc']
```

5. To fetch the dataset, we use the following lines of code:

```
news_data = fetch_20newsgroups(subset='train',
categories=categories,shuffle=True, random_state=42, download_if_
missing=True)
```

6. To view the data of the fetched content, add the following code:

```
news_data['data'][:5]
```

The preceding code generates the following output:

```
['From: Steve@Busop.cit.wayne.edu (Steve Teolis)\nSubject: Re: *** TurboGrafx System For SALE ***\nOrganiz
ation: Wayne State University\nLines: 38\nDistribution: na\nNNTP-Posting-Host: 141.217.75.24\n\n>TurboGraf
x-16 Base Unit (works like new) with:\n>        1 Controller\n>         AC Adapter\n>         Antenna hookup\n>
* Games:\n>         Kieth Courage\n>         Victory Run\n>         Fantasy Zone\n>         Military Madne
ss\n>         Battle Royal\n>         Legendary Axe\n>         Blazing Lasers\n>         Bloody Wolf\n>\n>
-------------------------------------\n>* Will sell games separately at $25 each\n>  ---------------------
------------------\n\nYour kidding, $210.00, man o man, you can buy the system new for $49.00 at \nElectro
nic Boutique and those games are only about $15 - $20.00 brand new.  \nMaybe you should think about that p
rice again if you REALLY need the money.\n\n\n\n\n\n                                      \n                \n
-=-=-=-=-=-=-=-=-=-=-=-\n                    Wayne State University        \n
\n                    Steve Teolis              \n                             6050 Cass Ave. #
238       \n                         Detroit, MI  48202         \n
\n                    Steve@Busop.cit.wayne.edu      \n                     -=-=-=-=-=-=-=-=-=
-=-=-=-\n',
```

Figure 3.1: The first five news articles

7. To check the categories of news articles, insert a new cell and add the following code:

```
news_data.target
```

The preceding code generates the following output:

$$array([0, 0, 1, ..., 0, 1, 0])$$

Figure 3.2: Enclosed target corresponding to news data

Here, **0** refers to **'misc.forsale'**, **1** refers to **'sci.electronics'**, and **2** refers to category **'talk.religion.misc'**.

8. To check the categories we are dealing with, add the following code:

```
news_data.target_names
```

The preceding code generates the following output:

```
['misc.forsale', 'sci.electronics', 'talk.religion.misc']
```

Figure 3.3: Target names corresponding to news data

9. To store **news_data** and the corresponding categories in a pandas DataFrame and view it, we write the following code:

```
news_data_df = pd.DataFrame({'text' : news_data['data'], 'category': news_data.target})
news_data_df.head()
```

The preceding code generates the following output:

	text	category
0	From: Steve@Busop.cit.wayne.edu (Steve Teolis)...	0
1	From: jks2x@holmes.acc.Virginia.EDU (Jason K. ...	0
2	From: wayne@uva386.schools.virginia.edu (Tony ...	1
3	From: lihan@ccwf.cc.utexas.edu (Bruce G. Bostw...	1
4	From: myoakam@cis.ohio-state.edu (micah r yoak...	0

Figure 3.4: Text corpus of news data corresponding to the categories in a dataframe

10. To count the number of occurrences of each category appearing in this dataset, we write the following code:

```
news_data_df['category'].value_counts()
```

The preceding code generates the following output:

```
1    591
0    585
2    377
Name: category, dtype: int64
```

Figure 3.5: The number of news articles present in each category

11. In the next step, we will use a lambda function to extract tokens from each 'text' of the **news_data_df** DataFrame, check whether any of these tokens are stop words, lemmatize them, and concatenate them side by side. We make use of the **join** function to concatenate a list of words into a single sentence. We use the regular expression (**re**) to replace anything other than alphabets, digits, and white spaces with blank space. Add the following code to do this:

```
news_data_df['cleaned_text'] = news_data_df['text'].apply(\
lambda x : ' '.join([lemmatizer.lemmatize(word.lower()) \
    for word in word_tokenize(re.sub(r'([^\s\w]|_)+', ' ', str(x))) if
word.lower() not in stop_words]))
```

12. Now, we'll create a **tf-idf** matrix and transform it to a DataFrame. Add the following code to do this:

```
tfidf_model = TfidfVectorizer(max_features=200)
tfidf_df = pd.DataFrame(tfidf_model.fit_transform(news_data_df['cleaned_
text']).todense())
tfidf_df.columns = sorted(tfidf_model.vocabulary_)
tfidf_df.head()
```

The preceding code generates the following output:

	00	10	100	12	14	15	16	20	25	30	...	well	wire	wiring	without	word	work	world	would
0	0.435655	0.0	0.000000	0.0	0.000000	0.127775	0.136811	0.127551	0.133311	0.0	...	0.0	0.0	0.0	0.0	0.0	0.113042	0.000000	0.000000
1	0.000000	0.0	0.000000	0.0	0.000000	0.294937	0.000000	0.000000	0.000000	0.0	...	0.0	0.0	0.0	0.0	0.0	0.000000	0.000000	0.000000
2	0.000000	0.0	0.000000	0.0	0.000000	0.000000	0.000000	0.000000	0.000000	0.0	...	0.0	0.0	0.0	0.0	0.0	0.000000	0.000000	0.000000
3	0.000000	0.0	0.000000	0.0	0.000000	0.000000	0.000000	0.000000	0.000000	0.0	...	0.0	0.0	0.0	0.0	0.0	0.000000	0.142267	0.106317
4	0.000000	0.0	0.207003	0.0	0.191897	0.182138	0.000000	0.000000	0.000000	0.0	...	0.0	0.0	0.0	0.0	0.0	0.000000	0.000000	0.000000

5 rows x 200 columns

Figure 3.6: TF-IDF representation as a DataFrame

13. In this step, we'll create a distance matrix by subtracting the cosine similarities of the **tf-idf** representation of documents from number 1. The **ward** function is used to create a linkage matrix, used in hierarchical clustering. Add the following code to do this:

```
dist = 1 - cosine_similarity(tfidf_df)
linkage_matrix = ward(dist)
```

14. Now, we'll truncate the **dendrogram** to keep the last four clusters. The leaves of a **dendrogram** refer to the individual instances that are data points. **leaf_rotation** denotes the angle by which leaf levels must be rotated. **leaf_font_size** denotes the font size of leaf labels. Add the following code to implement this:

```
#Truncating the Dendogram Truncation to show last 4 clusters
plt.title('Hierarchical Clustering using truncated Dendrogram')
plt.xlabel('clustered documents')
plt.ylabel('distance')
dendrogram(
    linkage_matrix,
    truncate_mode='lastp',   # showing only last p clusters after merging
    p=4,   # p is the number of cluster that should remain after merging
    leaf_rotation=90.,
    leaf_font_size=12.
    )
plt.show()
```

The preceding code generates the following output:

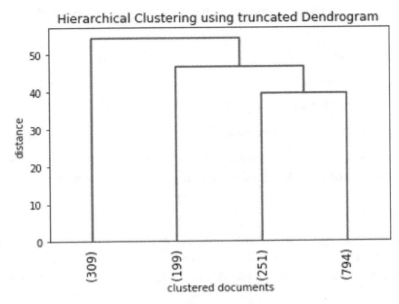

Figure 3.7: Truncated dendrogram

15. Now, we'll use the **fcluster()** function to obtain cluster labels of clusters obtained by hierarchical clustering:

```
k=4
clusters = fcluster(linkage_matrix, k, criterion='maxclust')
clusters
```

The preceding code generates the following output:

$$array([3, 3, 3, \ldots,4, 4, 1], dtype=int32)$$

Figure 3.8: Predicted cluster labels

16. Finally, we make use of the **crosstab** function of pandas to compare the clusters we have obtained with the actual categories of news articles. Add the following code to implement this:

```
news_data_df['obtained_clusters'] = clusters
pd.crosstab(news_data_df['category'].replace({0:'misc.forsale', 1:'sci.
electronics', 2:'talk.religion.misc'}),\
            news_data_df['obtained_clusters'].\
            replace({1 : 'cluster_1', 2 : 'cluster_2', 3 : 'cluster_3', 4:
'cluster_4'}))
```

The preceding code generates the following output:

obtained_clusters category	cluster_1	cluster_2	cluster_3	cluster_4
misc.forsale	155	0	230	200
sci.electronics	110	1	19	461
talk.religion.misc	44	198	2	133

Figure 3.9: Crosstab between actual categories and clusters obtained

You learned how to create clusters with the help of hierarchical clustering. In the next section, we will look at another form of clustering, that is, **K-means clustering**.

K-Means Clustering

In this algorithm, we segregate the given instances (data points) into k groups (here, k is a natural number). Firstly, we choose k centroids. We assign each instance to its nearest centroid, thereby creating k groups. This is the assignment phase. It is followed by the update phase.

In the update phase, new centroids for each of these k groups are calculated. The data points are reassigned to their nearest newly calculated centroids. The assignment phase and the update phase are carried on repeatedly until the assignment of data points no longer changes.

For example, suppose you have 10 documents. You want to group them into 3 categories based on their attributes, such as the number of words they contain, the number of paragraphs, punctuation, and so on. In this case, k is 3. Firstly, 3 centroids (means) need to be chosen. In the initialization phase, each of these 10 documents is assigned to one of these 3 categories, thereby forming 3 groups. In the update phase, the centroids of the 3 newly formed groups are calculated. To decide the optimal number of clusters, that is, k, we execute k-means clustering for various values of k and note down their performances (sum of squared errors). We try to select a small value for k having the lowest sum of squared errors. This method is called the **elbow method**.

In the next section, we will solve an exercise to get a better understanding of k-means clustering.

Exercise 30: K-Means Clustering

In this exercise, we will create four clusters from text documents in sklearn's "fetch_20 newsgroups" text dataset using k-means clustering. We will compare these clusters with the actual categories and use the elbow method to obtain the optimal number of clusters. Follow these steps to implement this exercise:

1. Open a Jupyter notebook.

2. Insert a new cell and add the following code to import the necessary packages:

```python
import pandas as pd
from sklearn.datasets import fetch_20newsgroups
import matplotlib.pyplot as plt
%matplotlib inline
import re
import string
from nltk import word_tokenize
from nltk.corpus import stopwords
from nltk.stem import WordNetLemmatizer
from sklearn.feature_extraction.text import TfidfVectorizer
from collections import Counter
from pylab import *
import nltk
import warnings
warnings.filterwarnings('ignore')
import seaborn as sns;
sns.set()
import numpy as np
from scipy.spatial.distance import cdist
from sklearn.cluster import KMeans
```

3. We will be using stop words from the English language only. Also, we will use the **wordnet** corpus for lemmatization. Add the following code to implement this:

```python
stop_words = stopwords.words('english')
stop_words = stop_words + list(string.printable)
lemmatizer = WordNetLemmatizer()
```

4. To specify the categories of news articles we want to fetch by, add the following code:

```python
categories= ['misc.forsale', 'sci.electronics', 'talk.religion.misc']
```

5. To fetch the dataset, we use the following lines of code:

```python
news_data = fetch_20newsgroups(subset='train', categories=categories,
shuffle=True, random_state=42, download_if_missing=True)
```

6. Now, we'll make use of the **lambda** function to extract tokens from each 'text' of the **news_data_df** dataframe. Also, we'll check whether any of these tokens are stop words, lemmatize them, and concatenate them side by side. We'll use the join function to concatenate a list of words into a single sentence. We'll use the regular expression (re) to replace anything other than alphabets, digits, and white spaces with blank space. Add the following code to do this:

```
news_data_df['cleaned_text'] = news_data_df['text'].apply(\
lambda x : ' '.join([lemmatizer.lemmatize(word.lower()) \
    for word in word_tokenize(re.sub(r'([^\s\w]|_)+', ' ', str(x))) if
word.lower() not in stop_words]))
```

7. The following lines of code are used to create a tf-idf matrix and transform it into a dataframe:

```
tfidf_model=TfidfVectorizer(max_features=200)tfidf_df=pd.DataFrame(tfidf_
model.fit_transform(news_data_df['cleaned_text']).todense())tfidf_
df.columns=sorted(tfidf_model.vocabulary_)tfidf_df.head()
```

The preceding code generates the following output:

	00	10	100	12	14	15	16	20	25	30	...	well	wire	wiring	without	word
0	0.435655	0.0	0.000000	0.0	0.000000	0.127775	0.136811	0.127551	0.133311	0.0	...	0.0	0.0	0.0	0.0	0.0
1	0.000000	0.0	0.000000	0.0	0.000000	0.294937	0.000000	0.000000	0.000000	0.0	...	0.0	0.0	0.0	0.0	0.0
2	0.000000	0.0	0.000000	0.0	0.000000	0.000000	0.000000	0.000000	0.000000	0.0	...	0.0	0.0	0.0	0.0	0.0
3	0.000000	0.0	0.000000	0.0	0.000000	0.000000	0.000000	0.000000	0.000000	0.0	...	0.0	0.0	0.0	0.0	0.0
4	0.000000	0.0	0.207003	0.0	0.191897	0.182138	0.000000	0.000000	0.000000	0.0	...	0.0	0.0	0.0	0.0	0.0

5 rows × 200 columns

Figure 3.10: TF-IDF representation as a DataFrame

8. In this step, we are using the **KMeans** function of sklearn to create four clusters from a tf-idf representation of news articles. Add the following code to do this:

```
kmeans = KMeans(n_clusters=4)
kmeans.fit(tfidf_df)
y_kmeans = kmeans.predict(tfidf_df)
news_data_df['obtained_clusters'] = y_kmeans
```

9. We use pandas' crosstab function to compare the clusters we have obtained with the actual categories of the news articles. Add the following code to do this:

```
pd.crosstab(news_data_df['category'].replace({0:'misc.forsale', 1:'sci.
electronics', 2:'talk.religion.misc'}),\
            news_data_df['obtained_clusters'].replace({0 : 'cluster_1', 1
: 'cluster_2', 2 : 'cluster_3', 3: 'cluster_4'}))
```

The preceding code generates the following output:

obtained_clusters	cluster_1	cluster_2	cluster_3	cluster_4
category				
misc.forsale	350	1	98	136
sci.electronics	9	0	420	162
talk.religion.misc	0	230	69	78

Figure 3.11: Crosstab between actual categories and obtained clusters

10. Finally, to obtain the optimal value of k, that is, the number of clusters, we execute the k-means algorithm for values of k ranging from **1** to **6**. For each value of **k**, we store the distortion, that is, the mean of distances of documents from their nearest cluster center. We look for the value of k where the slope of the plot changes rapidly. Add the following code to implement this:

```
distortions = []
K = range(1,6)
for k in K:
    kmeanModel = KMeans(n_clusters=k)
    kmeanModel.fit(tfidf_df)
    distortions.append(sum(np.min(cdist(tfidf_df, kmeanModel.cluster_
centers_, 'euclidean'), \
                       axis=1)) / tfidf_df.shape[0])

plt.plot(K, distortions, 'bx-')
plt.xlabel('k')
plt.ylabel('Distortion')
plt.title('The Elbow Method showing the optimal number of clusters')
plt.show()
```

The preceding code generates the following output:

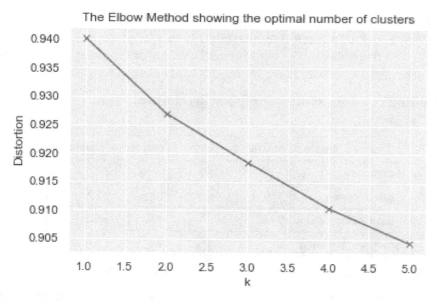

Figure 3.12: Optimal clusters represented in a graph using the elbow method

From the preceding figure, we can conclude that the optimal number of clusters is two. You have learned how to create clusters and find the optimal number of clusters with the help of k-means clustering. In the next section, you will learn about supervised learning.

Supervised Learning

Supervised learning algorithms need labeled data. They learn how to automatically generate labels or predict values by analyzing various features of the data provided. If you have already starred important text messages in your phone and want to automate the task of going through all your messages daily, considering they are important and marked already, then this is a use case for supervised learning. Here, messages starred previously can be used as labeled data. Using this data, we can create two types of models that are:

- Capable of classifying whether new messages are important

- Capable of predicting the probability of new messages being important

The first type is called classification, and the second type is called regression. You will learn more about them in the next section.

Classification

If you have two types of food—type 1 tastes sweet, and type 2 tastes salty—and you need to determine how an unknown food will taste—using various attributes of the food, such as color, fragrance, shape, and ingredients—this is an instance of classification.

Here, the two classes are: class 1, which tastes sweet, and class 2, which tastes salty. Features used in this classification are color, fragrance, the ingredients used to prepare the dish, and so on. These features are called independent variables. The class (according to whether the taste is sweet or salty) is called a dependent variable.

Formally, classification algorithms are those that learn patterns from a given dataset to determine classes of unknown datasets. Some of the most widely used classification algorithms are logistic regression, Naive Bayes, K-nearest neighbor, and tree methods. Let's learn about each of them in the next section.

Logistic Regression

Despite having the term "regression" in it, logistic regression is used for probabilistic classification. In this case, the dependent variable that is the outcome is qualitative. Generally, its values can be represented by 0 or 1. For example, you need to decide whether an email is spam or not. Here, the value of the decision (the dependent variable, that is, the outcome) can be considered to be 1 if the email is spam, otherwise it will be 0. The independent variables (that is, the features) will consist of various attributes of the email, such as the number of occurrences of certain keywords and so on.

Naive Bayes Classifiers

Just like logistic regression, a naive Bayes classifier is another kind of probabilistic classifier. It is based on Bayes' Theorem, which is shown here:

$$P(A/B) = \frac{P(B/A)P(A)}{P(B)}$$

In the preceding formula, A and B are events and $P(B)$ is not equal to 0. $P(A/B)$ is the probability of event A occurring given that event B is true. $P(B)$ is the probability of occurrence of event B.

Say there is an online platform where students register themselves and opt for elective books and these activities are handled by two different departments, a student facing difficulty with either of these two steps can raise an issue. The issues raised by students are raw texts that need to be classified into two classes (namely, registration issues and book-related issues) to assign them to the concerned department. This is a use case for a Naive Bayes classifier.

K-Nearest Neighbors

K-nearest neighbors is a type of non-parametric instance-based lazy learning. There is a saying that goes "birds of a feather flock together." This means that people who have similar interests prefer to stay close to each other and form groups. This characteristic is called **homophily**. We can make use of this fact for classification.

To classify an unknown object, k number of other objects located nearest to it with class labels will be looked into. The class occurring in majority among them will be assigned to it that is the object with unknown class. When dealing with text data, for a given document, we interpret "nearest neighbors" as other documents that are the most similar to it.

Now that we have an understanding of different types of classification, in the next section, we will solve an exercise based on text classification.

Exercise 31: Text Classification (Logistic regression, Naive Bayes, and KNN)

In this exercise, we will classify reviews of musical instruments on Amazon with the help of various classification algorithms, such as logistic regression, Naïve Bayes, and KNN. Follow these steps to implement this exercise:

1. Open a Jupyter notebook.

2. Insert a new cell and add the following code to import the necessary packages:

```
import pandas as pd
import matplotlib.pyplot as plt
%matplotlib inline
import re
import string
from nltk import word_tokenize
from nltk.stem import WordNetLemmatizer
from sklearn.feature_extraction.text import TfidfVectorizer
from collections import Counter
from pylab import *
import nltk
import warnings
warnings.filterwarnings('ignore')
```

3. Now, we will read the data file in JSON format using pandas. Add the following code to implement this:

```
review_data = pd.read_json('data_ch3/reviews_Musical_Instruments_5.json',
lines=True)
review_data[['reviewText', 'overall']].head()
```

The preceding code generates the following output:

	reviewText	overall
0	Not much to write about here, but it does exac...	5
1	The product does exactly as it should and is q...	5
2	The primary job of this device is to block the...	5
3	Nice windscreen protects my MXL mic and preven...	5
4	This pop filter is great. It looks and perform...	5

Figure 3.13: Data stored in a DataFrame

4. We'll use a lambda function to extract tokens from each **'reviewText'** of this DataFrame, lemmatize them, and concatenate them side by side. We use the **join** function to concatenate a list of words into a single sentence. We use the regular expression (**re**) to replace anything other than alphabets, digits, and white spaces with blank space. Add the following code to implement this:

```
lemmatizer = WordNetLemmatizer()
review_data['cleaned_review_text'] = review_data['reviewText'].apply(\
lambda x : ' '.join([lemmatizer.lemmatize(word.lower()) \
    for word in word_tokenize(re.sub(r'([^\s\w]|_)+', ' ', str(x)))]))
```

5. Now, we'll create a DataFrame from the TFIDF matrix representation of the cleaned version of **reviewText**. Add the following code to implement this:

```
review_data[['cleaned_review_text', 'reviewText', 'overall']].head()
```

The preceding code generates the following output:

	cleaned_review_text	reviewText	overall
0	not much to write about here but it doe exactl...	Not much to write about here, but it does exac...	5
1	the product doe exactly a it should and is qui...	The product does exactly as it should and is q...	5
2	the primary job of this device is to block the...	The primary job of this device is to block the...	5
3	nice windscreen protects my mxl mic and preven...	Nice windscreen protects my XML mic and preven...	5
4	this pop filter is great it look and performs ...	This pop filter is great. It looks and perform...	5

Figure 3.14: Review texts before and after cleaning, with their overall scores

6. Now, we'll create a tf-idf matrix and transform it into a DataFrame. Add the following code to do this:

```
tfidf_model = TfidfVectorizer(max_features=500)
tfidf_df = pd.DataFrame(tfidf_model.fit_transform(review_data['cleaned_
review_text']).todense())
tfidf_df.columns = sorted(tfidf_model.vocabulary_)
tfidf_df.head()
```

The preceding code generates the following output:

	10	100	12	20	34	able	about	accurate	acoustic	actually	...	won	work	worked	worth	would	wrong	year	yet	you	you
0	0.0	0.0	0.0	0.0	0.0	0.000000	0.159684	0.0	0.0	0.0	...	0.0	0.134327	0.0	0.0	0.000000	0.0	0.0	0.0	0.000000	0.00000
1	0.0	0.0	0.0	0.0	0.0	0.000000	0.000000	0.0	0.0	0.0	...	0.0	0.085436	0.0	0.0	0.000000	0.0	0.0	0.0	0.067074	0.00000
2	0.0	0.0	0.0	0.0	0.0	0.000000	0.000000	0.0	0.0	0.0	...	0.0	0.000000	0.0	0.0	0.115312	0.0	0.0	0.0	0.079880	0.11198
3	0.0	0.0	0.0	0.0	0.0	0.339573	0.000000	0.0	0.0	0.0	...	0.0	0.000000	0.0	0.0	0.000000	0.0	0.0	0.0	0.000000	0.00000
4	0.0	0.0	0.0	0.0	0.0	0.000000	0.000000	0.0	0.0	0.0	...	0.0	0.000000	0.0	0.0	0.000000	0.0	0.0	0.0	0.303608	0.00000

Figure 3.15: A TF-IDF representation as a DataFrame

7. The following lines of code are used to create a new column target, which will have 0 if the "**overall**" parameter is less than **4**, and 1 otherwise. Add the following code to implement this:

```
review_data['target'] = review_data['overall'].apply(lambda x : 0 if x<=4
else 1)
review_data['target'].value_counts()
```

The preceding code generates the following output:

```
1    6938
0    3323
Name: target, dtype: int64
```

Figure 3.16: The number of occurrences of each target value

8. Now, we will use sklearn's **LogisticRegression()** function to fit a logistic regression model on the TF-IDF representation of these reviews after cleaning. Add the following code to implement this:

```
from sklearn.linear_model import LogisticRegression
logreg = LogisticRegression()
logreg.fit(tfidf_df,review_data['target'])
predicted_labels = logreg.predict(tfidf_df)
logreg.predict_proba(tfidf_df)[:,1]
```

The preceding code generates the following output:

```
array([0.57128804, 0.68592538, 0.56024427, ..., 0.65982122, 0.55011385,
       0.21210023])
```

Figure 3.17: Output of logistic regression

9. We further use the **crosstab** function of pandas to compare the results of our classification model with the actual classes ('**target**' in this case) of the reviews. Add the following code to do this:

```
review_data['predicted_labels'] = predicted_labels
pd.crosstab(review_data['target'], review_data['predicted_labels'])
```

The preceding code generates the following output:

predicted_labels	0	1
target		
0	1543	1780
1	626	6312

Figure 3.18: Crosstab between actual target values and predicted labels

10. In this step, we'll be using sklearn's **GaussianNB()** function to fit a Gaussian Naive Bayes model on the TF-IDF representation of these reviews after cleaning. Add the following code to do this:

```
from sklearn.naive_bayes import GaussianNB
nb = GaussianNB()
nb.fit(tfidf_df,review_data['target'])
predicted_labels = nb.predict(tfidf_df)
nb.predict_proba(tfidf_df)[:,1]
```

The preceding code generates the following output:

```
array([9.97730158e-01, 3.63599675e-09, 9.45692105e-07, ...,
       2.46001047e-02, 3.43660991e-08, 1.72767906e-27])
```

Figure 3.19: Predicted values using a Naive Bayes model

11. We further use the **crosstab** function of pandas to compare the results of our classification model with the actual classes (**'target'** in this case) of the reviews. Add the following code to do this:

```
review_data['predicted_labels_nb'] = predicted_labels
pd.crosstab(review_data['target'], review_data['predicted_labels_nb'])
```

The preceding code generates the following output:

predicted_labels_nb	0	1
target		
0	2333	990
1	2380	4558

Figure 3.20: Crosstab between actual target values and predicted labels

12. Now, we'll be using sklearn's **KNeighborsClassifier()** function to fit a 3-Nearest Neighbour model on the TF-IDF representation of these reviews after cleaning. We'll further use the crosstab function of pandas to compare the results of our classification model with the actual classes (that is, **'target'** in this case) of the reviews:

```
from sklearn.neighbors import KNeighborsClassifier
knn = KNeighborsClassifier(n_neighbors=3)
knn.fit(tfidf_df,review_data['target'])
review_data['predicted_labels_knn'] = knn.predict(tfidf_df)
pd.crosstab(review_data['target'], review_data['predicted_labels_knn'])
```

The preceding code generates the following output:

predicted_labels_knn	0	1
target		
0	2594	729
1	375	6563

Figure 3.21: Crosstab between actual target values and predicted labels by KNN

Here, we see **2594** instances with the target label as 0 correctly classified and **729** such instances wrongly classified. Furthermore, **6563** instances with the target label as **1** are correctly classified, whereas 375 such instances are wrongly classified.

You have just learned how to perform text classification with the help of various classification algorithms. In the next section, you will learn about regression, which is another type of supervised learning.

Regression

Let's understand regression with a practical example. If you have photos of several people, along with their age, and need to predict the ages of some other people from their photos, this is a use case for regression.

In the case of regression, the dependent variable, that is, the age in this example, is continuous. The independent variables, that is, features, consist of attributes of the images such as the color intensity of each pixel. Formally, regression analysis refers to the process of learning a mapping function, which relates features or predictors (inputs) to the dependent variable (output).

There are various types of regression: **univariate**, **multivariate**, **simple**, **multiple**, **linear**, **non-linear**, **polynomial regression**, **stepwise regression**, **ridge regression**, **lasso regression**, and **elastic net regression**.

If there is just one dependent variable, then it is referred to as univariate regression. On the other hand, two or more dependent variables constitute multivariate regression. Simple regression has only one predictor variable, that is, a feature. Multivariate regression has more than one predictor variable. In the next section, we will cover linear regression in detail.

Linear Regression

Let's understand what the term "linear" means. Here, the term "linear" refers to the linearity of parameters. Parameters are the coefficients of predictor variables in the linear regression equation. The following formula represents the linear regression equation:

$$y = \beta_0 + \beta_1 X + \in$$

Here, y is termed a dependent variable (output); it is continuous. X is an independent variable or feature (input). 0 and 1 are parameters. is the error component, which is the difference between the actual and predicted values of y. In the next section, we will solve an exercise to get a better understanding of regression analysis.

Exercise 32: Regression Analysis Using Textual Data

In this exercise, we will use regression to predict the overall scores of reviews of musical instruments on Amazon. Follow these steps to implement this exercise:

1. Open a Jupyter notebook.

2. Insert a new cell and add the following code to import the necessary packages:

```
import pandas as pd
import matplotlib.pyplot as plt
%matplotlib inline
import re
import string
from nltk import word_tokenize
from nltk.stem import WordNetLemmatizer
from sklearn.feature_extraction.text import TfidfVectorizer
from collections import Counter
from pylab import *
import nltk
import warnings
warnings.filterwarnings('ignore')
```

3. Now, we'll read the given data file in the **json** format using **pandas**. Add the following code to implement this:

```
review_data = pd.read_json('data_ch3/reviews_Musical_Instruments_5.json',
lines=True)
review_data[['reviewText', 'overall']].head()
```

The preceding code generates the following output:

	reviewText	overall
0	Not much to write about here, but it does exac...	5
1	The product does exactly as it should and is q...	5
2	The primary job of this device is to block the...	5
3	Nice windscreen protects my XML mic and preven...	5
4	This pop filter is great. It looks and perform...	5

Figure 3.22: Reviews of musical instruments stored as a DataFrame

4. We make use of a lambda function to extract tokens from each **'reviewText'** of this DataFrame, lemmatize them, and concatenate them side by side. We use the join function to concatenate a list of words into a single sentence. We use the regular expression (re) to replace anything other than alphabets, digits, and white spaces with blank space. Add the following code to implement this:

```
lemmatizer = WordNetLemmatizer()
review_data['cleaned_review_text'] = review_data['reviewText'].apply(\
lambda x : ' '.join([lemmatizer.lemmatize(word.lower()) \
    for word in word_tokenize(re.sub(r'([^\s\w]|_)+', ' ', str(x)))]))
review_data[['cleaned_review_text', 'reviewText', 'overall']].head()
```

The preceding code generates the following output:

	cleaned_review_text	reviewText	overall
0	not much to write about here but it doe exactl...	Not much to write about here, but it does exac...	5
1	the product doe exactly a it should and is qui...	The product does exactly as it should and is q...	5
2	the primary job of this device is to block the...	The primary job of this device is to block the...	5
3	nice windscreen protects my mxl mic and preven...	Nice windscreen protects my XML mic and preven...	5
4	this pop filter is great it look and performs ...	This pop filter is great. It looks and perform...	5

Figure 3.23: Review texts before and after cleaning along with their overall scores

5. Now we'll create a DataFrame from the TFIDF matrix representation of cleaned **reviewText**. Add the following code to do this:

```
tfidf_model = TfidfVectorizer(max_features=500)
tfidf_df = pd.DataFrame(tfidf_model.fit_transform(review_data['cleaned_
review_text']).todense())
tfidf_df.columns = sorted(tfidf_model.vocabulary_)
tfidf_df.head()
```

The preceding code generates the following output:

	10	100	12	20	34	able	about	accurate	acoustic	actually	...	won	work	worked	worth	would	wrong	year	yet	you	you
0	0.0	0.0	0.0	0.0	0.0	0.000000	0.159684	0.0	0.0	0.0	...	0.0	0.134327	0.0	0.0	0.000000	0.0	0.0	0.0	0.000000	0.00000
1	0.0	0.0	0.0	0.0	0.0	0.000000	0.000000	0.0	0.0	0.0	...	0.0	0.085436	0.0	0.0	0.000000	0.0	0.0	0.0	0.067074	0.00000
2	0.0	0.0	0.0	0.0	0.0	0.000000	0.000000	0.0	0.0	0.0	...	0.0	0.000000	0.0	0.0	0.115312	0.0	0.0	0.0	0.079880	0.11198
3	0.0	0.0	0.0	0.0	0.0	0.339573	0.000000	0.0	0.0	0.0	...	0.0	0.000000	0.0	0.0	0.000000	0.0	0.0	0.0	0.000000	0.00000
4	0.0	0.0	0.0	0.0	0.0	0.000000	0.000000	0.0	0.0	0.0	...	0.0	0.000000	0.0	0.0	0.000000	0.0	0.0	0.0	0.303608	0.00000

5 rows x 500 columns

Figure 3.24: TF-IDF representation as a DataFrame

6. We will use sklearn's **LinearRegression()** function to fit a linear regression model on this TF-IDF dataframe. Add the following code to do this:

```
from sklearn.linear_model import LinearRegression
linreg = LinearRegression()
linreg.fit(tfidf_df,review_data['overall'])
linreg.coef_
```

The preceding code generates the following output:

```
array([-1.93271993e-01,   5.65226131e-01,   5.63243687e-01,  -1.84418658e-01,
        -6.32257431e-02,   3.05320627e-01,   4.95264614e-01,   5.21333693e-01,
         2.65736989e-01,   4.00058256e-01,   5.64020424e-01,   7.56022958e-01,
         1.00174846e-02,  -3.06429115e-01,  -3.12104234e-01,   3.38294736e-01,
        -6.05747380e-01,  -1.04123996e-01,   5.58669738e-02,  -1.13320890e-01,
         4.79471129e-01,   1.49528459e-01,   7.79094545e-01,  -3.63399268e-01,
         1.25993539e-01,  -6.29415062e-02,   4.94517373e-01,  -3.34989132e-01,
         2.55374355e-01,   8.84676972e-02,  -3.68013360e-01,  -1.09910777e-01,
        -7.09777794e-03,  -5.15547511e-02,   1.17415090e-01,  -8.89213726e-02,
         1.06398798e+00,  -1.19791236e+00,  -1.14906460e+00,   1.55215016e-01,
        -5.05283241e-01,   2.43200389e-01,   8.56413437e-02,  -3.74044994e-02,
        -7.31390217e-03,   9.63911076e-01,  -7.82062558e-02,   1.50616236e-01,
        -9.35299622e-02,   1.87239631e-02,   9.34145997e-02,   1.18038260e+00,
        -3.79855115e-01,   4.51076351e-02,   1.11808544e-01,   7.22506502e-03,
         3.60057791e-01,   2.35459334e-01,   1.15359278e-01,  -2.48993670e-01,
         1.34437898e-01,  -2.99424905e-01,  -1.00687767e-01,  -3.10436924e-01,
         2.44420457e-02,   1.34593395e-01,   1.52613968e-01,   1.14304224e-01,
         8.46643557e-02,  -9.06292369e-02,   1.88909690e-01,   1.71488133e-01,
```

Figure 3.25: Coefficients of the linear regression model

7. To check the intercept of the linear regression, type the following code:

```
linreg.intercept_
```

The preceding code generates the following output:

```
4.218882428983381
```

Figure 3.26: Intercept of the linear regression model

8. To check the prediction in a tf-idf DataFrame, we write the following code:

```
linreg.predict(tfidf_df)
```

```
array([4.19200071, 4.25771652, 4.23084868, ..., 4.40384767, 4.4936403,
       4.14797976])
```

Figure 3.27: Predictions of the linear regression model

9. Finally, we use this model to predict the 'overall' score and store it in a column called 'predicted_score_from_linear_regression'. Add the following code to implement this:

```
review_data['predicted_score_from_linear_regression'] = linreg.
predict(tfidf_df)
review_data[['overall', 'predicted_score_from_linear_regression']].
head(10)
```

The preceding code generates the following output:

	overall	predicted_score_from_linear_regression
0	5	4.192001
1	5	4.257717
2	5	4.230849
3	5	4.085927
4	5	4.851061
5	5	4.955069
6	5	4.446274
7	3	3.888593
8	5	4.941788
9	5	4.513824

Figure 3.28: Actual scores and predictions of the linear regression model

From the preceding table, we can see how the actual and predicted score varies for different instances. We will use this table later to evaluate the performance of the model.

You have just learned how to perform regression analysis on given data. In the next section, you will learn about tree methods.

Tree Methods

There are several algorithms that have both classification and regression forms. Tree-based methods are instances of such cases. What does tree mean here? In the context of machine learning, tree refers to a structure that aids decision-making. Thus, it is known as **decision tree**.

As before, if there is an online platform where students register themselves and opt for elective books, and these activities are handled by two different departments, a student facing difficulties with either of those two steps can raise an issue. The issues raised by students are raw texts that need be classified into two classes, namely, registration issues and book-related issues, to assign them to the concerned department. The following figure depicts a decision tree:

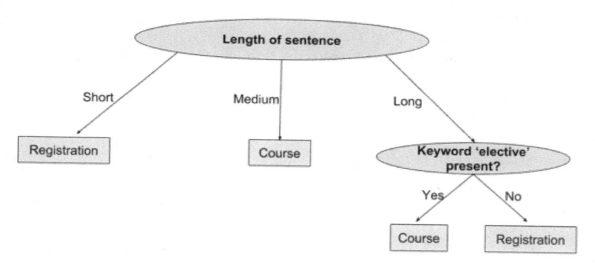

Figure 3.29: Decision tree

In the preceding figure, the first decision is made based on the length of sentence. If the length of the sentence is short it is classified as Registration and if it is medium then it is classified as Book. Similarly, if the length is long, we look for keywords present in it. If the 'elective' keyword is present, it belongs to **Course**, otherwise, it belongs to **Registration**.

Random Forest

Imagine you have to decide whether to join a particular university or not. In one scenario, you ask only one person about the quality of education the university provides. In another scenario, you ask several career counselors and academicians about this. Which scenario do you think would help you to make a better and the most stable decision? The second one, right? This is because, in the first case, the only person you are consulting may be biased. "Wisdom of the crowd" tends to remove biases, thereby aiding better decision-making.

In general terms, a forest is a collection of different types of trees. The same definition holds true in the case of machine learning as well. Instead of using a single decision tree for prediction, we use several of them.

In the scenario described earlier, the first case is equivalent to using a single decision tree, whereas the second one is equivalent to using several, that is, using a forest. In a random forest, an individual tree's vote impacts the final decision. Just like decision trees, random forest is capable of carrying out classification and regression tasks.

An advantage of the random forest algorithm is that it uses a sampling technique called bagging, which prevents **overfitting**. Overfitting refers to cases where a model learns the training dataset so well that it is unable to generalize or perform well on a validation/test dataset. They also aid in understanding the importance of predictor variables and features. However, building a random forest often takes a huge amount of time and memory.

GBM and XGBoost

There are various other tree-based algorithms, such as **gradient boosting machines** (GBM) and **extreme gradient boosting** (XGBoost). In GBM, weak learners are identified. It consists of key elements such as loss function and decision trees. Here, loss function needs to be optimized. Decision trees act as weak learners. More and more decision trees (weak learners) are added to the existing model, which often results in overfitting. To avoid this, an enhanced version of it, called XGBoost, is used. XGBoost uses various regularization parameters to avoid overfitting.

The main reasons for the popularity of XGBoost are the following:

- Capability to automatically deal with missing values

- High speed of execution

- High accuracy, if properly trained

- Support for distributed frameworks such as Hadoop and Spark

XGBoost uses a weighted combination of weak learners during the training phase. In the next section, we will look at an exercise wherein the practical implementation of all of the tree methods is provided.

Exercise 33: Tree-Based Methods (Decision Tree, Random Forest, GBM, and XGBoost)

In this exercise, we will use tree-based methods such as decision trees, random forests, GBM, and XGBoost to predict the overall scores and labels of reviews of patio, lawn, and garden on Amazon. Follow these steps to implement this exercise:

1. Open a Jupyter notebook.

2. Insert a new cell and add the following code to import the necessary packages:

```
import pandas as pd
import matplotlib.pyplot as plt
%matplotlib inline
import re
import string
from nltk import word_tokenize
from nltk.stem import WordNetLemmatizer
from sklearn.feature_extraction.text import TfidfVectorizer
from collections import Counter
from pylab import *
import nltk
import warnings
warnings.filterwarnings('ignore')
```

3. Now, we'll read the given data file in **json** format using **pandas**. Add the following code to implement this:

```
data_patio_lawn_garden = pd.read_json('data_ch3/reviews_Patio_Lawn_and_
Garden_5.json', lines = True)
data_patio_lawn_garden[['reviewText', 'overall']].head()
```

The preceding code generates the following output:

	reviewText	overall
0	Good USA company that stands behind their prod...	4
1	This is a high quality 8 ply hose. I have had ...	5
2	It's probably one of the best hoses I've ever ...	4
3	I probably should have bought something a bit ...	5
4	I bought three of these 5/8-inch Flexogen hose...	5

Figure 3.30: Storing reviews as a DdataFrame

4. We will be using WordNet corpus for lemmatization. Add the following code to do this:

```
lemmatizer = WordNetLemmatizer()
```

5. We'll make use of a lambda function to extract tokens from each '**reviewText**' of this DataFrame, lemmatize them, and concatenate them side by side. We'll use the join function to concatenate a list of words into a single sentence. We'll use the regular expression (re) to replace anything other than letters, digits, and white spaces with blank space. Add the following code to do this:

```
data_patio_lawn_garden['cleaned_review_text'] = data_patio_lawn_
garden['reviewText'].apply(\
lambda x : ' '.join([lemmatizer.lemmatize(word.lower()) \
    for word in word_tokenize(re.sub(r'([^\s\w]|_)+', ' ', str(x)))]))
data_patio_lawn_garden[['cleaned_review_text', 'reviewText', 'overall']].
head()
```

The preceding code generates the following output:

	cleaned_review_text	reviewText	overall
0	good usa company that stand behind their produ...	Good USA company that stands behind their prod...	4
1	this is a high quality 8 ply hose i have had g....	This is a high quality 8 ply hose. I have had ...	5
2	it s probably one of the best hose i ve ever h...	It's probably one of the best hoses I've ever ...	4
3	i probably should have bought something a bit ...	I probably should have bought something a bit ...	5
4	i bought three of these 5 8 inch flexogen hose...	I bought three of these 5/8-inch Flexogen hose...	5

Figure 3.31: Review text before and after cleaning, along with overall scores

6. We will be creating a DataFrame from the TFIDF matrix representation of the cleaned version of **reviewText**. Add the following code to do this:

```
tfidf_model = TfidfVectorizer(max_features=500)
tfidf_df = pd.DataFrame(tfidf_model.fit_transform(data_patio_lawn_
garden['cleaned_review_text']).todense())
tfidf_df.columns = sorted(tfidf_model.vocabulary_)
tfidf_df.head()
```

The preceding code generates the following output:

	10	20	34	8217	able	about	actually	add	after	again	...	work	worked	working	worth	would	yard	year	yet	you	you
0	0.0	0.0	0.0	0.0	0.0	0.000000	0.0	0.0	0.120568	0.0	...	0.0	0.0	0.0	0.0	0.0	0.000000	0.0	0.000000	0.161561	0.00000
1	0.0	0.0	0.0	0.0	0.0	0.000000	0.0	0.0	0.000000	0.0	...	0.0	0.0	0.0	0.0	0.0	0.000000	0.0	0.000000	0.000000	0.00000
2	0.0	0.0	0.0	0.0	0.0	0.000000	0.0	0.0	0.000000	0.0	...	0.0	0.0	0.0	0.0	0.0	0.116566	0.0	0.216988	0.000000	0.04935
3	0.0	0.0	0.0	0.0	0.0	0.000000	0.0	0.0	0.000000	0.0	...	0.0	0.0	0.0	0.0	0.0	0.000000	0.0	0.000000	0.000000	0.00000
4	0.0	0.0	0.0	0.0	0.0	0.064347	0.0	0.0	0.070857	0.0	...	0.0	0.0	0.0	0.0	0.0	0.083019	0.0	0.000000	0.000000	0.00000

5 rows x 500 columns

Figure 3.32: TF-IDF representation as a DataFrame

7. The following lines of code are used to create a new column target, which will have 0 if the 'overall' parameter is less than 4, otherwise, it will have 1:

```
data_patio_lawn_garden['target'] = data_patio_lawn_garden['overall'].
apply(lambda x : 0 if x<=4 else 1)
data_patio_lawn_garden['target'].value_counts()
```

The preceding code generates the following output:

```
1    7037
0    6235
Name: target, dtype: int64
```

Figure 3.33: Number of times each value of the target occurs

8. We will be using sklearn's **tree()** function to fit a decision tree classification model on the TF-IDF dataframe created earlier. Add the following code to do this:

```
from sklearn import tree
dtc = tree.DecisionTreeClassifier()
dtc = dtc.fit(tfidf_df, data_patio_lawn_garden['target'])
data_patio_lawn_garden['predicted_labels_dtc'] = dtc.predict(tfidf_df)
```

9. We'll use the crosstab function of pandas to compare the results of our classification model with the actual classes ('**target**' in this case) of the reviews. Add the following code to do this:

```
pd.crosstab(data_patio_lawn_garden['target'], data_patio_lawn_
garden['predicted_labels_dtc'])
```

The preceding code generates the following output:

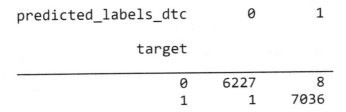

Figure 3.34: Crosstab between actual target values and predicted labels

Here, we see **6627** instances with a target label of **0** correctly classified, and **8** such instances wrongly classified. Furthermore, **7036** instances with a target label of **1** are correctly classified, whereas 1 such instance is wrongly classified.

10. We will use sklearn's **tree()** function to fit a decision tree regression model on the TF-IDF representation of these reviews after cleaning. We'll predict the overall scores using this model. Add the following code to do this:

```
from sklearn import tree
dtr = tree.DecisionTreeRegressor()
dtr = dtr.fit(tfidf_df, data_patio_lawn_garden['overall'])
data_patio_lawn_garden['predicted_values_dtr'] = dtr.predict(tfidf_df)
data_patio_lawn_garden[['predicted_values_dtr', 'overall']].head(10)
```

The previous code generates the following output:

	predicted_values_dtr	overall
0	4.0	4
1	5.0	5
2	4.0	4
3	5.0	5
4	5.0	5
5	5.0	5
6	5.0	5
7	5.0	5
8	5.0	5
9	4.0	4

Figure 3.35: Overall scores with predicted values

From the preceding table, we can see how the actual and predicted score varies for different instances. We will use this table later to evaluate the performance of the model.

11. Now, we'll define a generic function for all classifier models. Add the following code to do this:

```
def clf_model(model_type, X_train, y):
    model = model_type.fit(X_train,y)
    predicted_labels = model.predict(tfidf_df)
    return predicted_labels
```

12. We'll train three kinds of classifier models, namely: random forest, gradient boosting machines, and XGBoost. For random forest, we predict the class labels of the given set of review texts and compare it with their actual class, that is, the target using crosstabs. Add the following code to do this:

```
from sklearn.ensemble import RandomForestClassifier
rfc = RandomForestClassifier(n_estimators=20,max_depth=4,max_
features='sqrt',random_state=1)
data_patio_lawn_garden['predicted_labels_rfc'] = clf_model(rfc, tfidf_df,
data_patio_lawn_garden['target'])
pd.crosstab(data_patio_lawn_garden['target'], data_patio_lawn_
garden['predicted_labels_rfc'])
```

The preceding code generates the following output:

```
predicted_labels_rfc        0        1

        target

                    0      3302     2933
                    1      1557     5480
```

Figure 3.36: Crosstab between actual target values and predicted labels

Here, we see **3302** instances with a target label of **0** correctly classified, and **2933** such instances wrongly classified. Furthermore, **5480** instances with a target label of **1** are correctly classified, whereas **1557** such instances are wrongly classified.

13. For GBM, we predict the class labels of the given set of **reviewTexts** and compare it with their actual class, that is, the target using crosstabs. Add the following code to do this:

```
from sklearn.ensemble import GradientBoostingClassifier
gbc = GradientBoostingClassifier(n_estimators=2,max_depth=3,max_
features='sqrt',random_state=1)
data_patio_lawn_garden['predicted_labels_gbc'] = clf_model(gbc, tfidf_df,
data_patio_lawn_garden['target'])
pd.crosstab(data_patio_lawn_garden['target'], data_patio_lawn_
garden['predicted_labels_gbc'])
```

The preceding code generates the following output:

```
predicted_labels_gbc        0        1

        target

                    0       101     6134
                    1        26     7011
```

Figure 3.37: Crosstab between actual target values and predicted labels using GBM

Here, we see **101** instances with a target label of **0** correctly classified, and **6134** such instances wrongly classified. Furthermore, **7011** instances with a target label of **1** are correctly classified, whereas **26** such instances are wrongly classified.

14. For XGBoost, we predict the class labels of the given set of **reviewTexts** and compare it with their actual class, that is, the target using **crosstabs**. Add the following code to do this:

```
from xgboost import XGBClassifier
xgb_clf=XGBClassifier(n_estimators=20,learning_rate=0.03,max_
depth=5,subsample=0.6,colsample_bytree= 0.6,reg_alpha= 10,seed=42)
data_patio_lawn_garden['predicted_labels_xgbc'] = clf_model(xgb_clf, tfidf_
df, data_patio_lawn_garden['target'])
pd.crosstab(data_patio_lawn_garden['target'], data_patio_lawn_
garden['predicted_labels_xgbc'])
```

The preceding code generates the following output:

predicted_labels_xgbc	0	1
target		
0	4222	2013
1	2088	4949

Figure 3.38: Crosstab between actual target values and predicted labels using XGBoost

Here, we see **4222** instances with a target label of **0** correctly classified, and **2013** such instances wrongly classified. Furthermore, **4949** instances with a target label of **1** are correctly classified, whereas **2088** such instances are wrongly classified.

15. Now, we'll define a generic function for all regression models. Add the following code to do this:

```
def reg_model(model_type, X_train, y):
    model = model_type.fit(X_train,y)
    predicted_values = model.predict(tfidf_df)
    return predicted_values
```

16. We'll train three kinds of regression models, namely: random forest, gradient boosting machines, and XGBoost. For random forest, we predict the overall score of the given set of review texts. Add the following code to do this:

```
from sklearn.ensemble import RandomForestRegressor
rfg = RandomForestRegressor(n_estimators=20,max_depth=4,max_
features='sqrt',random_state=1)
data_patio_lawn_garden['predicted_values_rfg'] = reg_model(rfg, tfidf_df,
data_patio_lawn_garden['overall'])
data_patio_lawn_garden[['overall', 'predicted_values_rfg']].head(10)
```

The preceding code generates the following output:

	overall	predicted_values_rfg
0	4	4.236717
1	5	4.341767
2	4	4.219413
3	5	4.134852
4	5	4.147218
5	5	4.252751
6	5	4.190971
7	5	4.251688
8	5	4.251610
9	4	4.262498

Figure 3.39: Actual overall score and predicted values using a random forest regressor

From the preceding table, we can see how the actual and predicted score varies for different instances. We will use this table later to evaluate the performance of the model.

17. For GBM, we predict the overall score of the given set of **reviewTexts**. Add the following code to do this:

```
from sklearn.ensemble import GradientBoostingRegressor
gbr = GradientBoostingRegressor(n_estimators=20,max_depth=4,max_
features='sqrt',random_state=1)
data_patio_lawn_garden['predicted_values_gbr'] = reg_model(gbr, tfidf_df,
data_patio_lawn_garden['overall'])
data_patio_lawn_garden[['overall', 'predicted_values_gbr']].head(10)
```

The preceding code generates the following output:

	overall	predicted_values_gbr
0	4	4.354611
1	5	4.441782
2	4	4.329691
3	5	4.080094
4	5	4.145767
5	5	4.162901
6	5	4.227398
7	5	4.146231
8	5	4.269629
9	4	4.136460

Figure 3.40: Actual overall score and predicted values using a gradient boosting regressor

From the preceding table, we can see how the actual and predicted score varies for different instances. We will use this table later to evaluate the performance of the model.

18. For XGBoost, we predict the overall score of the given set of **reviewTexts**. Add the following code to do this:

```
from xgboost import XGBRegressor
xgbr = XGBRegressor(n_estimators=20,learning_rate=0.03,max_
depth=5,subsample=0.6,colsample_bytree= 0.6,reg_alpha= 10,seed=42)
data_patio_lawn_garden['predicted_values_xgbr'] = reg_model(xgbr, tfidf_df,
data_patio_lawn_garden['overall'])
data_patio_lawn_garden[['overall', 'predicted_values_xgbr']].head(2)
```

The preceding code generates the following output:

	overall	predicted_values_xgbr
0	4	2.220690
1	5	2.318871
2	4	2.235872
3	5	2.108017
4	5	2.108017
5	5	2.129134
6	5	2.193431
7	5	2.186514
8	5	2.178304
9	4	2.128875

Figure 3.41: Actual overall score and predicted values using an XGBoost regressor

From the preceding table, we can see how the actual and predicted score varies for different instances. We will use this table later to evaluate the performance of the model.

You have learned how to use tree-based methods to predict scores in data. In the next section, you will learn about sampling.

Sampling

Sampling is the process of creating a subset from a given set of instances. If you have 1,000 sentences in an article, out of which you choose 100 sentences for analysis, the subset of 100 sentences will be called a sample of the original article. This process is referred to as sampling. There are different kinds of sampling methods, such as the following:

- **Simple random sampling**

  In this process, each instance of the set has equal probability of being selected. For example, you have 10 balls of 10 different colors in a box. You need to select 4 out of 10 balls without looking at their color. In this case, each ball is equally likely to be selected. This is an instance of simple random sampling.

- **Stratified sampling**

  In this type of sampling, the original set is first divided into parts called "strata" based on a given criteria. Random samples are chosen from each of these "stratum." For example, you have 100 sentences, out of which 80 are non-sarcastic and 20 are sarcastic. To extract a stratified sample of 10 sentences, you need to select 8 from 80 non-sarcastic sentences and 2 from 20 sarcastic sentences. This will ensure that the ratio of non-sarcastic to sarcastic sentences, that is, 80:20, remains unaltered in the sample selected.

- **Multi-Stage Sampling**

  If you are analyzing social media posts of all the people in a particular country related to the current weather, the text data will be huge, as it will consist of the weather conditions of different cities. Drawing a stratified sample would be difficult. In this case, it is recommended to first extract a stratified sample by region, and then further sample it within regions, that is, by cities. This is basically performing stratified sampling at each and every stage.

In the next section, we will look at an exercise based on sampling, to get a better understanding of it.

Exercise 34: Sampling (Simple Random, Stratified, Multi-Stage)

In this exercise, we will extract samples from an online retail dataset, with the help of simple random sampling, stratified sampling, and multi-stage sampling. Follow these steps to implement this exercise:

1. Open a Jupyter notebook.

2. Insert a new cell and add the following code to import pandas and read the dataset:

```
import pandas as pd
data = pd.read_excel('data_ch3/Online Retail.xlsx')
data.head()
```

The preceding code generates the following output:

	InvoiceNo	StockCode	Description	Quantity	InvoiceDate	UnitPrice	CustomerID	Country
0	536365	85123A	WHITE HANGING HEART T-LIGHT HOLDER	6	2010-12-01 08:26:00	2.55	17850.0	United Kingdom
1	536365	71053	WHITE METAL LANTERN	6	2010-12-01 08:26:00	3.39	17850.0	United Kingdom
2	536365	84406B	CREAM CUPID HEARTS COAT HANGER	8	2010-12-01 08:26:00	2.75	17850.0	United Kingdom
3	536365	84029G	KNITTED UNION FLAG HOT WATER BOTTLE	6	2010-12-01 08:26:00	3.39	17850.0	United Kingdom
4	536365	84029E	RED WOOLLY HOTTIE WHITE HEART.	6	2010-12-01 08:26:00	3.39	17850.0	United Kingdom

Figure 3.42: Online retail data as a DataFrame

3. We use pandas' **sample** function to extract a sample from the DataFrame. Add the following code to do this:

```
data_sample_random = data.sample(frac=0.1,random_state=42) # selecting 10%
of the data randomly
data_sample_random.head()
```

The preceding code generates the following output:

	InvoiceNo	StockCode	Description	Quantity	InvoiceDate	UnitPrice	CustomerID	Country
209268	555200	71459	HANGING JAM JAR T-LIGHT HOLDER	24	2011-06-01 12:05:00	0.85	17315.0	United Kingdom
207108	554974	21128	GOLD FISHING GNOME	4	2011-05-27 17:14:00	6.95	14031.0	United Kingdom
167085	550972	21086	SET/6 RED SPOTTY PAPER CUPS	4	2011-04-21 17:05:00	0.65	14031.0	United Kingdom
471836	576652	22812	PACK 3 BOXES CHRISTMAS PANETTONE	3	2011-11-16 10:39:00	1.95	17198.0	United Kingdom
115865	546157	22180	RETROSPOT LAMP	2	2011-03-10 08:40:00	9.95	13502.0	United Kingdom

Figure 3.43: Random sample extracted from online retail data

4. Now, we'll use sklearn's **train_test_split** function to create stratified samples. Add the following code to do this:

```
from sklearn.model_selection import train_test_split
X_train, X_valid, y_train, y_valid = train_test_split(data,
data['Country'],test_size=0.2, random_state=42,stratify = data['Country'])
data.shape
```

The preceding code generates the following output:

```
(541909, 8)
```

Figure 3.44: The shape of the entire data

5. To check the shape of the training model, add the following code:

    ```
    X_train.shape
    ```

    The preceding code generates the following output:

    $$(433527, 8)$$

    Figure 3.45: The shape of the sample extracted

6. We filter out the data in various stages and extract random samples from it. We will extract a random sample of 2% from those transactions by country, which occurred in United Kingdom, Germany, or France and corresponding quantity is >= 2. Add the following code to implement this:

    ```
    data_ugf = data[data['Country'].isin(['United Kingdom', 'Germany',
    'France'])]
    data_ugf_q2 = data_ugf[data_ugf['Quantity']>=2]
    data_ugf_q2_sample = data_ugf_q2.sample(frac = .02, random_state=42)
    data_ugf_q2_sample.head()
    ```

    The preceding code generates the following output:

	InvoiceNo	StockCode	Description	Quantity	InvoiceDate	UnitPrice	CustomerID	Country
224900	556579	22987	WRAP SUMMER ROSE DESIGN	25	2011-06-13 14:16:00	0.42	15069.0	United Kingdom
479100	577137	21137	BLACK RECORD COVER FRAME	96	2011-11-18 08:59:00	3.39	14110.0	United Kingdom
78507	542888	22476	EMPIRE UNION JACK TV DINNER TRAY	3	2011-02-01 13:15:00	4.95	15687.0	United Kingdom
499283	578664	22593	CHRISTMAS GINGHAM STAR	7	2011-11-24 16:59:00	0.85	15910.0	United Kingdom
153888	549831	16156S	WRAP PINK FAIRY CAKES	25	2011-04-12 13:10:00	0.42	14844.0	United Kingdom

Figure 3.46: Multi-stage sample extracted from online retail data

Developing a Text Classifier

A text classifier is a machine learning model that is capable of labeling texts based on their content. For instance, a text classifier will help you understand whether a random text statement is sarcastic or not. Presently, text classifiers are gaining importance as manually classifying huge amounts of text data is impossible.

Feature Extraction

When dealing with text data, features denote its different attributes. Generally, they are numeric representations of the text. As discussed in *Chapter 2- Extraction Methods from Unstructured text*, TF-IDF representations of texts are one of the most popular ways of extracting features from them.

Feature Engineering

Feature engineering is the art of extracting new features from existing ones. Extracting novel features, which tend to capture variation in data better, requires sound domain expertise.

Removing Correlated Features

Regression models, including logistic regression, are unable to perform well when correlation between features exists. Thus, features with correlation beyond a certain threshold need to be removed.

Exercise 35: Removing Highly Correlated Features (Tokens)

In this exercise, we will remove highly correlated words from a tf-idf matrix representation of sklearn's "fetch_20newsgroups" text dataset. Follow these steps to implement this exercise:

1. Open a Jupyter notebook.

2. Insert a new cell and add the following code to import the necessary packages:

```
from sklearn.datasets import fetch_20newsgroups
import matplotlib as mpl
import pandas as pd
import numpy as np
import matplotlib.pyplot as plt
%matplotlib inline
import re
import string
from nltk import word_tokenize
from nltk.corpus import stopwords
from nltk.stem import WordNetLemmatizer
from sklearn.feature_extraction.text import TfidfVectorizer
from collections import Counter
from pylab import *
import nltk
import warnings
warnings.filterwarnings('ignore')
```

3. We will be using stop words from the English language only. **WordNet** states the **lemmatizer** we will be using. Add the following code to implement this:

```
stop_words = stopwords.words('english')
stop_words = stop_words + list(string.printable)
lemmatizer = WordNetLemmatizer()
```

4. To specify the categories of news articles we want to fetch by, add the following code:

```
categories= ['misc.forsale', 'sci.electronics', 'talk.religion.misc']
```

5. To fetch sklearn's "the 20 newsgroups" text dataset, corresponding to the categories mentioned earlier, we use the following lines of code:

```
news_data = fetch_20newsgroups(subset='train', categories=categories,
shuffle=True, random_state=42, download_if_missing=True)
news_data_df = pd.DataFrame({'text' : news_data['data'], 'category': news_
data.target})
news_data_df.head()
```

The preceding code generates the following output:

	text	category
0	From: Steve@Busop.cit.wayne.edu (Steve Teolis)...	0
1	From: jks2x@holmes.acc.Virginia.EDU (Jason K. ...	0
2	From: wayne@uva386.schools.virginia.edu (Tony ...	1
3	From: lihan@ccwf.cc.utexas.edu (Bruce G. Bostw...	1
4	From: myoakam@cis.ohio-state.edu (micah r yoak...	0

Figure 3.47: Texts of news data as a DataFrame

6. Now, make use of the lambda function to extract tokens from each 'text' of the **news_data_df** DataFrame. Check whether any of these tokens are stop words, lemmatize them, and concatenate them side by side. We'll use the join function to concatenate a list of words into a single sentence. We'll use the regular expression (re) to replace anything other than letters, digits, and white spaces with blank space. Add the following code to implement this:

```
news_data_df['cleaned_text'] = news_data_df['text'].apply(\
lambda x : ' '.join([lemmatizer.lemmatize(word.lower()) \
    for word in word_tokenize(re.sub(r'([^\s\w]|_)+', ' ', str(x))) if
word.lower() not in stop_words]))
```

7. The following lines of codes are used to create a tf-idf matrix and transform it to a DataFrame:

```
tfidf_model = TfidfVectorizer(max_features=20)
tfidf_df = pd.DataFrame(tfidf_model.fit_transform(news_data_df['cleaned_
text']).todense())
tfidf_df.columns = sorted(tfidf_model.vocabulary_)
tfidf_df.head()
```

The preceding code generates the following output:

	00	article	com	edu	good	host	know	like	line	new	nntp	one	organization	posting	sale	subject
0	0.719664	0.000000	0.000000	0.191683	0.0	0.124066	0.000000	0.153294	0.055931	0.520927	0.124370	0.0	0.068809	0.120711	0.161624	0.066888
1	0.000000	0.000000	0.000000	0.219265	0.0	0.000000	0.353598	0.350704	0.153124	0.000000	0.000000	0.0	0.157421	0.000000	0.739523	0.153025
2	0.000000	0.000000	0.000000	0.853563	0.0	0.000000	0.000000	0.000000	0.298044	0.000000	0.000000	0.0	0.306407	0.000000	0.000000	0.297852
3	0.000000	0.267175	0.255208	0.567867	0.0	0.245034	0.000000	0.302760	0.132190	0.000000	0.245634	0.0	0.135900	0.238407	0.000000	0.132105
4	0.000000	0.000000	0.000000	0.411807	0.0	0.266541	0.000000	0.000000	0.143793	0.000000	0.267194	0.0	0.147828	0.259333	0.694459	0.143700

Figure 3.48: TF-IDF representation as a DataFrame

8. We'll calculate the correlation matrix for this tf-idf representation. Add the following code to implement this:

```
correlation_matrix = tfidf_df.corr()
correlation_matrix.head()
```

The preceding code generates the following output:

	00	article	com	edu	good	host	know	like	line	new	nntp	one	organization	posting
00	1.000000	-0.113080	-0.081874	-0.116847	-0.053495	-0.078405	-0.096597	-0.084413	-0.161674	0.026696	-0.084632	-0.078635	-0.208121	-0.083772
article	-0.113080	1.000000	0.125853	0.076146	-0.008246	-0.055519	0.025570	-0.000201	-0.158956	-0.121483	-0.046249	0.029978	-0.201204	-0.038486
com	-0.081874	0.125853	1.000000	-0.471456	-0.016128	-0.178742	-0.036333	-0.037284	-0.110011	-0.071355	-0.175256	-0.037293	-0.084630	-0.168613
edu	-0.116847	0.076146	-0.471456	1.000000	-0.098067	0.242610	-0.100041	-0.103703	-0.043210	-0.059893	0.247395	-0.119432	0.023394	0.225912
good	-0.053495	-0.008246	-0.016128	-0.098067	1.000000	-0.098199	0.025899	0.045106	-0.186943	-0.046803	-0.098198	0.074548	-0.166908	-0.089622

Figure 3.49: Correlation matrix

9. Now, we'll plot the correlation matrix using seaborn's **heatmap** function. Add the following code to implement this:

```
import seaborn as sns
fig, ax = plt.subplots(figsize=(20, 20))
sns.heatmap(correlation_matrix,annot=True)
```

The preceding code generates the following output:

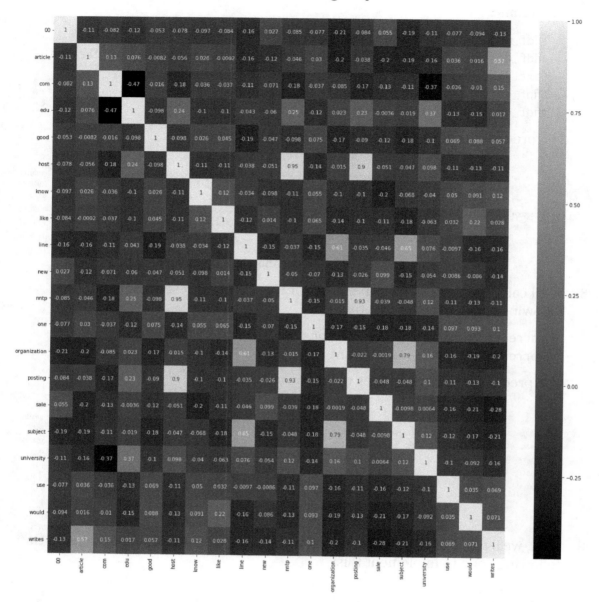

Figure 3.50: Heatmap representation of a correlation matrix

> **Note**
>
> You can find high-quality color for the preceeding figure at: https://github.com/ TrainingByPackt/Natural-Language-Processing-Fundamentals/blob/master/ Graphics/Lesson%2003/Figure%203.50.png.

10. To identify a pair of terms with high correlation, we created an upper triangular matrix from the correlation matrix. We also created a stacked array out of it and traversed it. Add the following code to do this:

```
import numpy as np
correlation_matrix_ut = correlation_matrix.where(np.triu(np.
ones(correlation_matrix.shape)).astype(np.bool))
correlation_matrix_melted = correlation_matrix_ut.stack().reset_index()
correlation_matrix_melted.columns = ['word1', 'word2', 'correlation']
correlation_matrix_melted[(correlation_matrix_melted['word1']!=\
                          correlation_matrix_melted['word2']) &
(correlation_matrix_melted['correlation']>.7)]
```

The preceding code generates the following output:

	word1	word2	correlation
95	host	nntp	0.953828
98	host	posting	0.986666
158	nntp	posting	0.934923
177	organization	subject	0.793946

Figure 3.51: Highly correlated tokens

11. In this step, we'll remove terms for which the coefficient of correlation is >.7 and create a separate DataFrame with the remaining terms. Add the following code to do this:

```
tfidf_df_without_correlated_word = tfidf_df.drop(['nntp', 'posting',
'organization'], axis = 1)
tfidf_df_without_correlated_word.head()
```

The preceding code generates the following output:

	00	article	com	edu	good	host	know	like	line	new	one	sale	subject	univerisity	use	would	writes
0	0.719664	0.000000	0.000000	0.191683	0.0	0.124066	0.000000	0.153294	0.066931	0.520927	0.0	0.161624	0.066888	0.255410	0.0	0.00000	0.000000
1	0.000000	0.000000	0.000000	0.219266	0.0	0.000000	0.353598	0.350704	0.153124	0.000000	0.0	0.739523	0.153025	0.292162	0.0	0.00000	0.000000
2	0.000000	0.000000	0.000000	0.853563	0.0	0.000000	0.000000	0.000000	0.298044	0.000000	0.0	0.000000	0.297852	0.000000	0.0	0.00000	0.000000
3	0.000000	0.267175	0.255208	0.567867	0.0	0.245034	0.000000	0.302760	0.132190	0.000000	0.0	0.000000	0.132105	0.252221	0.0	0.28648	0.270283
4	0.000000	0.000000	0.000000	0.411807	0.0	0.266541	0.000000	0.000000	0.143793	0.000000	0.0	0.694459	0.143700	0.274358	0.0	0.00000	0.000000

Figure 3.52: DataFrame after removing correlated tokens

After removing the highly correlated words from the TF-IDF DataFrame, it appears like this.

Dimensionality Reduction

There are some optional steps that are followed on a case-to-case basis. For example, sometimes the tf-idf matrix or bag-of-words representation of a text corpus is so big that it doesn't fit in memory. In this case, it would be necessary to reduce its dimension, that is, the number of columns in the feature matrix. The most popular method for dimension reduction is principal component analysis (PCA).

PCA uses orthogonal transformation to convert a list of features (which may be correlated) into a list of variables that are linearly uncorrelated. These linearly uncorrelated variables are known as principal components. These principal components are arranged in descending order of the amount of variability they capture in the dataset. In the next section, let's look at an exercise, to get a better understanding of this.

Exercise 36: Dimensionality Reduction (PCA)

In this exercise, we will reduce the dimensionality of a tf-idf matrix representation of sklearn's "fetch_20newsgroups" text dataset to two. Create a scatter plot of these documents. Each category should be colored differently. Follow these steps to implement this exercise:

1. Open a Jupyter notebook.

2. Insert a new cell and add the following code to import the necessary packages:

```
from sklearn.datasets import fetch_20newsgroups
import matplotlib as mpl
import pandas as pd
import numpy as np
import matplotlib.pyplot as plt
%matplotlib inline
import re
import string
from nltk import word_tokenize
from nltk.corpus import stopwords
from nltk.stem import WordNetLemmatizer
from sklearn.feature_extraction.text import TfidfVectorizer
from collections import Counter
from pylab import *
import nltk
import warnings
warnings.filterwarnings('ignore')
```

3. We will be using stop words from the English language only. WordNet states the lemmatizer we will be using. Add the following code to implement this:

```
stop_words = stopwords.words('english')
stop_words = stop_words + list(string.printable)
lemmatizer = WordNetLemmatizer()
```

4. To specify the categories of news articles we want to fetch by, add the following code:

```
categories= ['misc.forsale', 'sci.electronics', 'talk.religion.misc']
```

5. To fetch sklearn's dataset, corresponding to the categories mentioned earlier, we use the following lines of code:

```
news_data = fetch_20newsgroups(subset='train', categories=categories,
shuffle=True, random_state=42, download_if_missing=True)
news_data_df = pd.DataFrame({'text' : news_data['data'], 'category': news_
data.target})
news_data_df.head()
```

The preceding code generates the following output:

	text	category
0	From: Steve@Busop.cit.wayne.edu (Steve Teolis)...	0
1	From: jks2x@holmes.acc.Virginia.EDU (Jason K. ...	0
2	From: wayne@uva386.schools.virginia.edu (Tony ...	1
3	From: lihan@ccwf.cc.utexas.edu (Bruce G. Bostw...	1
4	From: myoakam@cis.ohio-state.edu (micah r yoak...	0

Figure 3.53: News texts and their categories

6. Now, we'll make use of a lambda function to extract tokens from each 'text' of the **news_data_df** DataFrame, check whether any of these tokens are stop words, lemmatize them, and concatenate them side by side. We'll use the join function to concatenate a list of words into a single sentence. We'll use a regular expression (re) to replace anything other than alphabets, digits, and white spaces with a blank space. Add the following code to implement this:

```
news_data_df['cleaned_text'] = news_data_df['text'].apply(\
lambda x : ' '.join([lemmatizer.lemmatize(word.lower()) \
    for word in word_tokenize(re.sub(r'([^\s\w]|_)+', ' ', str(x))) if
word.lower() not in stop_words]))
```

7. The following lines of code are used to create a tf-idf matrix and transform it into a DataFrame:

```
tfidf_model = TfidfVectorizer(max_features=20)
tfidf_df = pd.DataFrame(tfidf_model.fit_transform(news_data_df['cleaned_text']).todense())
tfidf_df.columns = sorted(tfidf_model.vocabulary_)
tfidf_df.head()
```

The preceding code generates the following output:

	00	10	100	12	14	15	16	20	25	30	...	well	wire	wiring	without
0	0.435655	0.0	0.000000	0.0	0.000000	0.127775	0.136811	0.127551	0.133311	0.0	...	0.0	0.0	0.0	0.0
1	0.000000	0.0	0.000000	0.0	0.000000	0.294937	0.000000	0.000000	0.000000	0.0	...	0.0	0.0	0.0	0.0
2	0.000000	0.0	0.000000	0.0	0.000000	0.000000	0.000000	0.000000	0.000000	0.0	...	0.0	0.0	0.0	0.0
3	0.000000	0.0	0.000000	0.0	0.000000	0.000000	0.000000	0.000000	0.000000	0.0	...	0.0	0.0	0.0	0.0
4	0.000000	0.0	0.207003	0.0	0.191897	0.182138	0.000000	0.000000	0.000000	0.0	...	0.0	0.0	0.0	0.0

Figure 3.54: TF-IDF representation as a DataFrame

8. In this step, we are using sklearn's **PCA** function to extract two principal components from the earlier data. Add the following code to do this:

```
from sklearn.decomposition import PCA
pca = PCA(2)
pca.fit(tfidf_df)
reduced_tfidf = pca.transform(tfidf_df)
reduced_tfidf
```

The preceding code generates the following output:

```
array([[ 0.2425953 ,  0.13326504],
       [ 0.23828348,  0.11497239],
       [ 0.21681333, -0.20598645],
       ...,
       [ 0.09494134,  0.15853317],
       [ 0.01106213, -0.09250798],
       [ 0.21498839, -0.194826  ]])
```

Figure 3.55: Principal components

9. Now, we'll create a **scatter** plot along these principal components and represent each category with a separate color. Add the following code to implement this:

```
plt.scatter(reduced_tfidf[:, 0], reduced_tfidf[:, 1], c=news_data_
df['category'], cmap='viridis')
plt.xlabel('dimension_1')
plt.ylabel('dimension_2')
plt.title('Representation of NEWS documents in 2D')
plt.show()
```

The preceding code generates the following output:

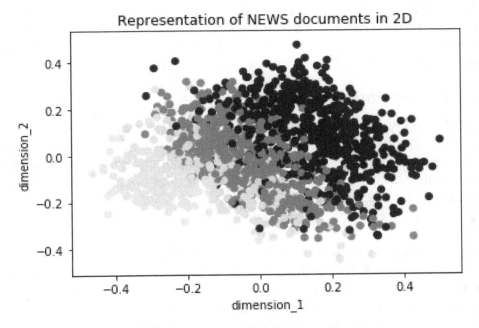

Figure 3.56: 2D representation of news documents

From the preceding figure, we can see that a scatter plot is created, where each category is represented by a different color.

> **Note**
>
> You can find high-quality color for the preeceding figure at: https://github.com/TrainingByPackt/Natural-Language-Processing-Fundamentals/blob/master/Graphics/Lesson%2003/Figure%203.56.png.

Deciding on a Model Type

Once the feature set is ready, it's necessary to decide on the type of model that will be used to deal with the problem. Usually, unsupervised models are chosen when data is not labeled. If we have a predefined number of clusters in mind, we go for clustering algorithms such as k-means, otherwise, we opt for hierarchical clustering. For labeled data, we generally follow supervised learning methods such as regression and classification.

If the outcome is continuous and numeric, we use regression. If it is discrete or categorical, we use classification. The Naive Bayes algorithm comes in handy for the fast development of simple classification models. More complex tree-based methods (such as decision trees, random forests, and so on) are needed when we want to achieve higher accuracy. In such cases, we sometimes compromise on model explainability and the time required to develop it. When the outcome of a model has to be the probability of the occurrence of a certain class, we use logistic regression.

Evaluating the Performance of a Model

Once a model is ready, it is necessary to evaluate its performance. This is because, without benchmarking it, we cannot be confident of how well or how badly it is functioning. It is not advisable to put a model into production without evaluating its efficiency. There are various ways to evaluate a model's performance. Let's work through them one by one.

- **Confusion Matrix**

  This is a two-dimensional matrix mainly used for evaluating the performance of classification models. Its columns consist of predicted values, and its rows consist of actual values. In other words, for a given confusion matrix, it is a crosstab between actual and predicted values. Entries of cells denote how many of the predicted values match with the actual values and how many don't.

- **Accuracy**

  Accuracy is defined as the ratio of correctly classified instances to the total number of instances. Whenever accuracy is used for model evaluation, we need to ensure that the data is balanced in terms of classes, meaning it should have an almost equal number of instances of each class. If a dataset is unbalanced, a model predicting that all instances have labels the same as the label of the class with the highest frequency of occurrence would be highly accurate. However, such a model does not serve any purpose.

- **Precision and Recall**

  Let's understand precision and recall with a real-life example. If your mother tells you to explore the kitchen of your house, find items that need to be replenished, and bring them back from the market, you will bring P number of items from the market and show it to your mother. Out of P items, she finds Q items to be relevant. The ratio Q/P is called precision. However, in this scenario, she was expecting you to bring R items relevant to her. The ratio, Q/R is referred to as recall.

  Precision = True Positive / (True Positive + False Positive)

  Recall = True Positive / (True Positive + False Negative)

- **F1-score**

  For a given classification model, F1 score is the harmonic mean of precision and recall.

  *F1 score = 2 * ((Precision * Recall) / (Precision + Recall))*

- **Receiver Operating Characteristic (ROC) Curve**

  To understand ROC curve, we need to get acquainted with True Positive Rate (TPR) and False Positive Rate (FPR).

  TPR = True Positive / (True Positive + False Negative)

  FPR = False Positive / (False Positive + True Negative)

  The output of a classification model can be probabilities. In that case, we need to set a threshold to obtain classes from those probabilities. ROC curve is a plot between the TPR and FPR for various values of the threshold. Area under the ROC curve (AUROC) represents the efficiency of the model. The higher the AUROC, the better the model is. The maximum value of AUROC is 1.

- **Root Mean Square Error (RMSE)**

  This is mainly used for evaluating the accuracy of regression models. We define it as described in the following formula:

  $$RMSE = \sqrt{\frac{\sum (P_i - O_i)^2}{n}}$$

  Here, n is the number of samples, Pi is the predicted value of the ith observation, and Oi is the observed value of the ith observation.

- **Maximum Absolute Percentage Error (MAPE)**

  Just like RMSE, this is another way to evaluate a regression model's performance. It is described in the following formula:

  $$\text{MAPE} = \left(\frac{1}{n}\sum \frac{|O_i - P_i|}{|O_i|}\right) * 100 \text{ for all i from i to n.}$$

  Here, n is the number of samples, Pi is the predicted value (that is, the forecast value) of the ith observation, andOi is the observed value (that is, the actual value) of the ith observation.

Exercise 37: Calculate the RMSE and MAPE

In this exercise, we will calculate the RMSE and MAPE of a given dataset. Follow these steps to implement this exercise:

1. Open a Jupyter notebook.

2. Now, we will use sklearn's **mean_squared_error** to calculate the RMSE. Add the following code to implement this:

```
from sklearn.metrics import mean_squared_error
from math import sqrt
y_actual = [0,1,2,1,0]
y_predicted = [0.03,1.2,1.6,.9,0.1]
rms = sqrt(mean_squared_error(y_actual, y_predicted))
print('Root Mean Squared Error (RMSE) is:', rms)
```

The preceding code generates the following output:

```
Root Mean Squared Error (RMSE) is: 0.21019038988498018
```

Figure 3.57: Calculated RMSE

3. We will use sklearn's **mean_absolute_error** to calculate the MAPE. Add the following code to implement this:

```
from sklearn.metrics import mean_absolute_error
y_actual = [0,1,2,1,0]
y_predicted = [0.03,1.2,1.6,.9,0.1]
mape = mean_absolute_error(y_actual, y_predicted) * 100
print('Mean Absolute Percentage Error (MAPE) is:', round(mape,2), '%')
```

The preceding code generates the following output:

```
Mean Absolute Percentage Error (MAPE) is: 16.6%
```

Figure 3.58: Calculated MAPE

In the next section, we will solve an activity based on classifying text.

Activity 5: Developing End-to-End Text Classifiers

In this activity, we will build an end-to-end classifier that classifies comments on Wikipedia articles. The classifier will classify comments as toxic or not. Follow these steps to implement this activity:

1. Import the necessary packages.

2. Read the dataset from https://github.com/TrainingByPackt/Natural-Language-Processing-Fundamentals/blob/master/Lesson3/data_ch3/train_comment_small.csv.zip and clean it.

3. Create a TF-IDF matrix out of it.

4. Divide the data into a training and validation set.

5. Develop classifier models for logistic regression, random forest, and XGBoost.

6. Evaluate the models developed using parameters such as confusion matrix, accuracy, precision, recall, F1 plot curve, and ROC curve.

> **Note**
>
> The solution for this activity can be found on page 269.

You have learned how to build end-to-end classifiers. Developing an end-to-end classifier was done in phases. Firstly, the text corpus was cleaned and tokenized, features were extracted using TF-IDF, then the dataset was divided into training and validation sets. Several machine learning algorithms, such as logistic regression, random forest, and XGBoost were used to develop classification models. Finally, their performances were measured using parameters such as confusion matrix, accuracy, precision, recall, F1 plot curve, and ROC curve. In the next section, you will learn how to build pipelines for NLP projects.

Building Pipelines for NLP Projects

What does the word pipeline refer to? In general, pipeline refers to a structure that allows a streamlined flow of air, water, or something similar. In this context, pipeline has a similar meaning. It helps to streamline various stages of an NLP project.

An NLP project is done in various stages, such as tokenization, stemming, feature extraction (tf-idf matrix generation), and model building. Instead of carrying out each stage separately, we create an ordered list of all these stages. This list is known as a pipeline. Let's solve a text classification problem using a pipeline in the next section.

Exercise 38: Building Pipelines for NLP Projects

In this exercise, we will develop a pipeline that will allow us to create a TF-IDF matrix representation from sklearn's **fetch_20newsgroups** text dataset. Follow these steps to implement this exercise:

1. Open a Jupyter notebook.

2. Insert a new cell and add the following code to import the necessary packages:

```
from sklearn.pipeline import Pipeline
from sklearn.feature_extraction.text import TfidfTransformer
from sklearn import tree
from sklearn.datasets import fetch_20newsgroups
from sklearn.feature_extraction.text import CountVectorizer
import pandas as pd
```

3. Here, we specify categories of news articles we want to fetch by. Add the following code to do this:

```
categories = ['misc.forsale', 'sci.electronics', 'talk.religion.misc']
```

4. To fetch sklearn's 20newsgroups dataset, corresponding to the categories mentioned earlier, we use the following lines of code:

    ```
    news_data = fetch_20newsgroups(subset='train', categories=categories,
    shuffle=True, random_state=42, download_if_missing=True)
    ```

5. Here, we'll define a pipeline consisting of two stages: **CountVectorizer** and **TfidfTransformer**. We'll fit it on the news_data mentioned earlier and use it to transform that data. Add the following code to implement this:

    ```
    text_classifier_pipeline = Pipeline([('vect', CountVectorizer()), ('tfidf',
    TfidfTransformer())])
    text_classifier_pipeline.fit(news_data.data, news_data.target)
    pd.DataFrame(text_classifier_pipeline.fit_transform(news_data.data, news_
    data.target).todense()).head()
    ```

    The preceding code generates the following output:

	0	1	2	3	4	5	6	7	8	9	...	26016	26017	26018	26019	26020	26021	26022	26023	26024	26025
0	0.165523	0.000000	0.0	0.0	0.0	0.0	0.0	0.0	0.0	0.0	...	0.0	0.0	0.0	0.0	0.0	0.0	0.0	0.0	0.0	0.0
1	0.000000	0.000000	0.0	0.0	0.0	0.0	0.0	0.0	0.0	0.0	...	0.0	0.0	0.0	0.0	0.0	0.0	0.0	0.0	0.0	0.0
2	0.000000	0.000000	0.0	0.0	0.0	0.0	0.0	0.0	0.0	0.0	...	0.0	0.0	0.0	0.0	0.0	0.0	0.0	0.0	0.0	0.0
3	0.000000	0.000000	0.0	0.0	0.0	0.0	0.0	0.0	0.0	0.0	...	0.0	0.0	0.0	0.0	0.0	0.0	0.0	0.0	0.0	0.0
4	0.000000	0.081279	0.0	0.0	0.0	0.0	0.0	0.0	0.0	0.0	...	0.0	0.0	0.0	0.0	0.0	0.0	0.0	0.0	0.0	0.0

5 rows x 26026 columns

Figure 3.59: TF-IDF representation of the DataFrame created using a pipeline

Here, we created a pipeline consisting of the count vectorizer and TF-IDF transformer. The outcome of this pipeline is the TF-IDF representation of the text data that has been passed to it as an argument.

Saving and Loading Models

After a model has been built and its performance matches our expectations, we may want to save it for future use. This eliminates the time needed for rebuilding it. Models can be saved in the hard disk by using **joblib** and **pickle**.

To deploy saved models, we need to load them from the hard disk to the memory. In the next section, we will solve an exercise based on this to get a better understanding.

Exercise 39: Saving and Loading Models

In this exercise, first we will create a tf-idf representation of sentences. Then, we will save this model on disk. Later, we will load it from the disk. Follow these steps to implement this exercise:

1. Open a Jupyter notebook.

2. Insert a new cell and the following code to import the necessary packages:

```
import pickle
from joblib import dump, load
from sklearn.feature_extraction.text import TfidfVectorizer
```

3. Defining a corpus consisting of four sentences, add the following code:

```
corpus = [
'Data Science is an overlap between Arts and Science',
'Generally, Arts graduates are right-brained and Science graduates are
left-brained',
'Excelling in both Arts and Science at a time becomes difficult',
'Natural Language Processing is a part of Data Science'
]
```

4. Then, we'll fit a tf-idf model to it. Add the following code to do this:

```
tfidf_model = TfidfVectorizer()
print(tfidf_model.fit_transform(corpus).todense())
```

The preceding code generates the following output:

```
[[0.40332811 0.25743911 0.         0.25743911 0.         0.
  0.40332811 0.         0.         0.31798852 0.         0.
  0.         0.         0.         0.31798852 0.         0.
  0.         0.         0.40332811 0.         0.         0.
  0.42094668 0.         ]
 [0.         0.159139   0.49864399 0.159139   0.         0.
  0.         0.         0.49864399 0.         0.         0.
  0.24932199 0.49864399 0.         0.         0.         0.24932199
  0.         0.         0.         0.         0.         0.24932199
  0.13010656 0.         ]
 [0.         0.22444946 0.         0.22444946 0.35164346 0.35164346
  0.         0.35164346 0.         0.         0.         0.35164346 0.35164346
  0.         0.         0.35164346 0.         0.         0.
  0.         0.         0.         0.         0.
  0.18350214 0.35164346]
 [0.         0.         0.         0.         0.         0.
  0.         0.         0.         0.30887228 0.         0.
  0.         0.         0.         0.30887228 0.39176533 0.
  0.39176533 0.39176533 0.         0.39176533 0.39176533 0.
  0.2044394  0.         ]]
```

Figure 3.60: TF-IDF representation as a matrix

5. Save this tf-idf model on disk using **joblib**. Add the following code to do this:

```
dump(tfidf_model, 'tfidf_model.joblib')
```

6. Finally, we'll load this model from the disk to the memory and use it. Add the following code to do this:

```
tfidf_model_loaded = load('tfidf_model.joblib')
print(tfidf_model_loaded.fit_transform(corpus).todense())
```

The preceding code generates the following output:

```
[[0.40332811 0.25743911 0.         0.25743911 0.         0.
  0.40332811 0.         0.         0.31798852 0.         0.
  0.         0.         0.         0.31798852 0.         0.
  0.         0.         0.40332811 0.         0.         0.
  0.42094668 0.         ]
 [0.         0.159139   0.49864399 0.159139   0.         0.
  0.         0.         0.49864399 0.         0.         0.
  0.24932199 0.49864399 0.         0.         0.         0.24932199
  0.         0.         0.         0.         0.         0.24932199
  0.13010656 0.         ]
 [0.         0.22444946 0.         0.22444946 0.35164346 0.35164346
  0.         0.35164346 0.         0.         0.35164346 0.35164346
  0.         0.         0.35164346 0.         0.         0.
  0.         0.         0.         0.         0.         0.
  0.18350214 0.35164346]
 [0.         0.         0.         0.         0.         0.
  0.         0.         0.         0.30887228 0.         0.
  0.         0.         0.         0.30887228 0.39176533 0.
  0.39176533 0.39176533 0.         0.39176533 0.39176533 0.
  0.2044394  0.         ]]
```

Figure 3.61: TF-IDF representation as a matrix

7. Save this tf-idf model on disk using **pickle**. Add the following code to do this:

```
pickle.dump(tfidf_model, open("tfidf_model.pickle.dat", "wb"))
```

8. Load this model from the disk to the memory and use it. Add the following code to do this:

```
loaded_model = pickle.load(open("tfidf_model.pickle.dat", "rb"))
print(loaded_model.fit_transform(corpus).todense())
```

The preceding code generates the following output:

```
[[0.40332811 0.25743911 0.        0.25743911 0.        0.
  0.40332811 0.        0.        0.31798852 0.        0.
  0.        0.        0.        0.31798852 0.        0.
  0.        0.        0.40332811 0.        0.        0.
  0.42094668 0.        ]
 [0.        0.159139   0.49864399 0.159139   0.        0.
  0.        0.        0.49864399 0.        0.        0.
  0.24932199 0.49864399 0.        0.        0.        0.24932199
  0.        0.        0.        0.        0.        0.24932199
  0.13010656 0.        ]
 [0.        0.22444946 0.        0.22444946 0.35164346 0.35164346
  0.        0.35164346 0.        0.        0.35164346 0.35164346
  0.        0.        0.35164346 0.        0.        0.
  0.        0.        0.        0.        0.        0.
  0.18350214 0.35164346]
 [0.        0.        0.        0.        0.        0.
  0.        0.        0.        0.30887228 0.        0.
  0.        0.        0.35164346 0.30887228 0.39176533 0.
  0.39176533 0.39176533 0.        0.39176533 0.39176533 0.
  0.2044394  0.        ]]
```

Figure 3.62: TF-IDF representation as matrix

You have learned how to save and load models.

Summary

In this chapter, you learned about different types of machine learning techniques, such as supervised and unsupervised learning. Various kinds of supervised learning algorithms, such as K-Nearest Neighbor and a Naive Bayes classifier have been explored. Moreover, different kinds of sampling techniques for splitting a given dataset into training and validation sets have also been elucidated with examples. This chapter focused mainly on developing machine learning models using features extracted from text data.

As you progressed through the chapter, you were introduced to various metrics used for evaluating the performance of these models. Finally, we covered the process of saving a model on the hard disk and loading it back to the memory for future use.

In the next chapter, you will learn several techniques with which data can be collected from various sources.

Collecting Text Data from the Web

Learning Objectives

By the end of this chapter, you will be able to:

- Extract and process data from web pages

- Describe different kinds of semi-structured data, such as JSON and XML

- Extract real-time data using Application Programming Interfaces

- Extract data from various file formats

In this chapter, you will learn how to collect data from different file formats.

Introduction

In the last chapter, we learned about developing a simple classifier using feature extraction methods. We also covered different algorithms that fall under supervised and unsupervised learning. In this chapter, you will learn about collecting data by scraping web pages and then processing it. You will also learn how to handle various kinds of semi-structured data, such as JSON and XML. We will cover different methods for extracting data using **Application Programming Interfaces** (**APIs**). Finally, we will explore different ways to extract data from different types of files.

Collecting Data by Scraping Web Pages

The process of gathering data from web pages and extracting information from them is known as **web scraping**. More than 85% of websites are created using HTML, that is, **Hypertext Markup Language**. A markup language is one in which text content is embedded between tags. Apart from this, additional information can be added by using attributes within tags. A web page can be considered to be a document written using HTML. Thus, we need to know the basics of HTML to scrape web pages effectively. The following figure depicts the contents that are included within an HTML tag:

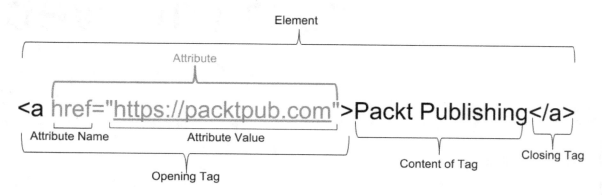

Figure 4.1: Tags and attributes of HTML

As you can see in the preceding figure, we can easily identify different elements within an HTML tag. In the next section, we will walk through an exercise in which we'll extract tag-based information from HTML files.

Exercise 40: Extraction of Tag-Based Information from HTML Files

In this exercise, we will extract the addresses, quotes, and text written in bold and the table present in **sample_doc.html**. Follow these steps to implement this exercise:

1. Open a Jupyter notebook.

2. Insert a new cell and add the following code to import the **BeautifulSoup** library:

   ```
   from bs4 import BeautifulSoup
   ```

3. Then, we create an object of the **BeautifulSoup** class and pass the location of the HTML file to it:

   ```
   soup = BeautifulSoup(open('data_ch4/sample_doc.html'), 'html.parser')
   ```

4. Add the following code to check the **text** contents of the **sample_doc.html** file:

   ```
   soup.text
   ```

   The preceding code generates the following output:

   ```
   '\n\n\n A sample HTML Page \n\n\nI am staying at  Mess on No. 72, Banamali Naskar Lane, Kolkata. \nSherlock  stays at
   221B, Baker Street, London, UK. \nHamlet said to Horatio,   There are more things in heaven and earth, Horatio,  Than
   are dreamt of in your philosophy. \n A table denoting details of students\n\n\nname\nqualification\nadditional qualif
   ication\nother qualification\n\n\nGangaram\nB.Tech\nNA\nNA\n\n\nGanga\nB.A.\nNA\nNA\n\n\nRam\nB.Tech\nM.Tech\nNA\n\n
   \nRamlal\nB.Music\nNA\nDiploma in Music\n\n\n\n'
   ```

   Figure 4.2: Text content of an HTML file

5. To check the **address** tag, we insert a new cell and add the following code:

   ```
   soup.find('address')
   ```

   The preceding code generates the following output:

   ```
   <address> Mess on No. 72, Banamali Naskar Lane, Kolkata.</address>
   ```

   Figure 4.3: Contents of one address tag

6. To locate all the **address** tags within the given content, write the following code:

   ```
   soup.find_all('address')
   ```

   The preceding code generates the following output:

   ```
   [<address> Mess on No. 72, Banamali Naskar Lane, Kolkata.</address>,
    <address>221B, Baker Street, London, UK.</address>]
   ```

   Figure 4.4: Contents of all the address tags

7. To check **quotes** within the content, we write the following code:

```
soup.find_all('q')
```

The preceding code generates the following output:

```
[<q> There are more things in heaven and earth, Horatio, <br> Than are dreamt of in your philosophy. </br></q>]
```

Figure 4.5: Contents of the q tag

8. To check all the **bold** items, we write the following command:

```
soup.find_all('b')
```

The preceding code generates the following output:

```
[<b>Sherlock </b>, <b>Hamlet</b>, <b>Horatio</b>]
```

Figure 4.6: Contents of all the b tags

9. To check all the contents inside the **table** tag, we write the following command:

```
table = soup.find('table')
```

The preceding code generates the following output:

```
<table>
<tr>
<th>name</th>
<th>qualification</th>
<th>additional qualification</th>
<th>other qualification</th>
</tr>
<tr>
```

Figure 4.7: Contents of the table tag

10. We can also view the content of **table** by looping through it. Insert a new cell and add the following code to implement this:

```
for row in table.find_all('tr'):
    columns = row.find_all('td')
    print(columns)
```

The preceding code generates the following output:

```
[]
[<td>Gangaram</td>, <td>B.Tech</td>, <td>NA</td>, <td>NA</td>]
[<td>Ganga</td>, <td>B.A.</td>, <td>NA</td>, <td>NA</td>]
[<td>Ram</td>, <td>B.Tech</td>, <td>M.Tech</td>, <td>NA</td>]
[<td>Ramlal</td>, <td>B.Music</td>, <td>NA</td>, <td>Diploma in Music</td>]
```

Figure 4.8: Table contents

11. We can also locate specific content in the table. If we want to locate the value of the third row and the second column, we write the following command:

```
table.find_all('tr')[3].find_all('td')[2]
```

The preceding code generates the following output:

```
<td>M.Tech</td>
```

Figure 4.9: Value of the third row of the second column

We have just learned how to extract tag-based information from an HTML file. In the next section, we will focus on fetching content from web pages.

Requesting Content from Web Pages

Whenever you visit a web page from your web browser, you actually send a request to fetch its content. This can be done using Python scripts. Packages such as **urllib3** and **requests** are used to do so. Let's look at an exercise to get a better understanding of this concept.

Exercise 41: Collecting Online Text Data

In this exercise, we will collect online data, with the help of **requests** and **urllib3**. Follow these steps to implement this exercise:

1. Use the **requests** library to request the content of a book available online with the following set of commands:

```
import requests
r = requests.post('https://www.gutenberg.org/files/766/766-0.txt')
r.status_code
```

The preceding code generates the following output:

```
200
```

Figure 4.10: HTTP status code

> **Note**
>
> Here, 200 indicates that we received a proper response from the URL.

2. To locate the text content of the fetched file, write the following code:

```
r.text[:1000]
```

The preceding code generates the following output:

```
'\ufeffThe Project Gutenberg EBook of David Copperfield, by Charles Dickens\r\n\r\nThis eBook is for the use of anyone anywhere
at no cost and with\r\nalmost no restrictions whatsoever. You may copy it, give it away or\r\nre-use it under the terms of the
Project Gutenberg License included\r\nwith this eBook or online at www.gutenberg.org\r\n\r\n\r\n\nTitle: David Copperfield\r\n\r
\nAuthor: Charles Dickens\r\n\r\n\nRelease Date: December, 1996 [Etext #766]\r\nPosting Date: November 24, 2009\r\nLast Updated:
September 25, 2016\r\n\r\nLanguage: English\r\n\r\nCharacter set encoding: UTF-8\r\n\r\n\n*** START OF THIS PROJECT GUTENBERG EBO
OK DAVID COPPERFIELD ***\r\n\r\n\r\n\r\n\r\n\nProduced by Jo Churcher\r\n\r\n\r\n\r\n\r\n\r\n\nDAVID COPPERFIELD\r\n\r\n\r\n\nBy Char
les Dickens\r\n\r\n\r\n\r\n               AFFECTIONATELY INSCRIBED TO\r\n              THE HON.  Mr. AND Mrs. RICHARD WATSO
N,\r\n         OF ROCKINGHAM, NORTHAMPTONSHIRE.\r\n\r\n\r\n\r\nCONTENTS\r\n\r\n\r\n\r\n      I.      I Am Born\r\n      II.      I O
bserve\r\n      III.     I Have a Change\r\n      IV.      I Fall into Disgrace\r\n      V.      '
```

Figure 4.11: Text contents of the file

3. Now we'll write the fetched content to a text file. To do that, add the following code:

```
open("data_ch4/David_Copperfield.txt", 'w').write(r.text)
```

The preceding code generates the following output:

```
1992581
```

Figure 4.12: Total lines

4. Now we'll make use of the **urllib3** library to request the content of the book, available online. Add the following code to do so:

```
import urllib3
http = urllib3.PoolManager()
rr = http.request('GET', 'https://www.gutenberg.org/files/766/766-0.txt')
rr.data[:1000]
```

The preceding code generates the following output:

```
b'\xef\xbb\xbfThe Project Gutenberg EBook of David Copperfield, by Charles Dickens\r\n\r\nThis eBook is for the use of anyone a
nywhere at no cost and with\r\nalmost no restrictions whatsoever.  You may copy it, give it away or\r\nre-use it under the term
s of the Project Gutenberg License included\r\nwith this eBook or online at www.gutenberg.org\r\n\r\n\r\nTitle: David Copperfie
ld\r\n\r\nAuthor: Charles Dickens\r\n\r\nRelease Date: December, 1996  [Etext #766]\r\nPosting Date: November 24, 2009\r\nLast
Updated: September 25, 2016\r\n\r\nLanguage: English\r\n\r\nCharacter set encoding: UTF-8\r\n\r\n*** START OF THIS PROJECT GUTE
NBERG EBOOK DAVID COPPERFIELD ***\r\n\r\n\r\n\r\n\r\n\r\nProduced by Jo Churcher\r\n\r\n\r\n\r\n\r\n\r\nDAVID COPPERFIELD\r\n\r\n\r
\nBy Charles Dickens\r\n\r\n\r\n\r\n\r\n                 AFFECTIONATELY INSCRIBED TO\r\n                THE HON. Mr. AND Mrs. RICHARD
WATSON,\r\n                OF ROCKINGHAM, NORTHAMPTONSHIRE.\r\n\r\n\r\n\r\nCONTENTS\r\n\r\n\r\n\r\n         I.    I Am Born\r\n        II.
I Observe\r\n       III.   I Have a Change\r\n      IV.    I Fall into Disgrace\r\n      V.     '
```

Figure 4.13: Content of the book, available online

5. Once the content is fetched properly, we write it to a text file using the following code:

```
open("data_ch4/David_Copperfield_new.txt", 'wb').write(rr.data)
```

The preceding code generates the following output:

```
2033139
```

Figure 4.14: Total lines

We have just learned how to collect data from online sources with the help of requests and the urllib3 library.

Exercise 42: Analyzing the Content of Jupyter Notebooks (in HTML Format)

In this exercise, we will analyze the content of **text_classifier.html**. Here, we will focus on things such as counting the number of images, listing the packages that have been imported, and checking models and their performance. Follow these steps to implement this exercise:

1. Import **BeautifulSoup** and pass the location of the given HTML file using the following commands:

```
from bs4 import BeautifulSoup
soup = BeautifulSoup(open('data_ch4/text_classifier.html'), 'html.parser')
soup.text[:100]
```

The preceding code generates the following output:

```
'\n\n\nCh3_Activity7_Developing_end_to_end_Text_Classifiers\n\n\n  /*!\n*\n* Twitter Bootstrap\n*\n*/\n/*!\n *'
```

Figure 4.15: Text content of the HTML file

2. To count the number of images, we make use of the **img** tag:

```
len(soup.find_all('img'))
```

The output shows that there are three **img** tags:

3

Figure 4.16: The number of images in the HTML file

3. To list all the packages that are imported, we add the following code:

```
[i.get_text() for i in soup.find_all('span',attrs={"class":"nn"})]
```

The preceding code generates the following output:

```
['pandas',
 'pd',
 'seaborn',
 'sns',
 'matplotlib.pyplot',
 'plt',
 're',
 'string',
 'nltk',
 'nltk.corpus',
 'nltk.stem',
 'sklearn.feature_extraction.text',
 'sklearn.model_selection',
 'pylab',
 'nltk',
 'warnings',
 'sklearn.metrics',
 'sklearn.linear_model',
 'sklearn.ensemble',
 'xgboost']
```

Figure 4.17: List of libraries imported

4. To extract the models and their performances, look for the **h2** and **div** tags with the **class** attribute:

```
for md,i in zip(soup.find_all('h2'), soup.find_
all('div',attrs={"class":"output_subarea output_stream output_stdout
output_text"})):
    print("Model: ",md.get_text())
    print(i.get_text())
    print("------------------------------------------------------------\n\
n\n")
```

The preceding code generates the following output:

```
Model:  Logistic Regression

confusion matrix:
 [[28705   151]
 [ 1663  1396]]

accuracy:  0.943161522794924

classification report:
              precision    recall  f1-score   support

           0       0.95      0.99      0.97     28856
           1       0.90      0.46      0.61      3059

   micro avg       0.94      0.94      0.94     31915
   macro avg       0.92      0.73      0.79     31915
weighted avg       0.94      0.94      0.93     31915


Area under ROC curve for validation set: 0.911224422146723
```

Figure 4.18: Models and their performance

Note

The preceding code also displays the performance of other models such as **Random Forest** and **XGBoost**. The updated output can be viewed at the following location: https://bit.ly/2OxEJwu.

To collect data that's available online, we need to know how HTML pages can be scraped. For instance, if you come across an article on Wikipedia, you may want to extract certain information from it. Since the data is too huge to be processed manually, it would be difficult to deal with this situation. In the next section, we will fetch data from a Wikipedia page.

Activity 6: Extracting Information from an Online HTML Page

In this activity, we will extract data about Rabindranath Tagore from a Wikipedia page. After extracting the data, we will analyze things such as the list of headings under the Works section, the list of his works, and the list of universities named after him. Follow these steps to implement this activity:

1. Import the requests and BeautifulSoup libraries.

2. Fetch the Wikipedia page from https://bit.ly/1ZmRIPC the **get** method of the **requests** library.

3. Convert the fetched content into HTML format using an HTML parser.

4. Print the list of headings under the Works section.

5. Print the list of works by Tagore.

6. Print the list of universities named after Tagore.

> **Note**
>
> The solution for this activity can be found on page 276.

Activity 7: Extracting and Analyzing Data Using Regular Expressions

In this activity, we will extract data from Packt's website. The data to be extracted includes FAQs and their answers, phone numbers, and emails. Follow these steps to implement this activity:

1. Import the necessary libraries.

2. Extract data from https://bit.ly/2uw0Avf the urllib3 library.

3. Fetch questions and answers from the data.

4. Create a DataFrame consisting of questions and answers.

5. Fetch email addresses and phone numbers with the help of regular expressions.

> **Note**
>
> The solution for this activity can be found on page 278.

In this section, we learned how to fetch data from online sources and analyze it in various ways. In the next section, we will discuss dealing with semi-structured data.

Dealing with Semi-Structured Data

We learned about various types of data in *Chapter 2, Feature Extraction from Texts*. Let's quickly recapitulate what semi-structured data refers to. A dataset is said to be semi-structured if it is not in a row-column format but can be converted into a structured format that has a definite number of rows and columns. Often, we come across data that is stored as key-value pairs or embedded between tags, as is the case with **JSON** and **XML** files. These are instances of semi-structured data. The popular semi-structured data formats are JSON and XML.

JSON

JavaScript Object Notation, or JSON, files are used for storing and exchanging data. It is human-readable and easy to interpret. Just like text files and CSV files, JSON files are language independent. This means that different programming languages such as Python, Java, and so on can work with JSON files effectively. In Python, a built-in data structure called **dictionary** is capable of storing JSON objects as is. Generally, data in JSON objects is present in the form of key-value pairs. The datatype of values of JSON objects must be any of the following:

- A string
- A number
- Another JSON object
- An array
- A Boolean
- Null

NoSQL databases such as MongoDB store data in the form of JSON objects. Most APIs return JSON objects. The following figure depicts what a JSON file looks like:

```
{
  "stones":[
    {
      "name": "Space Stone",
      "movies": ["Thor", "Captain America", "The
        Avengers"]
    },
    {
      "name": "Mind Stone",
      "movies": ["The Avengers", "The Winter Soldier",
        "Age of Ultron", "Civil War"]
    },
    {
      "name": "Reality Stone",
      "movies": ["The Dark World"]
    },
    {
      "name": "Power Stone",
      "movies": ["Guardians of the Galaxy"]
    },
    {
      "name": "Time Stone",
      "movies": ["Dr. Strange"]
    },
    {
      "name": "Soul Stone"
    }
  ]
}
```

Figure 4.19: A sample JSON file

Often, the response we get when requesting a URL is in the form of JSON objects. To deal with a JSON file effectively, we need to know how to parse it. The following exercise throws light on this.

Exercise 43: Dealing with JSON Files

In this exercise, we will extract details such as the names of students, their qualifications, and additional qualifications from a JSON file. Follow these steps to implement this exercise:

1. Open a Jupyter notebook.

2. Insert a new cell and import **json**. Pass the location of the file mentioned using the following commands:

```
import json
from pprint import pprint
data = json.load(open('data_ch4/sample_json.json'))
pprint(data)
```

The preceding code generates the following output:

```
{'students': [{'name': 'Gangaram', 'qualification': 'B.Tech'},
              {'name': 'Ganga', 'qualification': 'B.A.'},
              {'additional qualification': 'M.Tech',
               'name' : 'Ram',
               'qualification': 'B.Tech'},
              {'name' : 'Ramlal',
               'other qualification': 'Diploma in Music',
               'qualification': 'B.Music'}]}
```

Figure 4.20: Dictionary form of fetched data

3. To extract the names of the students, add the following code:

    ```
    [dt['name'] for dt in data['students']]
    ```

    The preceding code generates the following output:

```
['Gangaram', 'Ganga', 'Ram', 'Ramlal']
```

Figure 4.21: Names of students extracted

4. To extract their qualifications, enter the following code:

    ```
    [dt['qualification'] for dt in data['students']]
    ```

    The preceding code generates the following output:

```
['B.Tech', 'B.A.', 'B.Tech', 'B.Music']
```

Figure 4.22: Qualifications of students extracted

5. To extract their additional qualifications, enter the following code. Remember: not every student will have additional qualifications. Thus, we need to check this separately. Add the following code to implement this:

    ```
    [dt['additional qualification'] if 'additional qualification' in dt.keys()
    else None for dt in data['students']]
    ```

    The preceding code generates the following output:

```
[None, None, 'M.Tech', None]
```

Figure 4.23: The additional qualifications of students

As JSON objects are similar to the dictionary data structure of Python, they can be effectively stored in a pandas DataFrame in most cases. In the following activity, we will learn how to store JSON files in a pandas DataFrame and extract sentiment scores from them.

Activity 8: Dealing with Online JSON Files

In this activity, we will fetch JSON files from online, extract comments, and evaluate the sentiment scores of each of them. We will make use of the TextBlob library. Follow these steps to implement this activity:

1. Import the necessary libraries.

2. Fetch the data from https://bit.ly/2TJ1T4H the requests library.

3. Create a DataFrame from the fetched data.

4. Translate the comments in the data into English.

5. Make use of the TextBlob library to find the sentiment of each comment and display it.

> **Note**
>
> The solution for this activity can be found on page 281.

We just learned how to detect the sentiments of comments present in a fetched JSON file. In the next section, we will learn about XML.

XML

Just like HTML, XML is another kind of markup language that stores data in between tags. XML stands for Extensible Markup Language. It is human-readable and extensible, that is, we have the liberty to define our own tags. Attributes, elements, and tags in the case of XML are similar to those of HTML. An XML file may or may not have a declaration. But, if it has a declaration, then that must be the first line of the XML file. This declaration statement has three parts: **Version**, **Encoding**, and **Standalone**. Version states which version of the XML standard is being used; Encoding states the type of character encoding being used in this file; Standalone tells the parser whether external information is needed for interpreting the content of the XML file. The following figure depicts what an XML file looks like:

```
<?xml version="1.0" encoding="UTF-8" ?>          ◄──────── XML declaration
<stones>   ◄────────────────────────────────────────────── Start Tag
        <name>Space Stone</name>
        <movies>Thor</movies>
        <movies>Captain America</movies>
        <movies>The Avengers</movies>
</stones>  ◄────────────────────────────────────────────── End Tag
<stones>
        <name>Mind Stone</name>
        <movies>The Avengers</movies>
        <movies>The Winter Soldier</movies>
        <movies>Age of Ultron</movies>
        <movies>Civil War</movies>   ◄──────────────────── Element
</stones>
<stones>
        <name>Reality Stone</name>
        <movies>The Dark World</movies>
</stones>
<stones>
        <name>Power Stone</name>
        <movies>Guardians of the Galaxy</movies>
</stones>
<stones>
        <name>Time Stone</name>
        <movies>Dr. Strange</movies>
</stones>
<stones>
        <name>Soul Stone</name>
</stones>
```

Figure 4.24: A sample XML file

An XML file can be represented as a tree called an XML tree. This XML tree begins with the root element (parent). This root element further branches into child elements. Each element of the XML file is a node in the XML tree. Those elements that don't have any children are leaf nodes. The following figure clearly differentiates between an original XML file and a tree representation of an XML file:

```
<?xml version="1.0" encoding="UTF-8"?>
<datascientists>
    <ds type="A">
        <title>A for Analysis</title>
        <work>Presents insights from data</work>
        <salary>8 LPA</salary>
    </ds>
    <ds type="B">
        <title>B for Building Products</title>
        <work>Uses Machine Learning based algorithms to
            create data driven products</work>
        <salary>12 LPA</salary>
```

```
datascientists ..
  ds ..
    @type: A
    title A for Analysis
    work Presents insights from data
    salary 8 LPA
  ds ..
    @type: B
    title B for Building Products
    work Uses Machine Learning based algorithms to create data driven products
```

Figure 4.25: Comparison of an XML structure

To deal with XML files effectively, we need to comprehend their structure. Let's learn how to parse XML files in the following exercise.

Exercise 44: Dealing with a Local XML File

In this exercise, we will parse an XML file and print various things, such as the names of employees, the organizations they work for, and the total salaries of all employees. Follow these steps to implement this exercise:

1. Open a Jupyter notebook.

2. Insert a new cell, import **xml.etree.ElementTree**, and pass the location of the XML file using the following code:

```
import xml.etree.ElementTree as ET
tree = ET.parse('data_ch4/sample_xml_data.xml')
root = tree.getroot()
root
```

The preceding code generates the following output:

```
<Element 'records' at 0x106512e08>
```

Figure 4.26: Root element

3. To check the tag of the fetched element, type the following code:

```
root.tag
```

The preceding code generates the following output:

```
'records'
```

Figure 4.27: Tag of the element

4. Look for the **name** and **company** tags in the XML and print the data enclosed within them:

```
for record in root.findall('record')[:20]:
    print(record.find('name').text, "---",record.find('company').text)
```

The preceding code generates the following output:

```
Peter Brewer --- Erat Ltd
Wallace Pace --- Sed Nunc Industries
Arthur Ray --- Amet Faucibus Corp.
Judah Vaughn --- Nunc Quis Arcu Inc.
Talon Combs --- Leo Elementum Ltd
Hall Bruce --- Proin Non Massa Consulting
Ronan Grant --- Scelerisque Sed Inc.
Dennis Whitaker --- Scelerisque Neque Foundation
Bradley Oconnor --- Aliquet Corporation
Forrest Alvarez --- Et Eros Institute
Ignatius Meyers --- Facilisis Lorem Limited
Bert Randolph --- Facilisis LLP
Victor Stevenson --- Lacinia Vitae Sodales Incorporated
Jamal Cummings --- Litora Ltd
Samson Estrada --- Lacinia Vitae Sodales Industries
Ira Spencer --- Duis Associates
Kevin Henson --- Sagittis Limited
Melvin Mccarthy --- Ipsum Suspendisse Company
Kieran Underwood --- Quisque Porttitor Eros Ltd
Cedric Phelps --- Lorem Vehicula Corp.
```

Figure 4.28: Data of the name and company tags printed

5. Create a list consisting of the salaries of all employees. Use **numpy** to find out the sum of the salaries:

```
import numpy as np
np.sum([int(record.find('salary').text.replace('$','').replace(',','')) for record in root.findall('record')])
```

The preceding code generates the following output:

745609

Figure 4.29: Sum of salaries

We just learned how to deal with a local XML file. When we request data, many URLs return XML files. Extracting information from a raw XML file is an art. In the next section, we will look at how APIs can be used to retrieve real-time data.

Using APIs to Retrieve Real-Time Data

API stands for Application Programming Interface. Let's understand what an API is, using a real-life example. Suppose you have a socket plug in the wall and you need to charge your cellphone using it. How will you do it? You will have to use a charger/adapter, which will enable you to connect the cellphone to the socket. Here, this adapter is acting as a mediator that connects the cellphone and the socket, thus enabling the smooth transfer of electricity between them. Similarly, some websites do not provide their data directly. Instead, they provide APIs, using which we can extract data from them. Just like the cellphone charger, an API acts as a mediator, enabling the smooth transfer of data between those websites and us. Let's do an exercise to get hands-on experience of collecting data using APIs.

Exercise 45: Collecting Data Using APIs

In this exercise, we will extract carbon intensities from December 30, 2018, to January 3, 2019, using an API. Follow these steps to implement this exercise:

1. Open a Jupyter notebook.

2. Import the necessary packages. Construct the corresponding URL and call it:

```
http = urllib3.PoolManager()
start_dt = '2018-12-30T12:35Z'
end_dt = '2019-01-03T12:35Z'
rrq = http.request('GET', 'https://api.carbonintensity.org.uk/
intensity/'+start_dt+'/'+end_dt, \
                    headers = {'Accept': 'application/json'})
rrq.status
```

The preceding code generates the following output:

200

Figure 4.30: HTTP status code

3. Load the **json** data, insert a new cell, and add the following code to implement this:

```
data = json.loads(rrq.data)
pprint(data)
```

The preceding code generates the following output:

```
{'data': [{'from': '2018-12-30T12:30Z',
           'intensity': {'actual': 203, 'forecast': 202, 'index': 'moderate'},
           'to': '2018-12-30T13:00Z'},
          {'from': '2018-12-30T13:00Z',
           'intensity': {'actual': 208, 'forecast': 201, 'index': 'moderate'},
           'to': '2018-12-30T13:30Z'},
          {'from': '2018-12-30T13:30Z',
           'intensity': {'actual': 217, 'forecast': 205, 'index': 'moderate'},
           'to': '2018-12-30T14:00Z'},
          {'from': '2018-12-30T14:00Z',
           'intensity': {'actual': 225, 'forecast': 214, 'index': 'moderate'},
           'to': '2018-12-30T14:30Z'},
          {'from': '2018-12-30T14:30Z',
           'intensity': {'actual': 235, 'forecast': 220, 'index': 'moderate'},
           'to': '2018-12-30T15:00Z'},
          {'from': '2018-12-30T15:00Z',
           'intensity': {'actual': 247, 'forecast': 231, 'index': 'moderate'},
           'to': '2018-12-30T15:30Z'},
          {'from': '2018-12-30T15:30Z',
```

Figure 4.31: Dictionary of fetched data

4. To create the **DataFrame** of the fetched data and print it, add the following code:

```
pd.DataFrame(data['data'])
```

The preceding code generates the following output:

	from	intensity	to
0	2018-12-30T12:30Z	{'forecast':202,'actual': 203,'index': 'mod…	2018-12-30T13:00Z
1	2018-12-30T13:00Z	{'forecast':201,'actual': 208,'index': 'mod…	2018-12-30T13:30Z

Figure 4.32: DataFrame showing details of carbon intensities

We just learned how to collect data using APIs. In the next section, we will see how to create an API.

API Creation

Often, we need to create our own APIs. The main utilities of APIs are for deploying models and exchanging information between heterogeneous platforms. Popular Python libraries that are used for creating APIs include Flask, Sanic, Bottle, and Django.

Some websites, such as Twitter, provide ready-made APIs for extracting data from them. You just need to have a developer account. In the next section, let's see how we can collect data from Twitter using their Python API, Tweepy.

Activity 9: Extracting Data from Twitter

In this activity, we will extract tweets using the Tweepy library, calculate sentiment scores, and visualize the tweets using a word cloud. Follow these to implement this activity:

1. Log in to your Twitter account with your credentials.

2. Visit https://dev.twitter.com/apps/new and fill in the form by completing the necessary fields.

3. Submit the form and receive the keys and tokens.

4. Use these keys and tokens in your application when making an API call for #WorldWaterDay.

5. Import the necessary libraries.

6. Fetch the data using the keys and tokens.

7. Create a DataFrame consisting of tweets.

8. Filter out those tweets written in English.

9. Calculate sentiment scores for each tweet using the TextBlob library.

10. Visualize the tweets using a word cloud.

> **Note**
>
> The solution for this activity can be found on page 283.

We just learned how to extract data from twitter, analyze tweets, and create a word cloud out of them. In the next section, we will look at how to extract data from local files.

Extracting Data from Local Files

Data exists in various kinds of formats, such as PDF, DOCX, Excel, PPTX, and images. Extracting content from such files is often a tedious job. Let's do an exercise to learn how we can effectively retrieve data from these files.

Exercise 46: Extracting Data from Local Files

In this exercise, we will extract data from different local files, such as a PDF file, an image file, an Excel file, and a Word file. Follow these steps to implement this exercise:

1. Open a Jupyter notebook.

2. Import the **textract** library to extract text from a PDF file:

```
import textract
text = textract.process("data_ch4/Flowchart_Selecting_Model_Type.pdf")
text
```

The preceding code generates the following output:

```
b'Is data\nlabeled?\n\nNo\n\nUnsupervised Methods (Clustering,\nAssociation Rule Mining)\n\nYes\n\nDo
the label(s) have\ncontinuous (numeric)\nvalues or discrete\n(categorical) values?\n\nDiscrete\nCLASS
IFICATION\n\nOutput\nprobability(ies) of\na class(es) or\nclass labels?\n\nContinuous REGRESSION\nCla
ss Labels\n\nNumber of\nresponse\nvariables?\n\nOne\n\nLogistic\nRegression\nor\n\nNaive Bayes\n\nK-NN or
\nLogistic\nRegression\n(with\nthreshold)\n\nNumber of\nexplanatory\nvariables?\n\nOne\n\nTwo or more\n
Univariate\nRegression\n\n\nProbability\n\nMultivariate\nRegression\n\n\nTwo or more\nSimple\nRegression
\n\nAre parameters\nlinearly related?\n\nMultiple\nRegression\nYes\nLinear\nRegression\n\nNo\nNon-Lin
ear\nRegression\n\n\x0c'
```

Figure 4.33: Extracted text from PDFs

3. Import the **PIL** and **pytesseract** libraries to extract text from the image file:

```
from PIL import Image
import pytesseract

print(pytesseract.image_to_string(Image.open('data_ch4/ChatBot.png')))
```

The preceding code generates the following output:

```
Customer Care ChatBot

Customer

ChatBot

Customer

ChatBot

Customer

ChatBot

ustomer
ChatBot:
```

Figure 4.34: Extracted text from the image file

4. To extract text from the image file using **textract**, add the following code:

```
import textract
textract.process("data_ch4/ChatBot.png")
```

The preceding code generates the following output:

```
b' \n\n \n\nCustomer Care ChatBot\n\nCustomer\n\nChatBot\n\nCustomer\n\nChatBot\n\nCustomer\n\nChatBot\n\nustomer\nCh
atBot:\n\n|\n\n \n\n \n\xOc'
```

Figure 4.35: Text extracted using textract

5. To extract data from an Excel file, add the following code:

```
import pandas as pd
data = pd.read_excel('data_ch4/sample_excel.xlsx', sheet=1)
data.head()
```

The preceding code generates the following output:

	name	qualification	additional qualification	other qualification
0	Gangaram	B.Tech	NaN	NaN
1	Ganga	B.A	NaN	NaN
2	Ram	B.Tech	M.Tech	NaN
3	Ramlal	B.Music	NaN	Diploma in Music

Figure 4.36: Data extracted from an Excel file

6. To extract data from a Word document, add the following code:

```
import textract
textract.process("data_ch4/sample_word_document.docx")
```

The preceding code generates the following output:

```
b'Hamlet said to Horatio, There are more things in heaven and earth, Horatio, Than are dreamt of in your philosophy.'
```

Figure 4.37: Data extracted from a Word document

We just learned how to extract data from different local files with the help of different libraries. In the next section, we will walk through an exercise in which we perform various operations on local files.

Exercise 47: Performing Various Operations on Local Files

In this exercise, we will perform various file operations, such as open, write, read, append, and close, on local files. Follow these steps to implement this exercise:

1. Open a Jupyter notebook.

2. First, we create a text file and write a little content in it. Add the following code to implement this:

```
fp = open('data_ch4/sample_text.txt', 'w')
fp.write("I love text mining\n")
fp.close()
```

3. To add more text into an existing text file, add the following code:

```
fp = open('data_ch4/sample_text.txt', 'a')
fp.write("I am learning Natural Language Processing\n")
fp.close()
```

4. To read the content from the text file, add the following code:

```
fp = open('data_ch4/sample_text.txt', 'r')
fp.readlines()
```

The preceding code generates the following output:

```
['I love text mining\n', 'I am learning Natural Language Processing\n']
```

Figure 4.38: Content of the text file

5. To open text files with various encodings, add the following code:

```
import nltk
nltk.download('unicode_samples')
file_location = nltk.data.find('corpora/unicode_samples/polish-lat2.txt')
fp = open(file_location,'r', encoding='latin2')
fp.readlines()
```

The preceding code generates the following output:

```
['Pruska Biblioteka Państwowa. Jej dawne zbiory znane pod nazwą\n',
'"Berlinka" to skarb kultury i sztuki niemieckiej. Przewiezione przez\n',
'Niemców pod koniec II wojny światowej na Dolny Śląsk, zostały\n',
'odnalezione po 1945 r. na terytorium Polski. Trafiły do Biblioteki\n',
'Jagiellońskiej w Krakowie, obejmują ponad 500 tys. zabytkowych\n',
'archiwaliów, m.in. manuskrypty Goethego, Mozarta, Beethovena, Bacha.\n']
```

Figure 4.39: View of the open text file

6. To read these files line by line, insert a new cell and add the following code:

```
for line in open(file_location,'r', encoding='latin2'):
    print(line)
```

The preceding code generates the following output:

```
Pruska Biblioteka Państwowa. Jej dawne zbiory znane pod nazwą

"Berlinka" to skarb kultury i sztuki niemieckiej. Przewiezione przez

Niemców pod koniec II wojny światowej na Dolny Śląsk, zostały

odnalezione po 1945 r. na terytorium Polski. Trafiły do Biblioteki

Jagiellońskiej w Krakowie, obejmują ponad 500 tys. zabytkowych

archiwaliów, m.in. manuskrypty Goethego, Mozarta, Beethovena, Bacha.
```

Figure 4.40: Line-by-line text file

7. To close the opened file, add the following code:

```
fp.close()
```

We just learned how to perform various operations on a local file.

Summary

In this chapter, you have learned ways to collect data by scraping web pages. Moreover, you were introduced to various types of semi-structured data formats, namely JSON and XML. Different ways of retrieving data in real time from a website such as Twitter have been explained with examples. Finally, you were introduced to various methods to deal with different kinds of local files, such as PDF, Word documents, text files, and Excel files.

In the next chapter, you will learn about topic modeling, which is an unsupervised natural language processing technique. It helps in grouping the documents according to the topic detected in them.

5

Topic Modeling

Learning Objectives

By the end of this chapter, you will be able to:

- Describe topic modelling and its various use cases
- Describe topic modeling algorithms
- Describe the workings of LSA and LDA
- Describe topic fingerprinting
- Implement topic modeling using LSA and LDA

In this chapter, you will learn about different topic modeling algorithms and how we can use them to perform topic modeling on any dataset.

Introduction

In the previous chapter, we learned about different ways to collect data from local files and online resources. In this chapter, we will focus on **topic modeling**, which is a popular concept within natural language processing. Topic modeling is a simple way to capture meaning from a collection of documents. Note that, in this case, documents are any coherent collection of words, which could be as short as a tweet or as long as an article, based on the project at hand.

A topic model captures information about the concepts contained in a set of texts. Using these concepts, documents can be organized into different categories or topics.

Topic modeling is mostly done using unsupervised learning algorithms, which detect topics on their own. Topic modeling algorithms operate by doing statistical analysis of words or tokens in documents, and then they use those statistics to automatically assign documents to topics.

In this chapter, we will look at a few popular topic modeling algorithms, such as **Latent Semantic Analysis** (**LSA**) and **Latent Dirichlet Allocation** (**LDA**), and learn how to implement them.

As mentioned earlier, topic modeling uses unsupervised learning algorithms, as opposed to supervised learning algorithms. This means that, during training, we do not have to provide examples with topics from which to learn. This not only helps us discover interesting topics that might exist, but also reduces the manual effort spent labeling texts with topics. However, *unsupervised* does not mean completely unguided, as we often provide algorithms with some parameters with which they can operate.

Topic Discovery

The main goal of topic modeling is to find a set of topics that can be used to classify a set of documents. These topics are implicit because we do not know what they are beforehand, and they are unnamed. We just generally assume that some documents are similar to each other and that we can organize them into topics.

The number of topics is usually small; that is, from 2 to 10. However, there are some use cases in which you may want to have up to 100 (or even more) topics. Since it is the computer algorithm that discovers the topics, the number is generally arbitrary. These topics may not always directly correspond to topics a human would identify. In practice, the number of topics should be much smaller than the number of documents. This helps the topic modeling algorithm in the sorting process. The more examples of documents that we provide, the better the accuracy with which the algorithm can sort and place the documents into categories.

The number of topics chosen depends on the documents and the objectives of the project. You may want to increase the number of topics, if you have a large number of documents or if the documents are fairly diverse. Conversely, if you are analyzing a narrow set of documents, you may want to decrease the number of topics. This generally flows from your assumptions about the documents. If you think that the document set might inherently contain a large number of topics, you should configure the algorithm to look for a similar number of topics. Essentially, here, you are guiding the algorithm to discover what is already inherent in the documents, and you may have already gained a fair idea of that from sampling a few documents and seeing what types of topics they contain.

Discovering Themes

Often, when looking at a collection of text documents, you would like to get a general idea of what themes or topics are contained in the documents. The themes that you uncover can then be used to classify the documents, perhaps to help with further analysis. This can be helpful in legal discovery, which involves examining large numbers of documents, and topic modeling can be used to sort those documents by themes.

In addition to forensic analysis, you can also use topic modeling to discover themes in online text sources. The World Wide Web contains large amounts of data that prove challenging to organize. For example, we have Wikipedia, which is a collection of documents containing facts about the world.

Exploratory Data Analysis

It is recommended to do exploratory data analysis prior to performing any machine learning project. This helps you to learn about the data and the probability distributions of the items within it. You will then be in a better position to choose the specific algorithms to use. When starting a natural language processing project, you can do an exploratory data analysis of the text sources. This would usually involve topic modeling, which uses unsupervised methods such as **Latent Dirichlet Allocation** (**LDA**). This will give you a sense of how the documents can be grouped, and also of the statistical properties of the text dataset.

For example, you might want to know whether the text dataset is skewed to any set of topics, or whether the sources are uniform or disparate. This data further allows us to choose appropriate algorithms for the actual project. For natural language processing, topic modeling is a great way to explore text data and see the ways in which it is naturally grouped. Topic modeling can help you understand whether data is balanced or skewed in any particular way.

Document Clustering

Clustering involves grouping a set of items in such a way that similar items are grouped together. The result of a clustering project is a set of automatically assigned cluster IDs and the data items that they are associated with. For example, you can cluster customers on the basis of features such as buying habits, income, location, and age. Once this is done, you can use these clusters for predictions for general data analysis. There are two types of clustering, namely **hard clustering** and **soft clustering**.

Hard clustering associates each instance with only one cluster. However, a document often tends to have more than one topic within it. Topic modeling allows for soft clustering, meaning that each document can be associated with more than one topic. This gives you a richer understanding of a document and a way to build search indexes that can have documents in multiple categories.

Dimensionality Reduction

One of the challenges of machine learning is the handling of high-dimensional data. A **dimension** is an axis on which your data varies. Documents are highly dimensional in nature, because they contain many different words. Each word can be considered a feature on which the document would vary from another document. For example, if you look at the document for this chapter, you can see that it is inherently complex, once you start focusing on each individual word and what that word could possibly mean. If you instead tried to summarize this chapter by the topics that it focuses on, you would see that there are fewer topics than words. By working with topics, you reduce the number of dimensions with which to work. So, topic modeling is one way to perform dimensionality reduction in preparation for machine learning projects.

Historical Analysis

More recently, some enterprising historians have begun to use natural language processing techniques to aid historical analysis. History is literally dimensionality reduction. Historians take a vast amount of written information and construct themes and stories that help us understand what happened in the past. It turns out that topic modeling can be a really useful tool for historians.

One project that demonstrates this was performed by Dr. Robert K. Nelson of the University of Richmond. He used topic modeling to uncover the historical themes and topics in two newspapers on opposing sides of the American Civil War. He examined the archives of the Richmond Daily Dispatch, a Confederate newspaper; and the New York Times, a Union newspaper; where both sought to raise the level of patriotic support for their respective causes. The more popular topics in the Richmond Daily Dispatch were poetry, patriotism, and anti-Northern diatribes. The analysis also tracked changes in the topics over a period of time, as well as the intensity of difference between the two newspapers.

Thus, topic modeling is a tool that has proven to be useful for historians. It will be used more often in the future, given that we are producing so much digital data.

Bag of Words

Before we understand what a modeling algorithm is, we should make a few simplifying assumptions. Firstly, we treat a document as a **bag of words**, meaning we ignore the structure and grammar of the document and just use the counts of words in the document to infer patterns about it. Ignoring structure, sequences, and grammar allows us to use certain algorithms that rely on counts and probability to make inferences. On the other hand, we do lose some information when we ignore sequences and structure. A bag of words is a dictionary containing each unique word and the integer count of the occurrences of the word in the document.

> **Note**
>
> We will look at approaches that explicitly model sequences in later chapters.

Topic Modeling Algorithms

Topic modeling algorithms operate on the following assumptions:

- Topics contain a set of words
- Documents are made up of a set of topics

Topics are not observed but are assumed to be hidden generators of words. After these assumptions, different algorithms diverge in how they go about discovering topics. In this chapter, we will cover two topic modeling algorithms, namely **LSA** and **LDA**. Both models will be discussed in detail in the coming sections.

Latent Semantic Analysis

We will start by looking at LSA. LSA actually predates the **World Wide Web**. It was first described in 1988. LSA is also known by an alternative acronym, **Latent Semantic Indexing** (**LSI**), particularly when it is used for semantic searches of document indexes. The goal of LSA is to uncover the latent topics that underlie documents and words. The assumption is that these latent topics drive the distribution of words in the document. In the next section, we will learn about the workings of LSA.

LSA – How It Works

Let's start at the very beginning: we have a collection of documents, and these documents are made up of words. Our goal is to perform statistical analysis in order to discover the latent topics in the documents. Note that, even though the documents are made up of words, we sometimes think of them as terms. So, when you see phrases such as term-to-document, just think of "term" as "word."

So, in the beginning, we have a collection of documents that we can represent as a term-to-document matrix. This term-to-document matrix has terms as rows and documents as columns. The following table gives a simplified illustration of a term-to-document matrix:

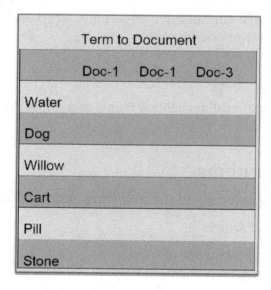

Figure 5.1: A simplified view of a term-to-document matrix

Now, we break this matrix down into separate matrices, namely a term-to-topics matrix, a topic-importance matrix, and a topic-to-documents matrix. This separation is done by **Singular Value Decomposition** (**SVD**). This is a matrix factorization technique used for separating a rectangular matrix into other matrices. We will discuss SVD in the next section. The following figure gives a better understanding of the concept:

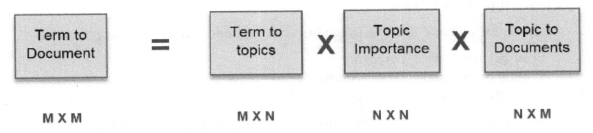

Figure 5.2: Document matrix and its broken matrices

As we can see in this diagram, the rectangular matrix is separated into the product of other matrices. Let's look at the equation for SVD. The process takes a matrix, M, and splits it, as shown in the following figure:

$$M = U\Sigma V^*$$

Figure 5.3: SVD equation

In the preceding figure:

- M is an m×m matrix
- U is an m×n left-singular matrix
- Σ is an n×n diagonal matrix with non-negative real numbers
- V is an m×n right-singular matrix
- V* is an n×m matrix, which is the transpose of V

The **gensim** library is probably the most popular Python library for topic modeling. It is easy to use and provides two popular topic modeling model classes, namely **LdaModel** (for LDA) and **LsiModel** (for LSI). There is also **CoherenceModel**, which is used to measure the accuracy of the topics that were chosen. Now that we have understood the workings of LSA, in the next section, we will solve an exercise to get an even better understanding.

Exercise 48: Analyzing Reuters News Articles with Latent Semantic Analysis

In this exercise, we will analyze a dataset of Reuters news articles. Specifically, we will perform topic modeling using LSI. For this, we will make use of the **LsiModel** class provided by the gensim library. Follow these steps to implement this exercise:

1. Open a Jupyter notebook.

2. Insert a new cell and add the following code to import the necessary libraries:

```
from gensim import corpora
from gensim.models import LsiModel
from gensim.parsing.preprocessing import preprocess_string
```

3. To clean the text, define the functions, then remove the non-alphanumeric characters and replace the numbers with the #character Insert a new cell and add the following code to implement this:

```
import re

def clean_text(x):
    pattern = r'[^a-zA-z0-9\s]'
    text = re.sub(pattern, '', x)
    return x

def clean_numbers(x):
    if bool(re.search(r'\d', x)):
        x = re.sub('[0-9]{5,}', '#####', x)
        x = re.sub('[0-9]{4}', '####', x)
        x = re.sub('[0-9]{3}', '###', x)
        x = re.sub('[0-9]{2}', '##', x)
    return x

def clean(x):
    x = clean_text(x)
    x = clean_numbers(x)
    return x
```

> **Note**
>
> The Reuters news articles are contained in files with the *.sgm extension and they can be found at this location: https://bit.ly/2YAQB5p. Each file contains multiple articles and the text is written within the <BODY></BODY> XML element.

4. The Reuters news articles are in XML format, and to read the articles into Python, we will make use of BeautifulSoup. Insert a new cell and add the following code to import the necessary libraries:

```
from pathlib import Path
from bs4 import BeautifulSoup
import re
```

> **Note**
>
> We can also use **ElementTree**, which is the built-in Python module for reading XML. As the Reuters SGM files have some characters that trip up the ElementTree parser, we'll use BeautifulSoup as it is considerably more forgiving of unusual characters.

5. Create a **load_articles()** function, which loops through each file, reads the contents, and creates a **BeautifulSoup** instance from them. Insert a new cell and add the following code to implement this:

```
def load_articles(data_dir):
    reuters = Path(data_dir)
    for path in reuters.glob('*.sgm'):
        with path.open() as sgm_file:
            contents = sgm_file.read()
            soup = BeautifulSoup(contents)
            for article in soup.find_all('body'):
                yield article.text
```

This yields the text of the **<BODY>** element.

6. Load all the documents into a list. Insert a new cell and add the following code:

```
def load_documents(document_dir):
    print(f'Loading from {document_dir}')
    documents = list(load_articles(document_dir))
    print(f'Loaded {len(documents)} documents')
    return documents
```

The **load_documents()** function uses the **load_articles()** function and returns the list of documents.

7. Prepare the documents for the model. For this, clean the text using the functions that we created earlier. Then, run each document through a series of text processing functions, which are often required for LSA and other similar models. Insert a new cell and add the following code:

```
def prepare_documents(documents):
    print('Preparing documents')
    documents = [clean(document) for document in documents]
    documents = [preprocess_string(doc) for doc in documents]
    return documents
```

8. Create a model that uses **LsiModel**. Insert a new cell and add the following code to implement this:

```
def create_lsa_model(documents, dictionary, number_of_topics):
    print(f'Creating LSI Model with {number_of_topics} topics')
    document_terms = [dictionary.doc2bow(doc) for doc in documents]
    return LsiModel(document_terms,
                    num_topics=number_of_topics,
                    id2word = dictionary)

def run_lsa_process(documents, number_of_topics=10):
    documents = prepare_documents(documents)
    dictionary = corpora.Dictionary(documents)
    lsa_model = create_lsa_model(documents, dictionary,
                                 number_of_topics)
    return documents, dictionary, lsa_model
```

9. Now we'll load the documents into the model and run the LSA process. Insert a new cell and add the following code to implement this:

```
document_dir ='data/reuters'
articles = list(load_articles(document_dir))
documents, dictionary, model = run_lsa_process(articles, number_of_
topics=8)
```

The code returns the following output:

```
Preparing documents
Creating LSA Model with 8 topics
```

Figure 5.4: This log output shows that we are training with eight topics

Once created, our model contains information about the topics that we specified and the word tokens that contributed to each topic.

10. The LSI model used the text data that we provided to separate the word tokens into the number of topics that we specified. Since we specified eight, you will see eight topics. The topics are unnamed, and they are overlapping. Due to this, if we were to examine the assignment of documents to topics, you would see some words assigned to multiple topics.

11. We can use the **print_topics** function to see the model's information. Insert a new cell and add the following code to implement this:

```
model.print_topics()
```

The code generates the following output:

```
[(0,
  '0.558*"said" + 0.279*"mln" + 0.258*"dlr" + 0.221*"reut" + 0.218*"reuter" + 0.192*"pct" + 0.164*"year" + 0.155*"march" + 0.13
6*"bank" + 0.130*"man"'),
 (1,
  '0.497*"apr" + -0.461*"mar" + -0.437*"march" + 0.412*"april" + 0.157*"june" + 0.155*"jun" + -0.106*"mln" + 0.074*"reut" + -0.
068*"ct" + 0.064*"said"'),
 (2,
  '0.647*"oct" + 0.308*"mln" + 0.243*"ct" + 0.228*"net" + 0.217*"shr" + -0.213*"march" + -0.191*"mar" + 0.178*"blah" + -0.138
*"said" + 0.126*"qtr"'),
 (3,
  '-0.487*"june" + -0.446*"jun" + 0.417*"apr" + 0.333*"april" + 0.216*"march" + 0.214*"mar" + -0.189*"said" + 0.088*"mln" + -0.
074*"compani" + -0.064*"juli"'),
 (4,
  '-0.298*"oct" + 0.266*"mln" + -0.252*"mar" + 0.252*"april" + -0.212*"reut" + -0.163*"sep" + 0.149*"usa" + -0.147*"jul" + -0.1
45*"jun" + -0.144*"close"'),
 (5,
  '-0.262*"jun" + -0.249*"reut" + 0.223*"japan" + -0.213*"june" + 0.210*"said" + 0.198*"bank" + 0.181*"trade" + 0.176*"oct" + -
0.175*"dlr" + -0.166*"usa"'),
 (6,
  '-0.309*"feb" + -0.214*"nil" + 0.208*"trade" + -0.188*"pct" + -0.185*"tonn" + -0.181*"price" + 0.173*"texaco" + 0.170*"man" +
0.145*"bank" + -0.130*"year"'),
 (7,
  '0.470*"feb" + -0.168*"rate" + 0.146*"texaco" + 0.126*"new" + 0.114*"januari" + -0.114*"blah" + 0.108*"report" + -0.107*"oct"
+ 0.105*"dlr" + -0.103*"nil"')]
```

Figure 5.5: Calling the print_topics function on LsiModel

12. To create our **LsiModel**, we had to decide upfront how many topics we wanted. This would not necessarily match the number of topics that are actually in the Reuters articles. There could, in fact, be more or fewer natural topics than the eight that we chose. In order to find a good number of topics, we can use **CoherenceModel**, which **gensim** provides, to see how well our model's topics were chosen and how well they fit together. Generally, we do not want topics to overlap too much, and the coherence score will let us know whether that is the case. Add the following code in a new cell to implement this:

```
from gensim.models.coherencemodel import CoherenceModel

def calculate_coherence_score(documents, dictionary, model):
    coherence_model = CoherenceModel(model=model,
                                     texts=documents,
                                     dictionary=dictionary,
                                     coherence='c_v')
```

```
    return coherence_model.get_coherence()

def get_coherence_values(start, stop):
    for num_topics in range(start, stop):
        print(f'\nCalculating coherence for {num_topics} topics')
        documents, dictionary, model = run_lsa_process(articles,
                                          number_of_
topics=num_topics)
        coherence = calculate_coherence_score(documents,
                                          dictionary,
                                          model)
        yield coherence
```

13. To calculate the coherence scores for a range between 20 and 25, insert a new cell and add the following code:

```
min_topics, max_topics = 20,25
coherence_scores = list(get_coherence_values(min_topics, max_topics))
```

The code generates the following output:

```
Calculating coherence for 20 topics
Preparing documents
Creating LSA Model with 20 topics

Calculating coherence for 21 topics
Preparing documents
Creating LSA Model with 21 topics

Calculating coherence for 22 topics
Preparing documents
Creating LSA Model with 22 topics

Calculating coherence for 23 topics
Preparing documents
Creating LSA Model with 23 topics

Calculating coherence for 24 topics
Preparing documents
Creating LSA Model with 24 topics
```

Figure 5.6: Calculating the coherence score on a different number of topics

14. Now we can plot the coherence scores in the chart to see how many topics would be best. We will make use of **Matplotlib's** `pyplot` library for this. Insert a new cell and add the following code to implement this:

```
%matplotlib inline

import matplotlib.pyplot as plt
import matplotlib.style as style

style.use('fivethirtyeight')
x = [int(i) for i in range(min_topics, max_topics)]

plt.figure(figsize=(10,8))
plt.plot(x, coherence_scores)
plt.xlabel('Number of topics')
plt.ylabel('Coherence Value')
plt.title('Coherence Scores by number of Topics')
```

The code generates the following output:

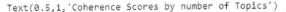

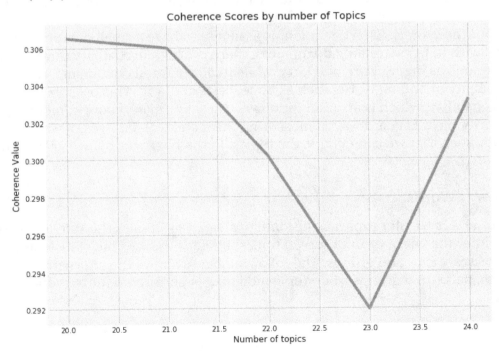

Figure 5.7: Chart of the coherence score by the number of topics

We have now performed topic modeling with the help of LSI. We also plotted the coherence scores of all the topics on the chart, which will help us make better decisions when selecting the best topics. In the next section, we will learn about another topic modeling algorithm: LDA.

Latent Dirichlet Allocation

LSA is prone to overfitting on training data. After you have trained your model and added new documents, the model will get progressively worse until you retrain it. This means that you have to pay attention to how you maintain an LSI model. Because of the potential of overfitting, as well as the fact that accuracy tends to be lower than that of LDA, the LDA model is used for topic modeling more often.

LDA is a generative statistical model that allows a set of items to be sorted into unobserved groups by similarity. LDA is applied to items that are each made up of various parts, and to which similarity sorting can be done using the statistical patterns of those parts. LDA can be performed on any collection of things that are made up of parts, such as employees and their skills, sports teams and their individual members, and documents and their words. Since this chapter is about natural language processing, we are primarily interested in documents and words.

In topic modeling, groups are unobserved. However, what we can observe are the words in documents and how we can reverse engineer statistical patterns about the words to figure out the groups. Each document is assumed to have a small number of topics associated with it. In cat-related documents, there is a high probability that you will find words such as meow, purr, and kitty, while in dog-related documents, there is a high probability of finding words such as bone, bark, and wag. This probability is called a **prior probability**, which is an assumption we can safely make about something before actually verifying it. LDA is a way of measuring the statistical patterns of words in documents, such that we can deduce the topics. In the next section, we will explore the workings of LDA.

LDA – How It Works

The goal of LDA is to infer topics using statistical analysis. It uses the statistical counts of data to infer the latent or unobserved topics. It keeps track of the statistical counts of the composites, parts, and groups. The following figure shows the alternative names for composites, parts, and groups when topic modeling is performed for text documents with LDA:

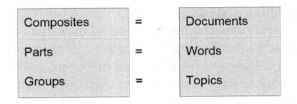

Figure 5.8: Alternative names for composites, parts, and groups

Let's look at a specific example. We have four documents that contain only three unique words: **Cat**, **Dog**, and **Hippo**. The following figure shows the documents and the number of times each word is found in each document:

	Cat	Dog	Hippo
Document 1	10	0	0
Document 2	0	10	0
Document 3	0	0	10
Document 4	10	10	10

Figure 5.9: Occurrence of words in different documents

As we can see from the figure, the word **Cat** is found **10** times in **Document 1** and **Document 4** and **0** times in documents **2** and **3**. **Document 4** contains all three words **10** times each. For its analysis, LDA maintains two probability tables. The first table tracks the probability of selecting a specific word when sampling a specific topic. The second table keeps track of the probability of selecting a specific topic when sampling a particular document:

Words vs Topics

	Topic 1	Topic 2	Topic 3
Cat	0.00	0.00	0.99
Dog	0.99	0.00	0.00
Hippo	0.00	0.99	0.00

Documents vs Topics

	Topic 1	Topic 2	Topic 3
Document 1	0.030	0.030	0.939
Document 2	0.939	0.030	0.030
Document 3	0.030	0.939	0.030
Document 4	0.33	0.33	0.33

Figure 5.10: Probability tables

These probability tables reflect how likely it is to get a particular word if you sampled from each topic. If you sampled a word from **Topic 3**, it would likely be **Cat** (probability 99%). If you sampled **Document 4**, then there is a one-third chance of getting each of the topics, since it contains all three words in equal proportions.

LDA is based on the **Dirichlet distribution**. The Dirichlet distribution is a multivariate distribution, meaning it describes the distribution of multiple variables. It is used for topic modeling since we are usually concerned with multiple topics. The Dirichlet distribution helps us specify our assumptions about the probability of distributions before doing analysis. In other words, it helps us with our prior assumptions. Now that we have learned about LDA and its workings, let's look at the exercise in the next section to get a better understanding.

Exercise 49: Topics in Airline Tweets

In this exercise, we will perform topic modeling on airline tweets in order to discover what topics are being discussed in them. We will use the LDA algorithm provided by the gensim library. Follow these steps to implement this exercise:

1. Open a Jupyter notebook.

2. We will use the **pandas** library to read the tweets into a DataFrame in order to do the text processing and build the LDA topic model. Insert a new cell and add the following code to import the necessary libraries:

```
import pandas as pd
import warnings
warnings.filterwarnings('ignore')
pd.set_option('display.max_colwidth', 900)
```

3. Now we'll read the **Tweets.csv** file into a DataFrame and then select only the **text** column by using the **usecols** parameter. We'll then look at the first 10 tweets using the **head()** function:

```
tweets = pd. read_csv('data/twitter-airline/Tweets.csv', usecols=['text'])
tweets.head(10)
```

The code generates the following output:

	text
0	@VirginAmerica What @dhepburn said.
1	@VirginAmerica plus you've added commercials to the experience... tacky.
2	@VirginAmerica I didn't today... Must mean I need to take another trip!
3	@VirginAmerica it's really aggressive to blast obnoxious "entertainment" in your guests' faces & they have little recourse
4	@VirginAmerica and it's a really big bad thing about it
5	@VirginAmerica seriously would pay $30 a flight for seats that didn't have this playing.\nit's really the only bad thing about flying VA
6	@VirginAmerica yes, nearly every time I fly VX this "ear worm" won't go away :)
7	@VirginAmerica Really missed a prime opportunity for Men Without Hats parody, there. https://t.co/mWpG7grEZP
8	@virginamerica Well, I didn't...but NOW I DO! :-D
9	@VirginAmerica it was amazing, and arrived an hour early. You're too good to me.

Figure 5.11: View of some of the tweets in a dataset as output in a Jupyter notebook

4. Now we need to clean the text. We will use the Python regex package, **re**, for this, and so we will add a number of regexes that will be used to clean the strings. Insert a new cell and the following code to implement this:

```
import re

HANDLE = '@\w+'
LINK = 'https://t\.co/\w+'
SPECIAL_CHARS = '&lt;|&lt;|&amp;|#'

def clean(text):
    text = re.sub(HANDLE, ' ', text)
    text = re.sub(LINK, ' ', text)
    text = re.sub(SPECIAL_CHARS, ' ', text)
    return text

tweets['text'] = tweets.text.apply(clean)
```

5. Now apply the **clean** function to the **tweets** DataFrame. We'll make use of the regexes that we defined previously and the **sub** function to replace the values with a blank string. At the end, we'll create a new column, called **CleanText**, which contains the values of the **text** column after applying the **clean** function. Insert a new cell and add the following code to implement this:

    ```
    tweets['text'] = tweets.text.apply(clean)
    ```

6. To display the results so far, use the **head** function. Insert a new cell and add the following code to implement this:

    ```
    tweets.head(10)
    ```

    The code generates the following output:

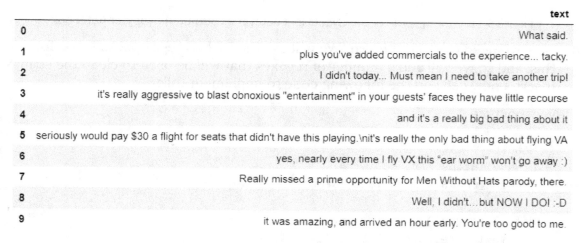

	text
0	What said.
1	plus you've added commercials to the experience... tacky.
2	I didn't today... Must mean I need to take another trip!
3	it's really aggressive to blast obnoxious "entertainment" in your guests' faces they have little recourse
4	and it's a really big bad thing about it
5	seriously would pay $30 a flight for seats that didn't have this playing.\nit's really the only bad thing about flying VA
6	yes, nearly every time I fly VX this "ear worm" won't go away :)
7	Really missed a prime opportunity for Men Without Hats parody, there.
8	Well, I didn't... but NOW I DO! :-D
9	it was amazing, and arrived an hour early. You're too good to me.

Figure 5.12: Tweet dataset after performing cleaning and preprocessing

7. After cleaning the text, we are ready to use the gensim library to build our model. But first, we need to convert the data into the form required for gensim. The gensim LDA model requires the data to be in a list of token lists, meaning each entry in the list is a list of the tokens that make up each individual document. This means that we need to tokenize each tweet by breaking it into individual words. Insert a new cell and add the following code to implement this:

    ```
    from gensim.parsing.preprocessing import preprocess_string
    tweets = tweets.text.apply(preprocess_string).tolist()
    ```

8. For the LDA model, we need to create a dictionary of each token in the dataset. The dictionary captures each unique word and gives it an index. Insert a new cell and the following code to implement this:

```
from gensim import corpora
from gensim.models.ldamodel import LdaModel

dictionary = corpora.Dictionary(tweets)
corpus = [dictionary.doc2bow(text) for text in tweets]
```

9. Now we will create an **LdaModel** instance that will learn on **10** topics. We specify that the model will make 15 passes through the data. To implement this, add the following code in a new cell:

```
NUM_TOPICS = 10
ldamodel = LdaModel(corpus,
                    num_topics = NUM_TOPICS,
                    id2word=dictionary, passes=15)
```

10. After training, we can access the topics as determined by the model. One method is by using the **print_topics** function. This gives us a list of each topic and the words that are attributed to each topic. Insert a new cell and add the following code:

```
ldamodel.print_topics(num_words=6)
```

The code generates the following output:

```
[(0,
  '0.046*"help" + 0.029*"book" + 0.029*"flight" + 0.028*"chang" + 0.026*"phone" + 0.023*"ticket"'),
 (1,
  '0.096*"servic" + 0.092*"custom" + 0.018*"answer" + 0.013*"person" + 0.013*"care" + 0.013*"agent"'),
 (2,
  '0.050*"flight" + 0.050*"wait" + 0.047*"hour" + 0.035*"plane" + 0.030*"delai" + 0.026*"gate"'),
 (3,
  '0.160*"thank" + 0.025*"great" + 0.019*"appreci" + 0.018*"follow" + 0.015*"respons" + 0.012*"gui"'),
 (4,
  '0.027*"work" + 0.027*"know" + 0.022*"fly" + 0.019*"let" + 0.019*"plane" + 0.018*"gui"'),
 (5,
  '0.054*"bag" + 0.028*"baggag" + 0.026*"check" + 0.023*"look" + 0.013*"free" + 0.012*"come"'),
 (6,
  '0.032*"fly" + 0.027*"worst" + 0.024*"time" + 0.023*"flight" + 0.022*"airlin" + 0.015*"updat"'),
 (7,
  '0.034*"ye" + 0.028*"luggag" + 0.021*"lost" + 0.018*"bag" + 0.015*"fleek" + 0.015*"fleet"'),
 (8,
  '0.186*"flight" + 0.069*"cancel" + 0.035*"flightl" + 0.025*"tomorrow" + 0.024*"late" + 0.023*"delai"'),
 (9,
  '0.021*"week" + 0.016*"point" + 0.016*"mile" + 0.015*"team" + 0.013*"offer" + 0.011*"dai"')]
```

Figure 5.13: Result of printing the topics from LdaModel

11. In order to decide on the correct number of topics, we will need a way to assess how well the model's topics were chosen. Gensim provides a **CoherenceModel** instance that you can use. Add the following code in a new code cell:

```
from gensim.models.coherencemodel import CoherenceModel

def calculate_coherence_score(documents, dictionary, model):
    coherence_model = CoherenceModel(model=model,
                                     texts=documents,
                                     dictionary=dictionary,
                                     coherence='c_v')
    return coherence_model.get_coherence()

def get_coherence_values(start, stop):
    for num_topics in range(start, stop):
        print(f'\nCalculating coherence for {num_topics} topics')
        ldamodel = LdaModel(corpus,
                       num_topics = num_topics,
                       id2word=dictionary, passes=2)
        coherence = calculate_coherence_score(tweets,
                                         dictionary,
                                         ldamodel)
        yield coherence
```

12. Now create a list of the coherence scores from 10 to 30 topics. Insert a new cell and add the following code to implement this:

```
min_topics, max_topics = 10,30
coherence_scores = list(get_coherence_values(min_topics, max_topics))
```

The code generates the following output:

```
Calculating coherence for 10 topics
Calculating coherence for 11 topics
Calculating coherence for 12 topics
Calculating coherence for 13 topics
Calculating coherence for 14 topics
Calculating coherence for 15 topics
Calculating coherence for 16 topics
Calculating coherence for 17 topics
Calculating coherence for 18 topics
Calculating coherence for 19 topics
Calculating coherence for 20 topics
Calculating coherence for 21 topics
Calculating coherence for 22 topics
Calculating coherence for 23 topics
Calculating coherence for 24 topics
Calculating coherence for 25 topics
Calculating coherence for 26 topics
Calculating coherence for 27 topics
Calculating coherence for 28 topics
Calculating coherence for 29 topics
```

Figure 5.14: Coherence scores

13. To plot the coherence scores, we insert a new cell and add the following code:

```python
import matplotlib.pyplot as plt
import matplotlib.style as style
from matplotlib.ticker import MaxNLocator

style.use('fivethirtyeight')

%matplotlib inline

x = [int(i) for i in range(min_topics, max_topics)]

ax = plt.figure(figsize=(10,8))
plt.xticks(x)
plt.plot(x, coherence_scores)
```

```
plt.xlabel('Number of topics')
plt.ylabel('Coherence Value')
plt.title('Coherence Scores', fontsize=10);
```

The code generates the following output:

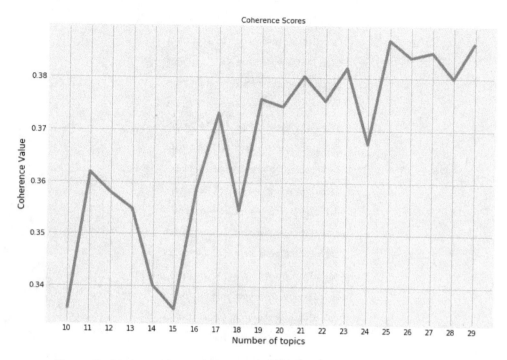

Figure 5.15: Chart of the coherence scores of the tweet topic model

We have performed topic modeling with the help of LDA. In the next section, we will focus on **topic fingerprinting**.

Topic Fingerprinting

Let's say you are required to perform a similarity search on a set of documents. Here, "similarity" refers to the closeness of a document's content to that of another document. For example, take a look at these two sentences:

- It was a week before we were to open our first show.

- It was the week before the final Christmas show.

These two sentences could be considered similar due to their similar topics, such as performing, shows, date, and time. If you analyzed them using topic modeling, you could discover those topics by creating a chart and finding how relevant each document was to each topic. Also, they are unrelated to other topics, such as cats and dogs, and so there would be a low score for those topics. If you had a fixed number of topics, then you could create a relevance chart and that would be a visualization of that document.

The first step is to represent documents as a set of numbers or a fingerprint. A document fingerprint is a set of numbers that summarizes a document's content and allows you to perform simple math functions. This further allows you to determine whether the documents are similar in content or not. To get a better understanding of topic fingerprinting, we will look at an exercise in the next section.

Exercise 50: Visualizing Documents Using Topic Vectors

In this exercise, we will make use of the LDA model to list the topics along with the score for the document. Using these topics, we will create a vector, which then will be converted into a chart. Follow these steps to implement this exercise:

1. Open a Jupyter notebook.

2. Insert a new cell and add the following code to import the necessary libraries:

```
import pandas as pd
pd.set_option('display.max_colwidth', 800)
```

3. We will use pandas to read the data into a DataFrame. We want to load only a few of the columns, including the **description_en** column, which we will use as the target for topic modeling. We will also drop rows that contain NA values in the **description_en** column. Insert a new cell and add the following code to implement this:

```
OPEN_DATA_URL = 'data/canada-open-data/inventory.csv'
COLUMNS = ['title_en', 'description_en','date_released']

catalog = pd.read_csv(OPEN_DATA_URL, usecols=COLUMNS)
catalog = catalog.dropna(subset=['description_en'])
```

4. You can now view the contents of the catalog. Insert a new cell and add the following code:

```
catalog
```

The code generates the following output:

	title_en	description_en	date_released
0	The AAFC Productivity Account for Canadian Agriculture	The AAFC Productivity Account for Canadian agriculture is an annual time-series database, covering the years 1961-2011, that is comprised of price index and constant dollar implicit quantity series for gross output and input aggregates. The data are defined at the national level only – i.e. for the whole of Canada. These data are used to estimate a total factor productivity (TFP) index for Canadian agriculture, which is the ratio of total gross output to total input, where both output and input are constant dollar implicit quantities. Average growth in the TFP index, referred to as TFP growth, can be estimated using a variety of methods; the growth rate reported in AAFC publications is estimated using OLS.\r\n\r\nFurther documentation provided in AAFC_PACA.odt	2018-08-10
1	Swift Current Water Chemistry - Long Term Tillage Study - 1962-2011	The Swift current water quantity and quality is an annual time-series database covering the period of 1962-2011. This database contains datasets for annual runoff volume, peak flow rates, water quality attributes, snow water equivalent and soil moisture from an edge of field study conducted at Swift Current, SK.	2018-11-23
2	Minor Use Pesticides Program Project Status by Crop	The Pest Management Centre's (PMC) Minor Use Pesticides Program is a joint initiative between Agriculture and Agri-Food Canada and Health Canada's Pest Management Regulatory Agency (PMRA) to improve the availability of reduced-risk products to agricultural producers and improve the access to a broad range of minor use pesticides. The PMC reviews the data resulting from field trials and laboratory analyses, and prepares a submission to PMRA to support the registration of the minor use pesticide. Upon receiving a finalized regulatory submission from PMC, PMRA reviews it and decides whether or not to accept the pesticide for use in Canada.\r\n\r\nThis is a complete list of PMC's projects with their statuses. For those projects with the status D.3.2 Review Complete, please check with the p...	2018-12-14

Figure 5.16: Sample records from the OpenData catalog

5. Now we are at the text processing stage. First, we convert the text to lowercase, then we remove the stop words, as they do not add any value to the model. Finally, we need to create a list of lists of tokens. Each item in the outer list is the description, split into individual tokens. For this, we make use of the gensim `simple_preprocess()` function. Insert a new cell and add the following code to implement this:

```
from gensim.parsing.preprocessing import remove_stopwords
from gensim.utils import import simple_preprocess

def text_to_tokens(text):
    text = text.lower()
    text = remove_stopwords(text)
    tokens = simple_preprocess(text)
    return tokens
```

6. Now we can create a new description dataset by applying the `text_to_tokens()` function. This will be the input for the topic model. Insert a new cell and add the following code to implement this:

```
dataset_descriptions = catalog.description_en.apply(text_to_tokens)
```

7. If you look at the contents of **dataset_descriptions**, you will see that it contains a list of the tokens extracted from each description using the **text_to_tokens()** function. Insert a new cell and add the following code to implement this:

```
dataset_descriptions
```

The code generates the following output:

```
0
[aafc, productivity, account, canadian, agriculture, annual, time, series, database, covering, years, comprised, price, inde
x, constant, dollar, implicit, quantity, series, gross, output, input, aggregates, data, defined, national, level, canada, da
ta, estimate, total, factor, productivity, tfp, index, canadian, agriculture, ratio, total, gross, output, total, input, outp
ut, input, constant, dollar, implicit, quantities, average, growth, tfp, index, referred, tfp, growth, estimated, variety, me
thods, growth, rate, reported, aafc, publications, estimated, ols, documentation, provided, aafc_paca, odt]
1
[swift, current, water, quantity, quality, annual, time, series, database, covering, period, database, contains, datasets, an
nual, runoff, volume, peak, flow, rates, water, quality, attributes, snow, water, equivalent, soil, moisture, edge, field, st
udy, conducted, swift, current, sk]
2                                                                        [pest, management, centre, pmc, minor, use,
pesticides, program, joint, initiative, agriculture, agri, food, canada, health, canada, pest, management, regulatory, agenc
y, pmra, improve, availability, reduced, risk, products, agricultural, producers, improve, access, broad, range, minor, use,
pesticides, pmc, reviews, data, resulting, field, trials, laboratory, analyses, prepares, submission, pmra, support, registra
tion, minor, use, pesticide, receiving, finalized, regulatory, submission, pmc, pmra, reviews, decides, accept, pesticide, us
e, canada, complete, list, pmc, projects, statuses, projects, status, review, complete, check, pesticide, manufacturer, visi
t, pmra, pesticide, label, database, pesticide, ready, use]
3                                                                         [pest, management, centre, m
inor, use, pesticides, program, joint, initiative, agriculture, agri, food, canada, health, canada, pest, management, regulat
```

Figure 5.17: Records from the description dataset after cleaning, preprocessing, and tokenization

8. Now we will use **LdaModel** and also create two objects – a **dictionary** instance containing the tokens from **dataset_descriptions**, and a **corpus** instance. Insert a new cell and add the following code to implement this:

```
import gensim
from gensim.models import LdaModel
from gensim.parsing.preprocessing import preprocess_string

dictionary = gensim.corpora.Dictionary(dataset_descriptions)
corpus = [dictionary.doc2bow(text)
for text in dataset_descriptions]
```

9. To get a sense of what is contained in **dictionary**, we can loop through the first **20** items by inserting a new cell and adding the following code:

```
for i in range(0, 20):
    print(i, dictionary[i])
```

The code generates the following output:

```
 0 aafc
 1 aafc_paca
 2 account
 3 aggregates
 4 agriculture
 5 annual
 6 average
 7 canada
 8 canadian
 9 comprised
10 constant
11 covering
12 data
13 database
14 defined
15 documentation
16 dollar
17 estimate
18 estimated
19 factor
```

Figure 5.18: The first 20 entries in the extracted dictionary from the OpenData catalog

10. For our topic vectors, we will choose a vector size of **50**. This means we will build a model with **50** topics. Insert a new cell and add the following code to implement this:

```
VECTOR_SIZE=50
lda_model:LdaModel = LdaModel(corpus,
                              num_topics=VECTOR_SIZE,
                              passes=4)
```

11. To illustrate how we will create topic vectors, let's look at the process for one description value. In the following code, we choose the first **catalog_description**, convert it to tokens, and then again convert the tokens into bags of words. The final step is to use the model to indicate which topic that description was associated with and the relevance of that topic. Insert a new cell and add the following code to implement this:

```
text = catalog.description_en[0]
tokens = text_to_tokens(text)
bag_of_words = dictionary.doc2bow(tokens)
pd.DataFrame(ldaModel[bag_of_words],
             columns=['Topic','Relevance']).set_index('Topic')
```

The code generates the following output:

Topic	Relevance
2	0.103467
4	0.049998
11	0.029675
16	0.040164
17	0.360627
22	0.027324
27	0.022355
29	0.032114
34	0.070352
40	0.059333
41	0.016863
42	0.177026

Figure 5.19: Topic IDs and the relevance scores from one description from the OpenData catalog

12. Now we create a function that takes a text description and converts it into a vector with 50 items. If the description fits a topic, then it will have a relevance score at that topic index. Otherwise, the value will be zero. Insert a new cell and add the following code to implement this:

```
def topic_vector(topic_model:LdaModel, text:str):
    processed_text = text_to_tokens(text)
    fingerprint = [0] * topic_model.num_topics
for topic, prob in topic_model[dictionary.doc2bow(processed_text)]:
        fingerprint[topic] = prob
    return fingerprint
```

13. The following code creates an image from a text description so we can visualize it. Insert a new cell and add the following code:

```
import matplotlib.pyplot as plt
import matplotlib.style as style
from IPython.display import display

style.use('fivethirtyeight')

VECTOR_SIZE=50
%matplotlib inline

def show_fingerprint(topic_model, text:str):
    display(text)
    vector = topic_vector(topic_model, text)
    plt.figure(figsize=(8,1))
    ax = plt.bar( range(len(vector)),
                  vector,
                  0.25,
                  linewidth=1)
    plt.ylim(top=0.4)
    plt.tick_params(axis='both',
                    which='both',
                    left=False,
                    bottom=False,
                    top=False,
                    labelleft=True,
                    labelbottom=True)
    plt.grid(False)
```

14. Now, if we run the **show_fingerprint()** function on a description, we can see it represented as an image. Insert a new cell and add the following code to implement this:

```
show_fingerprint(lda_model, catalog.description_en[0])
```

The code generates the following output:

Figure 5.20: Topic distribution image from one of the descriptions in the OpenData catalog

15. Now we will run the **show_fingerprint()** function for two similar descriptions. Insert a new cell and add the following code to implement this:

```
show_fingerprint(lda_model, catalog.description_en[3])
```

The code generates the following output:

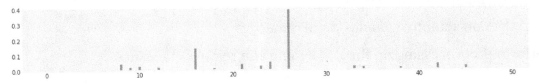

Figure 5.21: Topic distribution image from one of the descriptions in the OpenData catalog

16. Insert a new cell and add the following code to run the **show_fingerprint()** function for description ID **2**:

```
show_fingerprint(lda_model, catalog.description_en[2])
```

The code generates the following output:

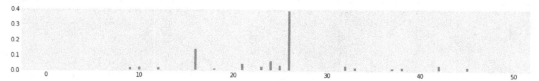

"The Pest Management Centre's (PMC) Minor Use Pesticides Program is a joint initiative between Agriculture and Agri-Food Canada and Health Canada's Pest Management Regulatory Agency (PMRA) to improve the availability of reduced-risk products to agricultural producers and improve the access to a broad range of minor use pesticides. The PMC reviews the data resulting from field trials and laboratory analyses, and prepares a submission to PMRA to support the registration of the minor use pesticide. Upon receiving a finalized regulatory submission from PMC, PMRA reviews it and decides whether or not to accept the pesticide for use in Canada.\r\n\r\nThis is a complete list of PMC's projects with their statuses. For those projects with the status D.3.2 Review Complete, please check with the pesticide manufacturer or visit PMRA's pesticide label database to find out if the pesticide is ready for use. "

Figure 5.22: Topic distribution image from one of the descriptions in the OpenData catalog

As you can see in the preceding two diagrams, when we run the **show_fingerprint()** function for two similar descriptions, we can see how they are almost identical except for slight differences in the topic relevance heights. This shows that we can use topic modeling to create topic vectors that can then be used to measure text similarity.

So far, we have learned about the LSA and LDA models and how they can be used for topic modeling. Using this knowledge, in the next section, we will look at an activity in which we have to perform topic modeling on a dataset.

Activity 10: Topic Modelling Jeopardy Questions

In this activity, you will do topic modeling on a dataset of Jeopardy questions. Follow these steps to implement this activity:

1. Load the dataset into a pandas DataFrame.

2. Perform preprocessing on the DataFrame and remove NA values.

3. Create an **LdaModel** instance using the **Question** column of the DataFrame.

4. Print the topics.

   After executing these steps, the expected output should look like the following:

```
[(0,
  '0.013*"king" + 0.013*"year" + 0.008*"countri" + 0.007*"centuri" + 0.007*"major" + 0.006*"number"'),
 (1,
  '0.028*"plai" + 0.022*"film" + 0.019*"titl" + 0.013*"star" + 0.011*"music" + 0.011*"song"'),
 (2,
  '0.028*"citi" + 0.021*"state" + 0.019*"new" + 0.016*"countri" + 0.013*"presid" + 0.012*"island"'),
 (3,
  '0.007*"short" + 0.006*"live" + 0.006*"best" + 0.006*"said" + 0.006*"court" + 0.005*"eat"'),
 (4,
  '0.008*"languag" + 0.007*"good" + 0.007*"author" + 0.006*"compani" + 0.005*"english" + 0.005*"fruit"'),
 (5,
  '0.022*"word" + 0.021*"clue" + 0.017*"crew" + 0.015*"mean" + 0.014*"type" + 0.013*"letter"'),
 (6,
  '0.007*"call" + 0.007*"queen" + 0.006*"seen" + 0.006*"color" + 0.006*"type" + 0.005*"franc"'),
 (7,
  '0.008*"war" + 0.007*"battl" + 0.007*"paint" + 0.007*"year" + 0.007*"man" + 0.006*"member"')]
```

Figure 5.23: Discovered topics and words

> **Note**
>
> The solution for this activity can be found on page 290.

We have learned how to apply topic modeling on any given dataset.

Summary

In this chapter, we discussed topic modeling in detail. We learned about two different algorithms, LSA and LDA, and how they can be used for topic modeling on any given dataset. We also learned about topic fingerprinting to check for similarity. In the next chapter, we will dig deep into concepts such as text summarization and text generation.

Text Summarization
and Text Generation

Learning Objectives

By the end of this chapter, you will be able to:

- Describe automated text summarization and its benefits

- Describe the TextRank algorithm

- Implement text summarization using Gensim

- Implement text summarization using word frequency

- Generate text using Markov chains

In this chapter, you will learn about the various ways in which text can be summarized and generated.

Introduction

One huge challenge when dealing with text data is that data can be huge in size and can come in various forms, such as documents, emails, and web pages. Reading and understanding such data is a cumbersome task. Also, people tend to be less patient when it comes to reading huge amounts of information; they prefer to consume information in bite-size chunks. For instance, Twitter has doubled its character limit, but it is still only 280 characters. Our interactions over Instagram, Facebook, Snapchat, and other social media platforms have got us accustomed to reading concise text.

Due to this change in habits, there is a need to reduce the volume of content that we ask people to read while still retaining the central ideas of the content. To aid this, content providers sport features such as text summaries that provide users with the gist of information.

Therefore, there is a big business need to automate text summarization. In the coming sections, we will explore text summarization.

> **Note**
>
> In 2016, BuzzSumo analyzed more than 800 million Facebook posts. Based on their findings, posts with fewer than 50 characters were found to be more engaging than long posts. According to another, more precise, study by Jeff Bullas, posts with 80 characters or fewer receive 66 percent higher engagement than other posts. For further details, you can refer to this link: https://buzzsumo.com/blog/facebook-engagement-guide/.

What is Automated Text Summarization?

Automated text summarization is the process of using natural language processing (NLP) tools to produce concise versions of text that preserve all the key information present in the original content.

Content providers have adapted to our change in reading habits and it's now quite conventional to see shorter articles and posts. The other key adaptation has been providing summaries and time estimates for content. These features are developed via NLP and there has been continuous progress in the development of techniques and tools for text summarization.

Some of these tools are frameworks, such as **Gensim** and **NLTK**, that contain algorithms for text summarization. They also have easy-to-use interfaces. These have become quite useful for machine learning engineers and data scientists, who are continuously looking at solving business problems without having to know too much about the research that happened behind the scenes. We will be looking at most of the algorithms in detail in later sections. In the next section, we will look at some of the benefits provided by automated text summarization.

Benefits of Automated Text Summarization

Automated text summarization provides benefits to do with the following:

- **Sampling:** An automated summary can be a sample of a document or article ahead of the article's actual release. This allows the reader to decide whether to read the full article or not.

- **Searching:** Summaries can assist in searches. They can be shown in search results for users to select.

- **Indexing:** Summaries can be used in search indexes, acting as a compressed representation of the original document. This also helps to reduce the amount of storage required.

- **Reading time:** If a summary is well constructed, it can be used instead of the actual document. This can result in a much shorter reading time and is acceptable as long as the reader gets the gist of the original document.

- **Answering questions:** Chatbots can provide automated summaries as responses to user questions.

It is for these reasons that research into text summarization using NLP tools has made its way into products and services that we use every day. One of these services is Google's Smart Reply, wherein our smartphones suggest short replies to emails. These short replies are composed based on what the tool thinks is the best reply for the user.

High-Level View of Text Summarization

We can look at the topic of text summarization from different angles. The following figure shows how we will proceed:

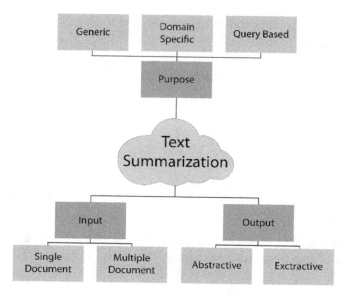

Figure 6.1: This diagram shows the ways in which we can classify text summarization

We will discuss each aspect of text suammarization in detail in the coming sections.

Purpose

There are a number of different angles from which we can view the topic of text summarization. First, we can look at the purpose of text summarization, where we are interested in knowing what people generally use it for. This is further divided into three parts:

- **Generic summarization:** Text summarizers can operate on any text input of sufficient length and they can perform adequately on sources from many different domains. If your project objectives do not care what the domain is and can accept sources from many different fields, then you can use generic summarizers, possibly provided in a tool such as Gensim.

- **Domain-specific summarization:** Text summarization can be specific to a domain, such as finance, shopping, medicine, and travel. So, the software needs to take into account certain terms that are important to the domain. You might not want to summarize a medical diagnosis in a way that removes key information. Thus, the text summarizer could be provided with specific weighted terms that it treats differently from the other terms.

- **Query-based summarization:** Query systems operate differently, in that they are centered around providing a response to user input, either in a search bar or from a chatbot. A response to a user could be related only to the question that was asked. For example, if a chatbot is answering a question where the response is contained in a terms and conditions document, it could tailor the response such that the summary contains only the text that is relevant to the initial question.

Input

The input sources to text summarization can be a single document or multiple documents:

- **Single document:** The input to text summarization can be a single document, such as an article, an email, a social media post, or even a single document with more content, such as a long Word document. This is the typical mode in which a user-centric summarization software operates. Here, a user is looking at a single source of content.

- **Multiple documents:** Text summarizers can also be used to summarize multiple documents and produce a single summary. This could be useful for businesses that need to save time analyzing multiple documents. For example, law firms could run a process to summarize multiple documents into a single summary.

Output

There are two ways to generate the output text for a summary: the extractive way and the abstractive way. Let's look at these in more detail.

Extractive Text Summarization

Extractive text summarization examines the original text and then extracts sentences or phrases from it that best convey the ideas contained in the text without losing too much of the meaning. There are many different algorithms that can perform extractive summarization. But they generally work on the same principle. This core principle is ranking the sentences of the text by importance.

We can interpret sentence importance by how much a sentence contributes to the overall meaning of the text document. After ranking, the summary can then be chosen by selecting the highest ranked sentence. There are different criteria, using which we can rank the sentence importance for the extraction. These could be the following:

- **Word frequency:** In this approach, sentences are ranked by how frequently the words in the sentence appear in the document. The general idea here is that a sentence that contains commonly used words is representative of the general meaning of the overall document. Note that, when ranking by word frequency, we sometimes ignore words that are way too frequent or that might be outliers and not truly representative of the document.

- **Sentence similarity:** This is a measure of how similar other sentences in a document are to a given sentence. The gist here is that if the sentence is selected for the summary, then it could represent a number of other sentences that do not appear, and so would represent much of the meaning of the document. This approach is used in the **TextRank** algorithm, which we will look at in more detail in later sections.

- **Clustering centricity:** In this, the sentences in the document are clustered into a group. Then, the sentences that are in the center of each cluster are selected for the summary. In this way, we select the sentences that are central to the meaning of the document.

Abstractive Text Summarization

This method creates an abstract summary, which is a piece of text that does not use the same words as the original document, but instead just has the same meaning. Abstracts are essentially rewrites of the original text in a more concise form.

Abstract summaries are much harder for algorithms to create, since they require the algorithm to learn the meaning of the original text and then to generate a summary. Because it is not easy to create abstracts, abstractive text summarization is now usually done with more advanced techniques such as neural network models.

Sequence to Sequence

As noted previously, the goal of abstractive text summarization is to take input text and create an abstract summary of that text. The input text can be considered a sequence of input words or characters, while the summary can be considered the output sequence. So, text summarization can be considered a **sequence-to-sequence** problem, where we translate one sequence into another. Sequence-to-sequence neural networks are commonly used to translate from one language to another, or from questions to answers. But they can also be used for text summarization with the aim of producing a smaller output sequence from the input.

Encoder Decoder

The most common way to perform sequence-to-sequence translation is by using an **encoder-decoder** network, consisting of the following:

- **An encoder**, which takes input word sequences and produces an internal representation.

- **A decoder**, which takes the input representation and produces an output sequence of words.

The encoder-decoder architecture is used by Google and other major companies that operate in the field of natural language translation.

TextRank

TextRank is a popular algorithm for extractive text summarization. It is based on one of the most well-known algorithms of all time: PageRank. It was the first search-ordering algorithm used by Google to order search results. It works on the principle of ranking pages based on the total number of other pages referring to a given page. Similarly, for TextRank, the text units – typically sentences – are ranked by how similar other sentences are to a given sentence. The TextRank algorithm works as follows:

1. Reads and extracts text from documents.

2. Splits text into sentences.

3. Converts sentences into vectors.

4. Converts each word in a sentence into a vector.

5. Finds the vector for the entire sentence – one approach would be averaging the word vectors.

6. Calculates a similarity matrix among sentences. This is a matrix that measures how similar sentences are to each other.

7. Creates a graph from the similarity matrix.

8. Ranks the sentences by graph importance.

9. Selects the top sentences by graph importance.

The flow of data through the TextRank process is described in this figure:

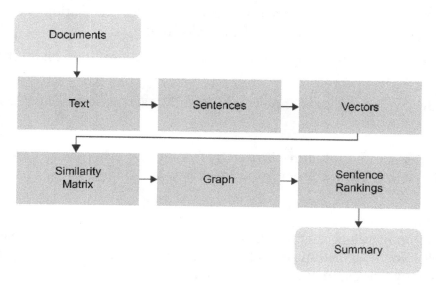

Figure 6.2: This figure shows the flow of data through the TextRank process

Now that we have gained some insight into TextRank, in the next section, let's look at an exercise based on it to get an even better understanding.

Exercise 51: TextRank from Scratch

This exercise takes you through the process of the TextRank algorithm. Here, we will fetch the dataset and summarize the articles present in it with the help of the TextRank algorithm. Follow these steps to implement this exercise:

1. Open a Jupyter notebook.

2. Add the following import statements:

```
import numpy as np
import pandas as pd
```

```
import nltk
import re
import contractions

nltk.download('punkt') # one time execution
pd.set_option('display.max_colwidth',1000)
```

The code also downloads the **nltk Punkt** tokenizer models. These will be used to tokenize the sentences and words in the articles.

3. In this step, we will load GloVe vector word representations, which are located in a ZIP file. The code given here is used to extract the file:

```
import zipfile

GLOVE_DIR = 'data/glove/'
GLOVE_ZIP = GLOVE_DIR + 'glove.6B.50d.zip'

zip_ref = zipfile.ZipFile(GLOVE_ZIP, 'r')
zip_ref.extractall(GLOVE_DIR)
zip_ref.close()
```

4. After extracting the glove vectors, we need to load them into a dictionary. With this dictionary, we can find the vector for each word. Insert a new cell and add the following code to implement this:

```
import numpy as np

def load_glove_vectors(fn):
    print("Loading Glove Model")
    with open( fn,'r', encoding='utf8') as glove_vector_file:
        model = {}
        for line in glove_vector_file:
            parts = line.split()
            word = parts[0]
            embedding = np.array([float(val) for val in parts[1:]])
            model[word] = embedding
        print("Loaded {} words".format(len(model)))
    return model

glove_vectors = load_glove_vectors('data/glove/glove.6B.50d.txt')
```

5. Now we can read the tennis articles, which are located in a CSV file in the **data** directory. Insert a new cell and add the following code to implement this:

```
articles = pd.read_csv("data/tennis_articles_v4.csv")
articles.head(2)
```

The code generates the following output:

	article_id	article_text	source
0	1	Maria Sharapova has basically no friends as tennis players on the WTA Tour. The Russian player has no problems in openly speaking about it and in a recent interview she said: 'I don't really hide any feelings too much. I think everyone knows this is my job here. When I'm on the courts or when I'm on the court playing, I'm a competitor and I want to beat every single person whether they're in the locker room or across the net.So I'm not the one to strike up a conversation about the weather and know that in the next few minutes I have to go and try to win a tennis match. I'm a pretty competitive girl. I say my hellos, but I'm not sending any players flowers as well. Uhm, I'm not really friendly or close to many players. I have not a lot of friends away from the courts.' When she said she is not really close to a lot of players, is that something strategic that she is doing? Is it different on the men's tour than the women's tour? 'No, not at all. I think just because you're in the sa...	https://www.tennisworldusa.org/tennis/news/Maria_Sharapova/62220/i-do-not-have-friends-in-tennis-says-maria-sharapova/
1	2	BASEL, Switzerland (AP), Roger Federer advanced to the 14th Swiss Indoors final of his career by beating seventh-seeded Daniil Medvedev 6-1, 6-4 on Saturday. Seeking a ninth title at his hometown event, and a 99th overall, Federer will play 93th-ranked Marius Copil on Sunday. Federer dominated the 20th-ranked Medvedev and had his first match-point chance to break serve again at 5-1. He then dropped his serve to love, and let another match point slip in Medvedev's next service game by netting a backhand. He clinched on his fourth chance when Medvedev netted from the baseline. Copil upset expectations of a Federer final against Alexander Zverev in a 6-3, 6-7 (6), 6-4 win over the fifth-ranked German in the earlier semifinal. The Romanian aims for a first title after arriving at Basel without a career win over a top-10 opponent. Copil has two after also beating No. 6 Marin Cilic in the second round. Copil fired 26 aces past Zverev and never dropped serve, clinching after 2 1/2 hours w...	http://www.tennis.com/pro-game/2018/10/copil-stuns-5th-ranked-zverev-to-reach-swiss-indoors-final/77721/

Figure 6.3: This image shows the first two tennis articles

6. Add the following code, which will download and load the NLTK English language **stopwords**:

```
nltk.download('stopwords')
from nltk.corpus import stopwords
stop_words = stopwords.words('english')
```

7. The code given here creates a number of functions that will clean the article text, as well as tokenizing it into words and sentences:

```
from nltk.tokenize import sent_tokenize, word_tokenize

CLEAN_PATTERN = r'[^a-zA-z\s]'

def clean(word):
    return re.sub(CLEAN_PATTERN, '', word)

def clean_sentence(sentence):
    sentence = [clean(word) for word in sentence]
    return [word for word in sentence if word]
```

```
def clean_sentences(sentences):
    return [clean_sentence(sentence) for sentence in sentences]

def lower(sentence):
    return [word.lower() for word in sentence]

def remove_stopwords(sentence):
    words = [word for word in sentence if word not in stop_words]
    return [word for word in words if len(word) >0]

def tokenize_words(sentences):
    return [word_tokenize(sentence)
                for sentence in sentences]

def fix_contractions(sentences):
    return [contractions.fix(sentence) for sentence in sentences]
```

8. Now apply the functions we just created to the articles. This will split each article into sentences and each sentence into words. Note that, because we are using DataFrames, we can apply the functions to each of the seven articles in the dataset:

```
articles['SentencesInArticle'] = articles.article_text.apply(sent_
tokenize)
articles['WordsInSentences'] = articles.SentencesInArticle \
                .apply(fix_contractions)\
                .apply(lower)\
                .apply(tokenize_words)\
                .apply(remove_stopwords)\
                .apply(clean_sentences)
```

9. Now subset the article columns to see the **SentencesInArticles** and **WordInSentences** columns. We will use the **head()** function to see the first two records:

```
articles = articles[['SentencesInArticle', 'WordsInSentences']]
articles.head(2)
```

The code generates the following output:

SentencesInArticle	WordsInSentences
0	[Maria Sharapova has basically no friends as tennis players on the WTA Tour., The Russian player has no problems in openly speaking about it and in a recent interview she said: 'I don't really hide any feelings too much., I think everyone knows this is my job here., When I'm on the courts or when I'm on the court playing, I'm a competitor and I want to beat every single person whether they're in the locker room or across the net.So I'm not the one to strike up a conversation about the weather and know that in the next few minutes I have to go and try to win a tennis match., I'm a pretty competitive girl., I say my hellos, but I'm not sending any players flowers as well., Uhm, I'm not really friendly or close to many players., I have not a lot of friends away from the courts.', When she said she is not really close to a lot of players, is that something strategic that she is doing?, Is it different on the men's tour than the women's tour?, 'No, not at all., i think just because you'...	[[maria, sharapova, has, basically, no, friends, as, tennis, players, on, the, wta, tour], [the, russian, player, has, no, problems, in, openly, speaking, about, it, and, in, a, recent, interview, she, said, i, do, not, really, hide, any, feelings, too, much], [i, think, everyone, knows, this, is, my, job, here], [when, i, am, on, the, courts, or, when, i, am, on, the, court, playing, i, am, a, competitor, and, i, want, to, beat, every, single, person, whether, they, are, in, the, locker, room, or, across, the, netso, i, am, not, the, one, to, strike, up, a, conversation, about, the, weather, and, know, that, in, the, next, few, minutes, i, have, to, go, and, try, to, win, a, tennis, match], [i, am, a, pretty, competitive, girl], [i, say, my, hellos, but, i, am, not, sending, any, players, flowers, as, well], [uhm, i, am, not, really, friendly, or, close, to, many, players], [i, have, not, a, lot, of, friends, away, from, the, courts], [when, she, said, she, is, not, really, close,...
1	[BASEL, Switzerland (AP), Roger Federer advanced to the 14th Swiss Indoors final of his career by beating seventh-seeded Daniil Medvedev 6-1, 6-4 on Saturday., Seeking a ninth title at his hometown event, and a 99th overall, Federer will play 93th-ranked Marius Copil on Sunday., Federer dominated the 20th-ranked Medvedev and had his first match-point chance to break serve again at 5-1., He then dropped his serve to love, and let another match point slip in Medvedev's next service game by netting a backhand., He clinched on his fourth chance when Medvedev netted from the baseline., Copil upset expectations of a Federer final against Alexander Zverev in a 6-3, 6-7 (6), 6-4 win over the fifth-ranked German in the earlier semifinal., The Romanian aims for a first title after arriving at Basel without a career win over a top-10 opponent., Copil has two after also beating No., 6 Marin Cilic in the second round., Copil fired 26 aces past Zverev and never dropped serve, clinching after 2 1...	[[basel, switzerland, ap, roger, federer, advanced, to, the, th, swiss, indoors, final, of, his, career, by, beating, seventhseeded, daniil, medvedev, on, saturday], [seeking, a, ninth, title, at, his, hometown, event, and, a, th, overall, federer, will, play, thranked, marius, copil, on, sunday], [federer, dominated, the, thranked, medvedev, and, had, his, first, matchpoint, chance, to, break, serve, again, at], [he, then, dropped, his, serve, to, love, and, let, another, match, point, slip, in, medvedev, s, next, service, game, by, netting, a, backhand], [he, clinched, on, his, fourth, chance, when, medvedev, netted, from, the, baseline], [copil, upset, expectations, of, a, federer, final, against, alexander, zverev, in, a, win, over, the, fifthranked, german, in, the, earlier, semifinal], [the, romanian, aims, for, a, first, title, after, arriving, at, basel, without, a, career, win, over, a, top, opponent], [copil, has, two, after, also, beating, no], [marin, cilic, in, the, se...

Figure 6.4: This figure shows the new columns we added – SentencesInArticle and WordInSentences

10. The next step is to create the sentence vectors. We define the following functions, namely **sentence_vector()** and **sentences_to_vectors()**. We will also use a vector size of **50**:

```
VECTOR_SIZE = 50
EMPTY_VECTOR = np.zeros(VECTOR_SIZE)


def sentence_vector(sentence):
    return sum([glove_vectors.get(word, EMPTY_VECTOR)
                for word in sentence])/len(sentence)


def sentences_to_vectors(sentences):
    return [sentence_vector(sentence)
            for sentence in sentences]
```

11. Now that we have the function to create sentence vectors, we can run it. It will create another column in the DataFrame, called **SentenceVectors**:

```
articles['SentenceVector'] = \
        articles.WordsInSentences.apply(sentences_to_vectors)
```

12. The next step is to create a similarity matrix. The similarity matrix captures the degree to which one sentence is similar to another for a given article. The function is as follows:

```
from sklearn.metrics.pairwise import cosine_similarity

def similarity_matrix(sentence_vectors):
    sim_mat = np.zeros([len(sentence_vectors), len(sentence_vectors)])
    for i in range(len(sentence_vectors)):
        for j in range(len(sentence_vectors)):
            element_i = sentence_vectors[i].reshape(1,VECTOR_SIZE)
            element_j = sentence_vectors[j].reshape(1,VECTOR_SIZE)
            sim_mat[i][j] = cosine_similarity(element_i,
                                              element_j)[0,0]

    return sim_mat
```

13. Now we run the function to create the similarity matrices for each article:

```
articles['SimMatrix'] = articles['SimMatrix'] = \
    articles.SentenceVector.apply(similarity_matrix)
```

14. The step after creating similarity matrices is to create a graph from the matrix. We use a Python library called **networkx** to create the graph. The graph will help us determine the relative importance of each sentence based on how much it is similar to other sentences:

```
import networkx as nx

def compute_graph(sim_matrix):
    nx_graph = nx.from_numpy_array(sim_matrix)
    scores = nx.pagerank(nx_graph)
    return scores
```

15. After creating the function, run the following code to create the new column with the graph for that article:

```
articles['Graph'] = articles.SimMatrix.apply(compute_graph)
```

16. Take a look at the articles using **articles.head()**. You can see each of the columns that we added, all the way to the Graph column:

```
articles.head(2)
```

The code generates the following output:

SentencesInArticle	WordsIn Sentences	SentenceVector	SimMatrix	Graph	Summary
[Maria Sharapova has basically no friends as tennis players on the WTA Tour., The Russian player has no problems in openly speaking about it and in a recent interview she said: 'I don't really hide any feelings too much., I think everyone knows this is my job here., When I'm on the courts or when I'm on the court playing, I'm a competitor and I want to beat every single person whether they're in the locker room or across the net.So I'm not the one to strike up a conversation about the weather and know that in the next few minutes I have to go and try to win a tennis match., I'm a pretty competitive girl., I say my hellos, but I'm not	[[maria, sharapova, has, basically, no, friends, as, tennis, players, on, the, wta, tour], [the, russian, player, has, no, problems, in, openly, speaking, about, it, and, in, a, recent, interview, she, said, i, do, not, really, hide, any, feelings, too, much], [i, think, everyone, knows, this, is, my, job, here], [when, i, am, on, the, courts, or, when, i, am, on, the, court, playing, i, am, a, competitor, and, i, want, to, beat, every, single, person, whether, they, are, in, the, netso, i, am, not, the, one, to, strike, up, a, conversation, about, the, weather, and, know, that, in, the, next, few, minutes, i,	[[0.07161230769230773, 0.5263353076923079, -0.22625407692307692, 0.4190584615384615, -0.0952153076923077, -0.10156600000000002, -0.40362538461538466, 0.400633476923077, -0.35831371000000006, -0.11500546153846154, 0.11607930769230769, -0.146259, -0.6847891923076924, 0.01432753846153846, 0.783284653846154, 0.046932615384615385, -0.10918245384615388, 0.054596461538461545, -0.29416438461538463, -0.1929796923076923, -0.2468181230769231, 0.310665846153846, 0.011112153846153848, 0.30192715384615376, 0.12148384615384614, -1.328529230769231, -0.2920881538461539, -0.07721707692307692, -0.3258306923076923,	[[0.0, 0.8804204422835109, 0.8400741992486218, 0.9129596149615926, 0.8445816500505545, 0.8497893583785374, 0.876852166283095, 0.886258925167321, 0.876688184230672, 0.9263429108619361, 0.8600162727238754, 0.88957833049645, 0.8313178033584998, 0.8565959297474462, 0.8824241286286072, 0.8868385761498727, 0.8136190246763892], [0.8804204422835109, 0.0, 0.9408964676641778, 0.9686965549113967, 0.8942781393973298, 0.9596334393985563, 0.9585076101382632, 0.9730773874995189, 0.987312380978821, 0.9125283526364883, 0.9594498058208407, 0.9640488970318378, 0.9632944418681554, 0.9732690670320119, 0.9616582246780772,	[0: 0.055286935618712896, 1: 0.05970578975658169, 2: 0.058379079199306204, 3: 0.05976056354283547, 4: 0.056304909154901626, 5: 0.05924913585736564, 6: 0.0594297063316984, 7: 0.05955702192007273, 8: 0.05966960309709363, 9: 0.056770439199444536, 10: 0.05907532875276158, 11:	I think just because you're in the same sport doesn't mean that you have to be friends with everyone just because you're categorized, you're a tennis player, so you're going to get along with tennis players. But ultimately tennis is just

Figure 6.5: This figure shows the additional columns that we added – SentenceVector, SimMatrix, and Graph

17. The graph contains a score and a numeric index to a sentence. We have to write a function that will rank the scores and return the top n sentences by their graph scores:

```python
def get_ranked_sentences(sentences, scores, n=3):
    top_scores = sorted(((scores[i],s)
                        for i,s in enumerate(sentences)),
                        reverse=True)
    top_n_sentences = [sentence
                        for score,sentence in top_scores[:n]]
    return " ".join(top_n_sentences)
```

18. After creating the function, we can apply it to the DataFrame to create a new column, called **Summary**. This will contain the top three sentences for each article:

```python
articles['Summary'] = articles.apply(lambda d:
                        get_ranked_sentences(d.
SentencesInArticle,
                        d.Graph), axis=1)
```

19. Now you can see the summary for each article:

```
articles.loc[0].Summary
```

The code generates the following output:

```
"I think just because you're in the same sport doesn't mean that you have to be friends with everyone just because you're categ
orized, you're a tennis player, so you're going to get along with tennis players. But ultimately tennis is just a very small pa
rt of what we do. I think everyone just thinks because we're tennis players we should be the greatest of friends."
```

Figure 6.6: Summary for the article with an ID of 0

To check the summary of ID 1, type the following code:

```
articles.loc[1].Summary
```

The code generates the following output:

```
'Federer had an easier time than in his only previous match against Medvedev, a three-setter at Shanghai two weeks ago. Federer
dominated the 20th-ranked Medvedev and had his first match-point chance to break serve again at 5-1. The Romanian aims for a fi
rst title after arriving at Basel without a career win over a top-10 opponent.'
```

Figure 6.7: Summary for the article with an ID of 1

We have learned how to use the TextRank algorithm to summarize the articles in a dataset. In the next section, we will look at how Gensim can be used to summarize text.

Summarizing Text Using Gensim

The Gensim NLP library actually contains a text summarizer. So, instead of writing your own text summarizer, you could actually use this already-available one in your project. As a bonus, Gensim is an excellent NLP library with many other features.

The text summarizer in Gensim is located in the **gensim.summarization** package. The main method, which is **summarize**, provides a number of options for returning the number of words, a percentage of the text, and more. The underlying implementation is the TextRank algorithm, which you are already familiar with. To get a better understanding of this concept, we will go through an activity in the next section.

Activity 11: Summarizing a Downloaded Page Using the Gensim Text Summarizer

Click is a Python project for creating beautiful command-line interfaces. In this activity, we will create a summary of the **Why Click** page. For this, we will make use of the Gensim Summarizer package. Follow these steps to implement this activity:

1. Download the web page using the **requests** library.

2. Using BeautifulSoup, find the contents of the **div** with the ID **#why-click** on the page.

3. Use the **summarize** function from the **gensim.summarization** package to summarize the text from the **why-click** div.

4. Use various parameters, such as **split**, **ratio**, and **word_count**, to limit the amount of text returns.

> **Note**
>
> The solution for this activity can be found on page 291.

We have learned how to summarize a downloaded page using Gensim's text summarizer. In the next section, we will look into a new concept—summarizing text using word frequency.

Summarizing Text Using Word Frequency

One of the simplest ways to do text summarization is to compute the frequency of words and extract sentences that contain the words that are most common in the text. This follows a certain process, which is discussed here:

1. **Ignore stop words**: Common words (known as stop words) are ignored.

2. **Determine top words**: The most frequently occurring words in the document are counted up.

3. **Select top words**: A small number of the top words are selected to be used for scoring.

4. **Select top sentences**: Sentences are scored on the basis of the total number of the top words they contain. The top four sentences are selected for the summary.

In the next section, we will go through an exercise to get a better understanding of this concept.

Exercise 52: Word Frequency Text Summarization

In this exercise, we will implement text summarization by ranking the sentences using word frequency. Follow these steps to implement this exercise:

1. Open a Jupyter notebook.

2. Insert a new cell and add the following code to import the necessary libraries:

```
from collections import Counter
from nltk.tokenize import sent_tokenize,word_tokenize
from nltk.corpus import stopwords
from string import punctuation
from heapq import nlargest
```

3. Add the following code to compute the word frequencies. The **compute_word_frequencies()** function will calculate the frequency of each word as a proportion of the frequency of the most common word. We will drop words that are really uncommon (whose proportion of use is less than **MIN_WORD_PROP**) or really common (whose proportion of use is greater than **MAX_WORD_PROP**):

```
STOPWORDS = set(stopwords.words('english') + list(punctuation))
MIN_WORD_PROP, MAX_WORD_PROP = 0.1, 0.9

def compute_word_frequencies(word_sentences):
    words = [word for sentence in word_sentences
                    for word in sentence
                        if word not in STOPWORDS]
    counter = Counter(words)
    limit = float(max(counter.values()))
    word_frequencies = {word: freq/limit
                            for word,freq in counter.items()}
```

```
    # Drop words if too common or too uncommon
    word_frequencies = {word: freq
                            for word,freq in word_frequencies.items()
                                if freq > MIN_WORD_PROP
                                and freq < MAX_WORD_PROP}
    return word_frequencies
```

4. Now add the following function to score each sentence by how frequent the words in it are:

```
def sentence_score(word_sentence, word_frequencies):
    return sum([ word_frequencies.get(word,0)
                    for word in word_sentence])
```

5. Now we can add the **summarize()** function. This will apply each of the functions we have written to summarize the text and return the top three sentences ranked by word frequency:

```
def summarize(text:str, num_sentences=3):
    """
    Summarize the text, by return the most relevant sentences
     :text the text to summarize
     :num_sentences the number of sentences to return
    """
    # Make the text lowercase
    text = text.lower()

    # Break text into sentences
    sentences = sent_tokenize(text)

    # Break sentences into words
    word_sentences = [word_tokenize(sentence)
                        for sentence in sentences]

    # Compute the word frequencies
    word_frequencies = compute_word_frequencies(word_sentences)

    # Calculate the scores for each of the sentences
    scores = [sentence_score(word_sentence, word_frequencies)
                    for word_sentence in word_sentences]
    sentence_scores = list(zip(sentences, scores))
```

```
# Rank the sentences
top_sentence_scores = nlargest(num_sentences,
                               sentence_scores,
                               key=lambda t: t[1])


# Return the top sentences
return [t[0] for t in top_sentence_scores]
```

6. To test our frequency summarizer, we will load a sample article, located in the **data** directory. Add the following code to implement this:

```
with open('data/PolarVortex.txt', 'r') as vortex_file:
    vortex_article = vortex_file.read()
```

7. Take a look at the original article. Add the following code in a new code cell:

```
vortex_article
```

The code generates the following output:

```
'On the coldest day in two decades on his fifth-generation dairy farm, Chris Pollack grabbed a thick black hose from the barn a
nd ventured into the subzero cold,\nwhere his beef cattle were chomping cud and waiting for water.\nThe power had briefly gone
out the previous morning, long enough to freeze the line that automatically fills the animals€™ heated water trough. Pollack w
as here to replace it.\n\n"Are you serious?" Pollack said, peering inside the black hose. "There€™s water frozen in the end al
ready."\nHe lifted it up to a small space heater and waited for it to thaw.\nSuch is life in the Deep Freeze of 2019.\nThe past
48 hours in the American Midwest have been about endurance, as a breathtaking cold settled in over a massive stretch of the cou
ntry. \nThe record-setting frigid temperatures, some of the coldest on the planet Thursday, have frozen the Great Lakes, taxed
electrical and natural gas infrastructure,\n endangered livestock and tested the mettle of millions who are used to the cold bu
t had never experienced anything like this.\nIn some areas Thursday, temperatures dropped below minus-50 degrees, and the extre
me weather was blamed for several deaths across the region,\n including people who appear to have frozen to death in Milwaukee,
Detroit and Rochester, Minn.\nFrom Minnesota to New York, the polar vortex again prompted school closures, mail service interru
ptions and thousands of flight cancellations, \nmany of them in and out of Chicago, which appeared otherworldly in a coating of
frost and ice. Eighteen factories run by General Motors, \nFiat Chrysler and Ford shut down Thursday because of the brutal weat
her and a fire at a natural gas compressor station.\n'
```

Figure 6.8: This figure shows the original vortex article

8. This is a short article about the experiences of some people in the American Midwest during the frigid conditions that were caused by the polar vortex in the winter of 2019. This article has 12 sentences, which we can verify by checking the length of the list of sentences after splitting using the **sent_tokenize()** function. Add the following code to check:

```
len(sent_tokenize(vortex_article))
```

The code generates the following output:

```
12
```

Figure 6.9: There are 12 sentences in the article

9. We can now summarize it using our frequency-based summarizer. This will, by default, return the top three most important sentences:

```
summarize(vortex_article)
```

The code generates the following output:

```
['in some areas thursday, temperatures dropped below minus-50 degrees, and the extreme weather was blamed for several deaths ac
ross the region,\n including people who appear to have frozen to death in milwaukee, detroit and rochester, minn.\nfrom minneso
ta to new york, the polar vortex again prompted school closures, mail service interruptions and thousands of flight cancellatio
ns, \nmany of them in and out of chicago, which appeared otherworldly in a coating of frost and ice.',
 'the record-setting frigid temperatures, some of the coldest on the planet thursday, have frozen the great lakes, taxed electr
ical and natural gas infrastructure,\n endangered livestock and tested the mettle of millions who are used to the cold but had
never experienced anything like this.',
 'on the coldest day in two decades on his fifth-generation dairy farm, chris pollack grabbed a thick black hose from the barn
and ventured into the subzero cold,\nwhere his beef cattle were chomping cud and waiting for water.']
```

Figure 6.10: A summary of the vortex article

10. You can also change the number of sentences being returned, from **3** to another number. Here is the result if you specify **num_sentences** as equal to **1**:

```
summarize(vortex_article, num_sentences=1)
```

The code generates the following output:

```
['in some areas thursday, temperatures dropped below minus-50 degrees, and the extreme weather was blamed for several deaths ac
ross the region,\n including people who appear to have frozen to death in milwaukee, detroit and rochester, minn.\nfrom minneso
ta to new york, the polar vortex again prompted school closures, mail service interruptions and thousands of flight cancellatio
ns, \nmany of them in and out of chicago, which appeared otherworldly in a coating of frost and ice.']
```

Figure 6.11: Summary of the vortex article, limited to only one sentence

This exercise showed how to extract the most important sentences from a text document using the criteria of word frequency. In the next section, we will learn about Markov chains.

Generating Text with Markov Chains

One of the more interesting uses of NLP is generating text, whether for amusement, for research, or for profit. The key concept in generating text is to take advantage of the statistical properties of the text. This makes the output text more realistic and, more importantly, we gain information about the text itself if we can rearrange it to identify interesting patterns in it. Text can be generated in many different ways. We will explore doing so using Markov chains.

Markov Chains

A Markov chain is a mathematical system for transitioning between states based on probabilities. No matter how a system arrives at its present state, the possible future states are all predetermined. Furthermore, the move to the next state is based on a set of probabilities. Markov chains operate in timesteps. After each timestep, the system selects a new state. This new state is chosen based on the current state and the probabilities of the future states.

Markov chains are quite useful in certain fields, such as finance, game theory, and economics. They have also started to find their way into NLP. In this field, the statistical patterns in text sources are used to create probability values for the state transitions. One statistical property is the probability of a given word following another.

> **Note**
>
> Using Markov chains is not the only way to generate text, but it is probably the simplest. Other ways include the use of recurrent neural networks.

In the next section, we will solve an exercise related to Markov chains to get a better understanding of them.

Exercise 53: Generating Text Using Markov Chains

In this exercise, we will generate text with the help of Markov chains. Follow these steps to implement this exercise:

1. Open a Jupyter notebook.

2. Insert a new cell and add the following code to import the necessary libraries:

   ```
   import glob
   import os
   import numpy as np
   ```

3. We will add a function to clean the text from the speeches. The **gensim** library contains utility functions that can perform text cleaning, including **strip_tags** and **strip_non_alphanum**:

   ```
   from gensim.parsing.preprocessing import preprocess_string,
   strip_non_alphanum, strip_tags

   def clean(text):
       text = strip_tags(text)
       text = strip_non_alphanum(text)
   ```

```
        return text

    def load_speeches(category, filename='*.txt'):
        """
            :param category: What type of speeches to load
                            - women or comedians
            :param filename: The filename pattern
        """
        category_dir = os.path.join(speeches_dir,category)
        for filename in glob.glob(os.path.join(category_dir, filename)):
            with open(filename, encoding='latin-1') as f:
                yield filename, clean(f.read())
```

We also add a function called **load_speeches** to load files from the **speeches** directory. The category corresponds to the subdirectory to load speeches from, such as those for women's speeches or comedians' speeches.

4. The **load_speeches** function is a generator and so loads lazily. Here, we can define two generators for **womens** speeches and **comedian** speeches, without actually loading anything just yet:

```
womens_speeches = load_speeches('women')
comedian_speeches = load_speeches('comedians')
```

5. Now we define a function to load a corpus, which is a list containing the words from the speeches:

```
from nltk.tokenize import word_tokenize

def load_corpus(speeches):
    corpus = []
    for filename, speech in speeches:
        print(f'Loading speech {filename}')
        tokens = word_tokenize(speech)
        corpus = corpus + tokens
    return corpus
```

6. In this step, we will make a list of word tuples containing all the consecutive word pairs. We will use these word pairs in our Markov chain to generate words that follow a given word:

```
def make_pairs(corpus):
    for i in range(len(corpus)-1):
        yield (corpus[i], corpus[i+1])
```

```
def load_word_dict(corpus):
    pairs = make_pairs(corpus)
    word_dict = {}
    for word_1, word_2 in pairs:
        if word_1 in word_dict.keys():
            word_dict[word_1].append(word_2)
        else:
            word_dict[word_1] = [word_2]
    return word_dict
```

7. The next step puts the functions together. First, we load **speeches**, then we load **corpus**, and finally, we create a word **dict**:

```
def load_markov_dict(category, filename='*.txt'):
    speeches = load_speeches(category, filename)
    corpus = load_corpus(speeches)
    return load_word_dict(corpus)
```

The word **dict** contains each word as a key, with the values being the list of words that follow the given word.

8. We can run the function for both speeches by women and speeches by comedians:

```
womens_speeches_word_dict = load_markov_dict('women')
```

The code generates the following output:

```
Loading speech data/speeches/women\AintIAWoman-SojournerTruth.txt
Loading speech data/speeches/women\FreedomFromFear-AungSuuKyi.txt
Loading speech data/speeches/women\FreedomOrDeath-EmmelinePankhurst.txt
Loading speech data/speeches/women\MisogynySpeech-JuliaGillard.txt
Loading speech data/speeches/women\PulseOfTheMorning-MayaAngelou.txt
Loading speech data/speeches/women\RoomOfOnesOwn-VirginiaWoolf.txt
Loading speech data/speeches/women\SpeechToTheTroopsAtTillsbury-ElizabethI.txt
Loading speech data/speeches/women\WellesleyCommencement-NoraEphron.txt
```

Figure 6.12: The logging output when loading the speeches by women

To check the logging output, while loading the speeches by comedians, type the following code:

```
comedians_word_dict = load_markov_dict('comedians')
```

The code generates the following output:

```
Loading speech data/speeches/comedians\Dartmouth-Conan.txt
Loading speech data/speeches/comedians\HardvardLawSchool-MindyKaling.txt
Loading speech data/speeches/comedians\Harvard-AmyPoehler.txt
Loading speech data/speeches/comedians\HarvardU-WillFerrell.txt
Loading speech data/speeches/comedians\TulaneGraduation-MayaRudolph.txt
Loading speech data/speeches/comedians\UniversityOfVirginia-StephenColbert.txt
Loading speech data/speeches/comedians\WilliamAndMary-JonStewart.txt
```

Figure 6.13: The logging output when loading speeches by comedians

9. Now, in the final step, we create a **get_sentence** function, which will construct a sentence from the word **dict**. It first chooses a random word to start with, then it chooses another random word, until it reaches the sentence length:

```
def get_sentence(word_dict, n_words=15):
    first_word = np.random.choice(list(word_dict.keys()))
    while first_word.islower():
        first_word = np.random.choice(corpus)
    chain = [first_word]
    for i in range(n_words):
        chain.append(np.random.choice(word_dict[chain[-1]]))
    return ' '.join(chain)
```

10. Generate a sample sentence from the women's speeches:

```
get_sentence(womens_speeches_word_dict)
```

The code generates the following output:

```
'I will have to find that the sort of itself for instance when the truth to'
```

Figure 6.14: A sample sentence from the speeches by women

11. Generate a sample sentence from the comedians' speeches:

```
get_sentence(comedians_word_dict)
```

The code generates the following output:

```
'Which some ways I was academics where you â Legally Blonde â He was a crushing'
```

Figure 6.15: A sample sentence from the speeches made by comedians

You have now learned how to generate text using Markov chains.

Summary

In this chapter, you have learned about text summarization and text generation. We also looked at various ways in which text summarization can be performed, such as the use of the TextRank algorithm, the Gensim library, and word frequency models. One approach we looked at during this chapter was the use of Markov chains to perform text generation. In the next chapter, we will learn about how text can be represented as vectors. We will also discuss various vector representations, such as Word2Vec and Doc2Vec, in detail.

Vector Representation

Learning Objectives

By the end of this chapter, you will be able to:

- Describe the need for vector representation in Natural Language Processing (NLP)
- Identify the various ways that text can be represented as vectors
- Describe word vectors and their various forms
- Implement vector arithmetic
- Describe document vectors

In this chapter, you will be learning about various encoding techniques using which a text can be represented as vector.

Introduction

The previous chapters laid a firm foundation for NLP. But now we will go deeper into a key topic – one that gives us surprising insights into how a language works and how some of the key advances in human computer interaction are facilitated. At the heart of NLP is the simple trick of representing text as numbers. This helps software algorithms to perform the sophisticated computations that are required to understand the meaning of text.

Text representation can be as simple as encoding each word as an integer. But it can also include using an array of numbers for each word. Each of these representations help machine learning programs to function effectively.

This chapter begins by discussing vectors, how text can be represented as vectors, and how vectors can be composed to represent complex speech. We will walk through the various representations in both directions – learning how to encode text as vectors as well as how to retrieve text from vectors. We will also look at some cutting-edge techniques used in NLP that are based on the idea of representing text as vectors. **Word2Vec**, for example, is used by Google as the main text representation technique in some of their deep learning models. The models support their consumer products, such as Google Home, which uses NLP for communicating with humans.

Vector Definition

There are various mathematical representations, such as **scalars**, **vectors**, **matrices**, and **tensors**. A scalar can be considered as a number, a decimal, or even a fraction. A matrix can be considered as a rectangular array of numbers. A vector is a collection of numbers that represent some real objects. You can think of a vector as a row in a matrix. A tensor is a general concept that can be comprised of scalars, vectors, and matrices.

The following diagram shows how scalars, vectors, matrices, and tensors are different from each other:

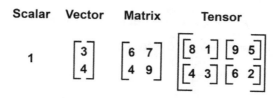

Figure 7.1: Scalars, vectors, matrices, and tensors

Now, try to think about text as follows::

- A letter that is a single unit of an alphabet
- A word that is a series of letters
- A sentence that is a series or words
- A paragraph that is a sequence of words
- A document that is a collection of words, possibly broken down into paragraphs

Each of the preceding units are in text format, and hence it becomes difficult for NLP algorithms to interpret them and perform different calculations. Thus, it is required to convert them into vectors, so that we can perform different computations on them and get better insights from the data.

> **Note**
>
> There are a few existing numeric representations of text that are used in computing. ASCII and Unicode are the most notably used techniques, but these are used only for general computing and not necessarily for NLP.

Throughout this chapter, we will be using the **NumPy** library. NumPy uses the array, which is a structure that can represent scalars, vectors, and matrices. We will use the term **array** interchangeably with vectors and matrices. There are different types of NumPy arrays, such as **one-dimensional**, **two-dimensional**, and **three-dimensional**. See the following diagram for an illustration of this:

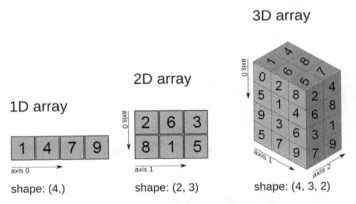

Figure 7.2: Different types of NumPy arrays

Why Vector Representations?

Computers natively understand 1s and 0s. Even the text displayed on computer screens is encoded in some numeric form. To make the processing easy, text is encoded as numbers. For the field of NLP, the demand is even more onerous. Here the computers are being taught to read, listen, and understand natural language. Mathematical functions are also being applied to the text data with the goal of detecting patterns.

NLP algorithms require large volumes of text data. However, the processing of this data takes a huge amount of time and eventually affects the performance of the algorithm. Thus, in order to make the processing faster and performance reasonable, we can take advantage of data structures. By representing data as vectors, we allow CPUs to operate over data in batches, which in turn improves performance. This is another key reason for representing text as vectors.

Encoding

The process of converting data into a specified format is called **encoding**. This is a process wherein we apply a code to change our original data into a form that can be used by any other processes. The most commonly used encoding scheme for files containing text is **American Standard Code for Information Interchange** (**ASCII**). In the next section, we will look into the different types of encoding that are required to convert text into vectors.

Character-Level Encoding

At its lowest level, text is simply a series of characters. Characters usually include letters of the alphabet along with punctuation. When it comes to NLP, the characters that are being encoded are the ones containing the linguistic meaning of the text. It is a common practice in preprocessing to remove those characters that do not assist the NLP program. This helps us understand the meaning of the text.

> **Note**
>
> There are exceptions, though. Sometimes, punctuation marks and spaces give additional meaning in the text. Thus, it's up to the data scientist whether to include and encode these characters or not.

The Roman alphabet is the most widely used alphabet and is the one on which ASCII encoding is based. So, one simple way to do character-level encoding is to simply use the ASCII code for that character. Let's improve our understanding of this with an exercise.

Exercise 54: Character Encoding Using ASCII Values

In this exercise, we will try a very simple method of encoding the text characters. Basically, we will write some code that will encode text characters using their ASCII values. We will make use of the **ord()** function, which in returns the ASCII value of a given character. Follow these steps to implement this exercise:

1. Open a Jupyter notebook.

2. Insert a new cell and enter the following code:

```
ord('A'), ord('a'), ord(',')
```

This code will generate the following output:

$$(65, 97, 44)$$

Figure 7.3: ASCII code of given inputs

3. From the preceding code, it is clear that the **ASCII** value for 'A' is **65**; for 'a', it is **97**; and for ',', it is **44**.

4. Now we are going to create a **to_vector_ascii()** function, which will take a text string as an input and return a vector of the ASCII characters for that text. Insert a new cell and enter the following code to create the function:

```
def to_vector_ascii(text):
    return [ord(a) for a in text]
```

In the function, we are looping through each character of the input text and adding its ASCII value to a list.

5. Pass a string, "**quick brown fox**", as an input to the **to_vector_ascii()** function. Insert a new cell and enter the following code to pass the input to the function we just created:

```
to_vector_ascii('quick brown fox')
```

6. The function, when executed, returns a Python list of length **15**. This list contains the ASCII values of each character. The output generated from this function looks like the following:

```
[113, 117, 105, 99, 107, 32, 98, 114, 111, 119, 110, 32, 102, 111, 120]
```

Figure 7.4: List of ASCII codes for a given statement

Thus, we have learned how to encode characters using ASCII values. However, the preceding list takes up a lot of memory space and is slow as far as performance is concerned. In order to overcome this shortcoming, we make use of the NumPy array, which is better than the normal Python list. We will explore this in the next exercise.

Exercise 55: Character Encoding with the Help of NumPy Arrays

In the preceding exercise, we saw basic character encoding of given text. In this exercise, we will make use of NumPy arrays to save a lot of memory space and improve performance. Follow these steps to implement this exercise:

1. Open a Jupyter notebook.

2. Insert a new cell and add the following code to import the **numpy** library:

    ```
    import numpy
    ```

3. After importing the **numpy** package, we make use of its **array()** function inside our **to_vector_ascii()** function. The **array()** function of NumPy converts any given list to a NumPy array. Insert a new cell and write the following code:

    ```
    def to_vector_ascii(text):
        return numpy.array([ord(a) for a in text])
    ```

4. To test the function, we again pass the same test string, "**quick brown fox**", as input. For that, insert a new cell and enter the following code:

    ```
    to_vector_ascii('quick brown fox')
    ```

    After executing the code, we get the following output:

    ```
    array([113, 117, 105,  99, 107,  32,  98, 114, 111, 119, 110,  32, 102,
           111, 120])
    ```

    Figure 7.5: List of ASCII codes converted into a NumPy array

5. The output generated is a NumPy array displayed in a horizontal manner. In order to change its shape, we make use of the **reshape()** function. The **reshape()** function provides a new shape to an array without changing its data. Insert a new cell and add the following code to modify the **to_vector_ascii()** function again:

    ```
    def to_vector_ascii(text):
        return numpy.array([ord(a) for a in text]).reshape(1, 18)
    ```

6. Now, in order to test the modified **to_vector_ascii()** function, we first pass a new text string, "**The world is round**", to the function, and then assign this function to the **my_vector** variable. Insert a new cell and add the following code:

```
my_vector = to_vector_ascii('The world is round')
```

7. To check the shape of the array, we need to print the variable. In order to do this, insert a new cell and add the following code:

```
my_vector
```

The code generates the following output:

```
array([[ 84],
       [104],
       [101],
       [ 32],
       [119],
       [111],
       [114],
       [108],
       [100],
       [ 32],
       [105],
       [115],
       [ 32],
       [114],
       [111],
       [117],
       [110],
       [100]])
```

Figure 7.6: NumPy array displayed in a particular shape

8. In NumPy, an array has a **shape** attribute, which contains the dimensions of the array. By using this attribute, we check the **shape** attribute of **my_vector**. Insert a new cell and add the following code:

```
my_vector.shape
```

The following output is generated:

$$(18, 1)$$

Figure 7.7: Dimensions of given NumPy array

In this exercise, we learned how to encode a character or text using ASCII values. We also learned how to convert a Python list into a NumPy array. The **reshape()** function and **shape** attribute help in dealing with the dimensions of NumPy arrays. In the next section, we will explore **Positional Character-Level Encoding** and understand how it is better than normal character-level encoding.

Positional Character-Level Encoding

In the previous exercise, we saw the **to_vector_ascii()** function being used to convert given text into a vector of numbers. But this function has its own limitation. Since this function is based on ASCII encoding, there are some characters that cannot be encoded using it. These characters are those that fall outside the range of the ASCII charset.

In order to overcome this limitation, we encode each character by its position. This can be done by giving each character a positional integer value, based on the position where that character is first encountered. For example, in the phrase "**sneeze epidemic**" the letter "**s**" would be **0**, "**n**" would be **1**, "**e**" would be **2**, and so on. Here, the repeated letters get the same integer value. So, as we can see in Figure 7.8, the letter "**e**" is always encoded as **2**. The following image shows how positional encoding is done for the phrase "**sneeze epidemic**":

s	n	e	e	z	e		e	p	i	d	e	m	i	c
0	1	2	2	3	2		4	2	5	6	7	2	8	6	9

Figure 7.8: Positional encoding of a phrase

To get a better understanding of how positional character-level encoding works, we will implement an exercise on it in the next section.

Exercise 56: Character-Level Encoding Using Positions

In this exercise, we will implement character-level encoding using the positions of characters in a given text. Given a string, we want to return a dictionary that contains the position where each character is first encountered. Follow these steps to implement this exercise:

1. Open a Jupyter notebook.

2. First, we need to import the **OrderedDict** class from the **collections** library. The **OrderedDict** class helps in preserving the order in which the keys are inserted. In order to do this, add a new cell and write the following code:

   ```
   from collections import OrderedDict
   ```

3. Now we create a function named **positional_encode_chars()**, which will help us in encoding characters using their positions. Add a new cell and write the following code to implement this:

   ```
   def positional_encode_chars(text):
       char_to_index = OrderedDict()
       index = 1
       for character in text:
           if character not in char_to_index:
               char_to_index[character] = index
               index +=1
       return char_to_index
   ```

4. In the preceding function, we created a **char_to_index** dictionary, which will map the characters in the given string to indices. We also looped through each characters in the string and provided a mapping between a character and an index, if the character is not present in the dictionary.

5. After creating the function, we need to test it by passing the "**The water was as wet as it could be**" string as a parameter. Add a new cell and write the following code to implement this:

   ```
   positional_encode_chars('The water was as wet as it could be')
   ```

The code produces the following output:

```
OrderedDict([('T', 1),
             ('h', 2),
             ('e', 3),
             (' ', 4),
             ('w', 5),
             ('a', 6),
             ('t', 7),
             ('r', 8),
             ('s', 9),
             ('i', 10),
             ('c', 11),
             ('o', 12),
             ('u', 13),
             ('l', 14),
             ('d', 15),
             ('b', 16)])
```

Figure 7.9: Python dictionary of each character encoded as an integer

Positional character-level encoding is rarely used as a final encoding step in machine learning. Instead, algorithms first positional-encode the characters (or words) and then convert them to **one-hot encoded** or **embedded** representations. We will cover one-hot encoding in the next section.

One-Hot Encoding

In NLP, a **one-hot vector** is a 1 x N matrix (vector) used to represent each word in a vocabulary. The vector is made up of all zeros except for a 1 in a single cell.

If we refer to the following figure, we can see that each word in the vocabulary has **1** in a different position, which is used to distinguish each word:

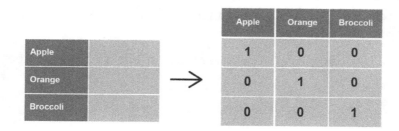

Figure 7.10: One-hot encoding of three items

So, when one-hot encoding is used to encode characters, the value of N for the vector will be the total number of characters that exist in the text. For example, if we want to one-hot encode the word "data," the total one-hot vectors created would be of length 4, since "data" comprises four characters only. In order to determine the size of each one-hot vector for the word "data," we enumerate the total number of characters in "data." For repeated characters, only one index is assigned. If we enumerate total characters in "data," the character "d" will be assigned index 0, the character "a" will be assigned index 1, and the character "t" will be assigned index 2. A better explanation of this is provided in the third exercise of this chapter.

One-hot encoding is such an accepted practice in machine learning and NLP that almost all machine learning and NLP libraries either provide utilities for one-hot encoding or accept input as one-hot encoded vectors.

> **Note**
>
> A **categorical variable** is a variable whose values are usually discrete, such as city or gender. In contrast, a **continuous variable** has values that vary continuously, such as temperature. One-hot encoding is applicable only for categorical variables, and not for continuous variables.

Key Steps in One-Hot Encoding

To one-hot encode text, the following steps are required:

1. Decide whether you want to encode characters or words.

2. Choose how to tokenize the text and decide what tokens are irrelevant for the project and can be removed.

3. Determine the total number of characters or words. This is simply the total number of unique tokens.

We have learned about one-hot encoding and the steps to implement it. Now we will try to solve an exercise to get a better insight into it.

Exercise 57: Character One-Hot Encoding – Manual

In this exercise, we will create our own function that can one-hot encode the characters of a given text. Follow these steps to implement this exercise:

1. Open a Jupyter notebook.

2. To one-hot encode the characters of a given text, we create a function named **onehot_word()**. Insert a new cell and add the following code to create the function:

    ```
    def onehot_word(word):
    ```

3. Within this function, we create a **lookup** table for each of the characters in the **word**. The **enumerate()** function takes the **word** and splits it into unique characters. Then we map each character to a positional index. Add following code to implement this:

    ```
    lookup = {v[1]: v[0] for v in enumerate(set(word))}
    print(lookup)
    word_vector = []
    ```

4. Next, we loop through the characters in the word and create a vector named **one_hot_vector** of the same size as the number of characters in the word. This vector is filled with zeros.

    Finally, we use the **lookup** table to find the position of the character and set that character's value to **1**. To implement this, add the following code:

    ```
    for c in word:
        one_hot_vector = [0] * len(lookup)
        one_hot_vector[lookup[c]] = 1
        word_vector.append(one_hot_vector)
    return word_vector
    ```

    The function we created earlier will return a word vector.

5. Once the **onehot_word()** function is ready, we test it by adding some input as a parameter. We add the text "**data**" as an input to the **onehot_word()** function. To implement this, add a new cell and write the following code:

    ```
    onehot_word('data')
    ```

The code generates the following output:

```
[[1, 0, 0], [0, 1, 0], [0, 0, 1], [0, 1, 0]]
```

Figure 7.11: One-hot encoding of the word "data"

As we pass "**data**" as input to the **onehot_word()** function, there will be four one-hot vectors , since "**data**" comprises four characters only. To determine the size of each one-hot vector for "**data**", we enumerate the total number of characters in "**data**". Only one index gets assigned for repeated characters. After enumerating through the total characters in "**data**", character "**d**" will be assigned index **0**, character "**a**" will be assigned index **1**, and character "**t**" will be assigned index **2**. Based on each character's index position, the elements in each one-hot vector will be marked as **1**, leaving other elements marked **0**. In this way, we manually one-hot encode any given text.

We have learned about how character-level one-hot encoding be performed manually, by developing our own function. We will focus on performing **character-level one-hot encoding** using **Keras** in the next exercise. Keras is a machine learning library that works along with **TensorFlow** to create deep learning models. Deep learning is being used more often nowadays in NLP, and so it is important to have a good understanding about common deep learning tools such as Keras.

Exercise 58: Character-Level One-Hot Encoding with Keras

In this exercise, we will make use of the **Tokenizer** class provided by the Keras library to perform character encoding. We will also explore a few functions and attributes provided by the **Tokenizer** class. Follow these steps to implement this exercise:

1. Open a Jupyter notebook.

2. Initially, we require a class that can transform the input text into vectors. The **keras.preprocessing.text** package provides a **Tokenizer** class, which caters to this need. Insert a new cell and the following code to import the necessary libraries:

```
from keras.preprocessing.text import Tokenizer
import numpy as np
```

3. Once we have imported the **Tokenizer** class, we need to create its instance. Insert a new cell and add the following code to create an instance:

```
char_tokenizer = Tokenizer(char_level=True)
```

In the code, we created a **char_tokenizer** instance. Since we are encoding at the character level, in the constructor, we need to set **char_level** to **True**.

> **Note**
>
> By default, **char_level** is set to **False**, if we are encoding words.

4. To test our **Tokenizer** instance, we require some text to work on. Insert a new cell and add the following code to assign a string to the **text** variable:

```
text = 'The quick brown fox jumped over the lazy dog'
```

5. After getting the text, we make use of the **fit_on_texts()** method provided by the **Tokenizer** class. It helps fit the tokenizer on the given text. Insert a new cell and add the following code to implement this:

```
char_tokenizer.fit_on_texts(text)
```

Under the hood, **char_tokenizer** will break **text** into characters and internally keep track of the tokens, the indices, and everything else needed to perform one-hot encoding.

6. Now that **char_tokenizer** has been fit to **text**, we can look at the possible output. One type of output is the sequence of the characters, that is, the integers assigned to each character in the text. The **texts_to_sequences()** method of the **Tokenizer** class helps assign integers to each character in the text. Insert a new cell and add the following code to implement this:

```
char_tokenizer.texts_to_sequences(text)
```

The code generates the following output:

```
[[4],
 [5],
 [2],
 [1],
 [9],
 [6],
 [10],
 [11],
 [12],
 [1],
 [13],
 [7],
 [3],
 [14],
 [15],
 [1],
 [16],
 [3],
 [17],
 [1],
 [18],
 [6],
 [19],
 [20],
 [2],
 [8],
 [1],
 [3],
 [21],
 [2],
 [7],
 [1],
 [4],
 [5],
 [2],
 [1],
 [22],
 [23],
 [24],
 [25],
 [1],
 [8],
 [3],
 [26]]
```

Figure 7.12: List of integers assigned to each character

As you can see, there were **44** characters in the **text** variable. From the output, we can see that for every unique character in **text**, an integer is assigned. For characters that are repetitive, the same integer is assigned.

7. Now we can look at the actual one-hot encoded values. For this, we make use of the **texts_to_matrix()** method provided by the **Tokenizer** class. This method takes text as input, processes it, and returns a NumPy array of one-hot encoded vectors. Insert a new cell and add the following code to implement this:

```
char_vectors = char_tokenizer.texts_to_matrix(text)
```

8. In this code, the results of the array are stored in the **char_vectors** variable. In order to view its values, just insert a new cell and add the following line:

```
char_vectors
```

The code, on being executed, displays the array of one-hot encoded vectors:

```
array([[0., 0., 0., ..., 0., 0., 0.],
       [0., 0., 0., ..., 0., 0., 0.],
       [0., 0., 1., ..., 0., 0., 0.],
       ...,
       [0., 0., 0., ..., 0., 0., 0.],
       [0., 0., 0., ..., 0., 0., 0.],
       [0., 0., 0., ..., 0., 0., 1.]])
```

Figure 7.13: Actual one-hot encoded values for the given text

9. In order to investigate the dimensions of the NumPy array, we make use of the **shape** attribute. Insert a new cell and add the following code to execute it:

```
char_vectors.shape
```

The following output is generated:

```
(44, 27)
```

Figure 7.14: Shape of the NumPy array

10. So, **char_vectors** is a NumPy array with **44** rows and **27** columns. In order to print an explanation of it, we insert a new cell and the following lines of code:

```
'char_vectors has shape {} because there are {} characters and there
are 26 letters of the alphabet plus space'.format(char_vectors.shape,
len(text))
```

The code generates the following output:

```
'char_vectors has shape (44, 27) because there are 44 characters and there are 26 letters of the alphabet
plus space'
```

Figure 7.15: Information about the NumPy array displayed in the form of a statement

The **len()** function returns the length of the characters inside the **text** variable.

11. To access the first row of the **char_vectors** NumPy array, we insert a new cell and write the following code:

```
char_vectors[0]
```

This returns a one-hot vector, which can be seen in the following figure:

```
array([0., 0., 0., 0., 1., 0., 0., 0., 0., 0., 0., 0., 0., 0., 0., 0.,
       0., 0., 0., 0., 0., 0., 0., 0., 0., 0.])
```

Figure 7.16: One-hot vector of first character

12. To access the index of this one-hot vector, we make use of the **argmax()** function provided by NumPy. Insert a new cell and write the following code to implement this:

```
np.argmax(char_vectors[0])
```

The code generates the following output:

```
4
```

Figure 7.17: Index of a one-hot vector

13. The `Tokenizer` class provides two dictionaries, namely **index_word** and **word_index**, using which we can view the contents of `Tokenizer` in key-value form. Insert a new cell and add the following code to view the **index_word** dictionary:

```
char_tokenizer.index_word
```

The code generates the following output:

```
{1: ' ',
 2: 'e',
 3: 'o',
 4: 't',
 5: 'h',
 6: 'u',
 7: 'r',
 8: 'd',
 9: 'q',
 10: 'i',
 11: 'c',
 12: 'k',
 13: 'b',
 14: 'w',
 15: 'n',
 16: 'f',
 17: 'x',
 18: 'j',
 19: 'm',
 20: 'p',
 21: 'v',
 22: 'l',
 23: 'a',
 24: 'z',
 25: 'y',
 26: 'g'}
```

Figure 7.18: The index_word dictionary

As you can see in this figure, the indices act as keys and the characters act as values. Now insert a new cell and the following code to view the **word_index** dictionary:

```
char_tokenizer.word_index
```

The code generates the following output:

```
{' ': 1,
 'a': 23,
 'b': 13,
 'c': 11,
 'd': 8,
 'e': 2,
 'f': 16,
 'g': 26,
 'h': 5,
 'i': 10,
 'j': 18,
 'k': 12,
 'l': 22,
 'm': 19,
 'n': 15,
 'o': 3,
 'p': 20,
 'q': 9,
 'r': 7,
 't': 4,
 'u': 6,
 'v': 21,
 'w': 14,
 'x': 17,
 'y': 25,
 'z': 24}
```

Figure 7.19: The word_index dictionary

In this figure, the characters act as keys and the indices act as values.

14. In the preceding steps, we saw how to access the index of a given one-hot vector by using the **argmax()** function provided by NumPy. Using this index as a key, we access its value in the **index_word** dictionary. To implement this, we insert a new cell and write the following code:

```
char_tokenizer.index_word[np.argmax(char_vectors[0])]
```

The preceding code generates the following output:

```
't'
```

Figure 7.20: Value of a one-hot vector in the index_word dictionary

In the code, **np.argmax(char_vectors[0])** produces an output of **4**. Once we get this output, this will act as a key in finding the value in the **index_word** dictionary. So, when **char_tokenizer.index_word[4]** is executed, it will scan through the dictionary, find that for key **4** the value is **t**, and finally print **t**.

We've understood how to one-hot encode characters using the Keras library. Before moving on to the next section, let's explore the advantages and disadvantages of one-hot encoding.

Until now, we have only performed one-hot encoding for characters. We can also do **one-hot encoding for words**, which we will cover in the next section followed by an exercise.

Word-Level One-Hot Encoding

Words are basic units of language and meaning in human language. They are the most efficient vector representations for allowing NLP algorithms to extract meaning from text. Most types of representations that are done at character level can also be done at word level. You can also one-hot encode words.

When one-hot encoding words, you also need to keep an eye on the **vocabulary** of words that you are dealing with. A vocabulary is the total number of unique words in the text sources for your project. So, if you have a large source, then you will end up with a huge vocabulary and large one-hot vector sizes, which will eventually consume a lot of memory. An exercise on word-level one-hot encoding will provide a better understanding of this.

Exercise 59: Word-Level One-Hot Encoding

In this exercise, we will one-hot encode words with the help of the **preprocessing** package provided by the **scikit-learn** library. For this, we shall make use of a file containing 100 movie lines. Follow these steps to implement this exercise:

1. Open a Jupyter notebook.

2. First, we need to load the file containing 100 movie lines. For this, we will make use of the **Path** class, provided by the **pathlib** library, to specify the location of the file. Insert a new cell and add the following code:

```
from pathlib import Path
data = Path('../data')
movie_lines_file = data / '100lines.txt'
```

From the code, we can see that the file details are stored in the **movie_lines_file** variable.

> **Note**
>
> The **100lines.txt** file can be found at this location: https://bit.ly/2tC5VAs.

3. Since we have got the file, we need to open it and read its contents. In order to open the file, we use the **open()** function. To reads the contents of the file, we make use of the **read()** function. We store the results in the `movie_lines_raw` variable. Insert a new cell and add the following code to implement this:

```
with movie_lines_file.open() as f:
    movie_lines_raw = f.read()
```

4. After reading the contents of the file, we load it by inserting a new cell and adding the following code:

```
movie_lines_raw
```

The code generates the following output:

```
'They do not!\nThey do to!\nI hope so.\nShe okay?\nLet\'s go.\nWow\nOkay -- you\'re gonna need to learn ho
w to lie.\nNo\nI\'m kidding.  You know how sometimes you just become this "persona"?  And you don\'t know
how to quit?\nLike my fear of wearing pastels?\nThe "real you".\nWhat good stuff?\nI figured you\'d get to
the good stuff eventually.\nThank God!  If I had to hear one more story about your coiffure...\nMe.  This
endless ...blonde babble. I\'m like, boring myself.\nWhat crap?\ndo you listen to this crap?\nNo...\nThen
Guillermo says, "If you go any lighter, you\'re gonna look like an extra on 90210."\nYou always been this
selfish?\nBut\nThen that\'s all you had to say.\nWell, no...\nYou never wanted to go out with \'me, did yo
u?\nI was?\nI looked for you back at the party, but you always seemed to be "occupied".\nTons\nHave fun to
night?\nI believe we share an art instructor\nYou know Chastity?\nLooks like things worked out tonight, hu
h?\nHi.\nWho knows?  All I\'ve ever heard her say is that she\'d dip before dating a guy that smokes.\nSo
that\'s the kind of guy she likes? Pretty ones?\nLesbian?  No. I found a picture of Jared Leto in one of h
er drawers, so I\'m pretty sure she\'s not harboring same-sex tendencies.\nShe\'s not a...\nI\'m workin\'
on it. But she doesn\'t seem to be goin\' for him.\nI really, really, really wanna go, but I can\'t.   Not
unless my sister goes.\nSure have.\nEber\'s Deep Conditioner every two days. And I never, ever use a blowd
ryer without the diffuser attachment.\nHow do you get your hair to look like that?\nYou\'re sweet.\nYou ha
ve my word.  As a gentleman\nI counted on you to help my cause. You and that thug are obviously failing. A
ren\'t we ever going on our date?\nYou got something on your mind?\nWhere?\nThere.\nWell, there\'s someone
I think might be --\nHow is our little Find the Wench A Date plan progressing?\nForget French.\nThat\'s be
cause it\'s such a nice one.\nI don\'t want to know how to say that though.  I want to know useful things.
Like where the good stores are.  How much does champagne cost?  Stuff like Chat.  I have never in my life
had to point out my head to someone.\nRight.   See?  You\'re ready for the quiz.\nC\'esc ma tete. This is m
y head\nLet me see what I can do.\nGosh, if only we could find Kat a boyfriend...\nThat\'s a shame.\nUnsol
ved mystery.  She used to be really popular when she started high school, then it was just like she got si
ck of it or something.\nWhy?\nSeems like she could get a date easy enough...\nThe thing is,  -- I\'m at th
e mercy of a particularly hideous breed of loser.  My sister.  I can\'t date until she does.\n.\nNo, no, i
t\'s my fault -- we didn\'t have a proper introduction ---\nForget it.\nYou\'re asking me out.  That\'s so
cute. What\'s your name again?\nOkay... then how \'bout we try out some French cuisine.  Saturday?  Night?
\nNot the hacking and gagging and spitting part.  Please.\nWell, I thought we\'d start with pronunciation,
if that\'s okay with you.\nCan we make this quick?  Roxanne Korrine and Andrew Barrett are having an incre
dibly horrendous public break- up on the quad.  Again.\nI did.\nYou think you \' re the only sophomore at
the prom?\nI don\'t have to be home \'til two.\nI have to be home in twenty minutes.\nAll I know is -- I
\'d give up my private line to go out with a guy like Joey.\nSometimes I wonder if the guys we\'re suppose
d to want to go out with are the ones we actually want to go out with, you know?\n, I don\'t think the hig
hlights of dating Joey Dorsey are going to include door-opening and coat-holding.\nCombination.  I don\'t
know -- I thought he\'d be different.  More of a gentleman...\nIs he oily or dry?\nHe practically proposed
when he found out we had the same dermatologist. I mean.  Dr. Bonchowski is great an all, but he\'s not exa
ctly relevant party conversation.\nWould you mind getting me a drink, ?\nGreat\nJoey.\nWho?\nWhere did he
go?  He was just here.\nYou might wanna think about it\nNo.\nDid you change your hair?\nYou know the deal.
  I can \' t go if Kat doesn\'t go --\nListen, I want to talk to you about the prom.\nYou\'re concentratin
g awfully hard considering it\'s gym class.\nHi, Joey.\nHey, sweet cheeks.\nMy agent says I\'ve got a good
shot at being the Prada guy next year.\nNeat...\nIt\'s a cruise line, but I\'ll be, like, wearing a unifor
m and stuff.\nQueen Harry?\nSo yeah, I\'ve got the Sears catalog thing going -- and the tube sock gig " th
at\'s gonna be huge.  And then I\'m up for an ad for Queen Harry next week.\nHopefully.\nExactly  So, you
going to Bogey Lowenbrau\'s thing on Saturday?\nExpensive?'
```

Figure 7.21: List of unique words in the file

If you take a look at the preceding figure, you will see a lot of newline characters. This happened because we loaded the entire content at once into a single variable instead of separate lines. You will also see a lot of non-alphanumeric characters.

5. The main objective is to create one-hot vectors for each word in the file. For that, we need to construct a **vocabulary**, which is the entire list of unique words in the file. We can achieve this by tokenizing the string into words and removing new lines and non-alphanumeric characters.

6. The `clean_tokenize()` function in the following code does the same thing. The vocabulary created using the `clean_tokenize()` function is stored in the variable `movie_lines` variable. Insert a new cell and add the following code to implement this:

```
import string
import re

alpha_characters = str.maketrans('', '', string.punctuation)

def clean_tokenize(text):
    text = text.lower()
    text = re.sub(r'\n', '*** ', text)
    text = text.translate(alpha_characters)
    text = re.sub(r' +', ' ', text)
    return text.split(' ')

movie_lines = clean_tokenize(movie_lines_raw)
```

7. Take a look at `movie_lines` now. It should look like a list. Insert a new cell and add the following code to view it:

```
movie_lines
```

The code generates the following output:

```
['they',
 'do',
 'not',
 'they',
 'do',
 'to',
 'i',
 'hope',
 'so',
 'she',
 'okay',
 'lets',
 'go',
 'wow',
 'okay',
 'youre',
 'gonna',
```

Figure 7.22: List of words in movie_lines

8. The next step is to convert the preceding list into a NumPy array. Insert a new cell and add the following code to convert the list to a NumPy array and print the shape of the array:

```
import numpy as np
movie_line_array = np.array([movie_lines])
movie_line_array = movie_line_array.reshape(-1, 1)
movie_line_array.shape
```

The code generates the following output:

$$(834, 1)$$

Figure 7.23: Shape of the NumPy array

As you can see in the preceding figure, our `movie_line_array` array consists of **834** rows and **1** column. Each row is a word in the original `movie_lines` file.

> **Note**
>
> NumPy arrays are more specific to NLP algorithms than Python lists. It is the format that is required for the scikit-learn library, which we will be using to one-hot encode words.

9. Now we can make use of encoders, such as the **LabelEncoder()** and **OneHotEncoder()** classes from the scikit-learn **preprocessing** package, to convert `movie_line_array` to one-hot encoded format. Insert a new cell and add the following lines of code to implement this:

```
from sklearn import preprocessing

labelEncoder = preprocessing.LabelEncoder()
movie_line_labels = labelEncoder.fit_transform(movie_line_array)

import warnings
warnings.filterwarnings('ignore')

wordOneHotEncoder = preprocessing.OneHotEncoder()

line_onehot = wordOneHotEncoder.fit_transform(movie_line_labels.reshape(-1,1))
```

10. In the code, the **LabelEncoder()** class encodes the labels, and the **fit_transform()** method of the **LabelEncoder()** class fits the label encoder and returns the encoded labels. If we want to check the list of encoded labels, then we insert a new cell and add the following code:

```
movie_line_labels
```

The preceding code generates the following output:

```
array([313,  77, 219, 313,  77, 322, 157, 151, 285, 278, 224, 184, 113,
       361, 224, 367, 118, 213, 322, 180, 154, 322, 185, 218, 161, 175,
       364, 177, 154, 290, 364, 173,  26, 317, 236,  10, 364,  80, 177,
       154, 322, 255, 188, 208,  99, 222, 342, 235, 309, 259, 364, 348,
       119, 297, 157, 100, 365, 109, 322, 309, 119, 297,  91, 306, 114,
       159, 157, 128, 322, 137, 226, 206, 296,   2, 366,  53, 200, 317,
        89,  31,  21, 161, 188,  35, 209, 348,  62,  77, 364, 191, 322,
       317,  62, 218, 310, 123, 268, 159, 364, 113,  12, 187, 367, 118,
       193, 188,   9,  96, 225,   0, 364,   8,  27, 317, 275,  40, 310,
       308,   7, 364, 128, 322, 267, 345, 218, 364, 214, 339, 322, 113,
       231, 354, 200,  72, 364, 157, 340, 157, 194, 102, 364,  22,  18,
       309, 234,  40, 364,   8, 273, 322,  24, 221, 324, 133, 106, 323,
       157,  30, 341, 277,   9,  15, 165, 364, 177,  48, 195, 188, 315,
       358, 231, 323, 156, 145, 352, 178,   7, 170,  92, 138, 141, 267,
       167, 307, 279,  76,  28,  67,   1, 124, 307, 284, 285, 308, 309,
       176, 222, 124, 278, 189, 244, 227, 181, 218, 157, 104,   1, 237,
       222, 171, 183, 162, 226, 222, 141,  84, 285, 161, 244, 300, 280,
       219, 130, 265, 304, 280, 219,   1, 161, 359, 225, 168,  40, 278,
        79, 272, 322,  24, 116, 102, 149, 157, 260, 260, 260, 337, 113,
        40, 157,  42, 219, 330, 208, 283, 115, 300, 133,  88,  70,  56,
        93, 328,  68,  10, 157, 214,  92, 334,   1,  32, 355, 309,  75,
        19, 154,  77, 364, 109, 366, 129, 322, 193, 188, 307, 367, 301,
       364, 133, 208, 357,  16,   1, 108, 157,  61, 225, 364, 322, 140,
       208,  44, 364,  10, 307, 320,  13, 220,  97,  14, 341,  92, 117,
       225, 230,  66, 364, 121, 289, 225, 366, 204, 351, 311, 345, 312,
       288, 157, 316, 203,  24, 154, 167, 230, 192, 101, 309, 346,   1,
        66, 238, 246, 103, 105, 308,  25, 169, 298,   1, 216, 226, 157,
        80, 338, 322, 177, 154, 322, 267, 307, 318, 157, 338, 322, 177,
       336, 315, 188, 351, 309, 119, 295,  13, 154, 207,  78,  46,  59,
       297, 188,  49, 157, 133, 214, 162, 208, 186, 128, 322, 240, 231,
       208, 136, 322, 288, 262, 271, 367, 258, 102, 309, 256,  45, 198,
       305, 317, 167, 208, 136, 182, 200, 271, 348, 157,  41,  77, 120,
       159, 228, 341,  60, 101, 174,   1,  37, 308,   1, 276, 331, 210,
       278, 335, 322,  24, 260, 241, 350, 278, 294, 147, 269, 310, 168,
       340, 173, 188, 278, 121, 282, 222, 168, 229, 289, 353, 274, 188,
       278,  60, 109,   1,  66,  87,  90, 309, 314, 167, 161,  18, 309,
       202, 222,   1, 233, 146,  39, 222, 196, 208, 283, 157,  42,  66,
       332, 278,  78, 218, 218, 169, 208,  98, 341,  73, 133,   1, 249,
       166, 103, 168, 367,  17, 200, 231, 308, 285,  65, 349, 366, 211,
         5, 224, 310, 154,  36, 341, 325, 231, 287, 105,  64, 266, 217,
       219, 309, 127,  10, 107,  10, 292, 232, 239, 345, 157, 319, 343,
       293, 354, 248, 159, 308, 224, 354, 364,  41, 341, 199, 317, 254,
       263, 179,  10,  11,  23,  13, 134,   9, 164, 153, 251,  38, 333,
       225, 309, 252,   5, 157,  72, 364, 316, 364, 257, 309, 228, 291,
        18, 309, 247, 157,  80, 133, 322,  24, 150, 321, 328, 157, 133,
       322,  24, 150, 162, 327, 205,   7, 157, 177, 167, 158, 112, 333,
       208, 245, 190, 322, 113, 231, 354,   1, 124, 188, 172, 290, 157,
       356, 159, 309, 125, 347, 299, 322, 338, 322, 113, 231, 354,  13,
       309, 227, 341,   3, 338, 322, 113, 231, 354, 364, 177, 157,  80,
       316, 309, 148, 222,  67, 172,  82,  13, 117, 322, 163,  81,  10,
        52,  54, 157,  80, 177, 157, 319, 139,  24,  74, 206, 222,   1,
       108, 167, 135, 223, 229,  86, 135, 242, 250, 350, 135, 104, 231,
       341, 128, 309, 264,  71, 157, 201,  83,  34, 167, 122,   9,   7,
        40, 143, 219,  94, 261, 234,  58, 360, 364, 204, 110, 200,   1,
        85, 122, 172, 352, 351,  72, 135, 113, 135, 340, 173, 142, 364,
       203, 337, 316,   2, 168, 218,  72, 364,  47, 366, 129, 364, 177,
       309,  69, 157,  41, 302, 113, 159, 174,  79, 113, 191, 157, 338,
       322, 303, 322, 364,   2, 309, 247, 367,  55,  20, 131,  57, 169,
       126,  51, 145, 172, 144, 301,  50, 208,   6, 268, 170, 121,   1,
       119, 281,  18,  29, 309, 243, 124, 215, 363, 212, 169,   1,  63,
       190,  40, 160,  24, 188, 342,   1, 329,  10, 297, 253, 132, 285,
       362, 170, 121, 309, 270,  43, 314, 117,  10, 309, 326, 286, 111,
       308, 118,  24, 155,  10, 310, 161, 333, 102,   9,   4, 102, 253,
       132, 215, 344, 152,  94, 285, 364, 117, 322,  33, 197, 314, 225,
       266,  95], dtype=int64)
```

Figure 7.24: List of encoded labels

11. The **OneHotEncoder()** class encodes encoding categorical integer features as a one-hot numeric array. The **fit_transform()** method of this class takes the **movie_line_labels** array as input. The **movie_line_labels** array is a numeric array, and each feature included in this array is encoded using the one-hot encoding scheme.

12. A binary column is created for each category, and a **sparse matrix** is returned as output. To view the matrix, insert a new cell and type the following code:

```
line_onehot
```

The code generates the following output:

```
<834x368 sparse matrix of type '<class 'numpy.float64'>'
        with 834 stored elements in Compressed Sparse Row format>
```

Figure 7.25: Sparse matrix

13. To convert the sparse matrix into a **dense array**, we make use of the **toarray()** function. Insert a new cell and add the following code to implement this:

```
line_onehot.toarray()
```

The code generates the following output:

```
array([[0., 0., 0., ..., 0., 0., 0.],
       [0., 0., 0., ..., 0., 0., 0.],
       [0., 0., 0., ..., 0., 0., 0.],
       ...,
       [0., 0., 0., ..., 0., 0., 0.],
       [0., 0., 0., ..., 0., 0., 0.],
       [0., 0., 0., ..., 0., 0., 0.]])
```

Figure 7.26: Dense array

The preceding figure shows that we have achieved our objective of one-hot encoding words. In the next section, we will focus on concepts such as embeddings and word embeddings.

Word Embeddings

An **embedding** is a mathematical structure that contains another structure. So, we can say that an embedding vector contains or represents a value of something. Now we will look at the area of **word embeddings**. Word embeddings are a special type of embedding where the word (and the meaning of the word) is embedded into a vector. The following diagram shows the transformation:

Figure 7.27: Transformation from word to embedding vector

We need to find a way to represent text as vectors so that they are useful for machine learning algorithms. One-hot encoding is one way to do this. But we need to find a way around the limitations of one-hot encoding, which include the following:

- One-hot vectors can get quite large.

- One-hot vectors are sparse.

- One-hot vectors contain no information about correlation between themselves. In other words, you cannot choose two vectors and determine whether they are close or far apart.

With these limitations in mind, the objective is to find a vector representation of words that complies with the following conditions:

- Is compressed in fewer dimensions.

- Contains more information.

- Each word vector contains some information in relation to other vectors. For example, you can find a correlation between the word vector for "man" and the word vector for "woman".

This leads us into word embeddings. **Word embeddings** are a special type of vector that try to achieve these objectives. Let's look generally at what an embedding is. An embedding is a structure into which we embed information. When we speak of a word embedding, we mean that we have a structure into which we embed the meaning of a word.

So, each individual embedding vector contains information about the meaning of a single word. For example, we can embed the meaning of the word "king" into a 100-dimension vector. We can then use that vector to represent the word "king" in machine learning programs or in search indexes. Word meanings are determined by looking at the word and other words that tend to surround it in the sentences. Word embeddings are trained to produce vectors that can predict what words might be used in the same context.

In the next section, we will learn about the **Word2Vec** algorithm, which is used to train word vectors. We will also solve an exercise, which will give us a better understanding about training word vectors.

Word2Vec

Word2Vec is an algorithm developed at Google for training word vectors. It takes a text corpus as input and produces word vectors as output. It learns from the output by using a predictive method. The exercise following shows how word vectors can be trained.

Exercise 60: Training Word Vectors

In this exercise, we will create word vectors using the **gensim** library. To create word vectors, we need a source of documents. For this, we will be using the books available on **Project Gutenberg**. We will write some code that will download the books from Project Gutenberg as the training dataset. We will also see the vector representation using Matplotlib's **pyplot** framework. Follow these steps to implement this exercise:

1. Open a Jupyter notebook.

2. We will be using the `requests` library to load books from the Project Gutenberg website, the `json` library to load a book catalog, and the `regex` package to clean the text by removing new lines. Insert a new cell and add the following code to implement this:

   ```
   import requests
   import json
   import re
   ```

3. After importing all the necessary libraries, we load the `json` file, which contains details of 10 books. Each book contains information about **title**, **author**, and **id**. Insert a new cell and add the following steps to implement this:

   ```
   with open('../ProjectGutenbergBooks.json', 'r') as catalog_file:
       catalog = json.load(catalog_file)
   ```

   > **Note**
   >
   > The book catalog file can be found at the following link: https://bit.ly/2U2jAR4.

4. To print the details of all the books, we insert a new cell and add the following code:

   ```
   catalog
   ```

The preceding code generates the following output:

```
[{'title': 'Pride and Prejudice', 'author': 'Jane Austen', 'id': 1342},
 {'title': 'A Christmas Carol in Prose',
  'author': 'Charles Dickens',
  'id': 46},
 {'title': 'A Tale of Two Cities', 'author': 'Charles Dickens', 'id': 98},
 {'title': 'Frankenstein; Or, The Modern Prometheus',
  'author': 'Mary Wollstonecraft Shelley',
  'id': 84},
 {'title': 'Dracula', 'author': 'Bram Stoker', 'id': 345},
 {'title': 'Heart of Darkness', 'author': 'Joseph Conrad', 'id': 219},
 {'title': 'Moby Dick; Or, The Whale',
  'author': 'Herman Melville',
  'id': 2701},
 {'title': "Alice's Adventures in Wonderland",
  'author': 'Lewis Carroll',
  'id': 11},
 {'title': 'The Adventures of Sherlock Holmes',
  'author': 'Arthur Conan Doyle',
  'id': 1661},
 {'title': 'A Modest Proposal', 'author': 'Jonathan Swift', 'id': 1080}]
```

Figure 7.28: Book details in catalog

From the figure, we can see that the **json** file contains details of 10 books.

5. We will make use of the Project Gutenberg website to load the book. For that, we will create our own **load_book()** function, which will take **book_id** as a parameter and, based on that **book_id**, will fetch the book and load it. Also, it will clean the text by removing the new lines. Insert a new cell and add the following code to implement this:

```
GUTENBERG_URL ='https://www.gutenberg.org/files/{}/{}-0.txt'

def load_book(book_id):
    url = GUTENBERG_URL.format(book_id, book_id)
    contents = requests.get(url).text
    cleaned_contents = re.sub(r'\r\n', ' ', contents)
    return cleaned_contents
```

6. Once we have defined our **load_book()** function, we will loop through the catalog and fetch all the **id** instances of the books and store them in the **book_ids** list. The **id** instances stored in the **book_ids** list will act as parameters for our **load_book()** function. The book information fetched for each book ID will be loaded in the **books** variable. Insert a new cell and add the following code to implement this:

```
book_ids = [ book['id'] for book in catalog ]
books = [ load_book(id) for id in book_ids]
```

To view the information of the **books** variable, we add the following code in a new cell:

```
Books
```

The code generates the following output:

```
["\ufeffThe Project Gutenberg EBook of Pride and Prejudice, by Jane Austen  This eBook is for the use of anyone anywhere at n
o cost and with almost no restrictions whatsoever.  You may copy it, give it away or re-use it under the terms of the Project
Gutenberg License included with this eBook or online at www.gutenberg.org   Title: Pride and Prejudice  Author: Jane Austen
Posting Date: August 26, 2008 [EBook #1342] Release Date: June, 1998 Last Updated: March 10, 2018  Language: English  Charact
er set encoding: UTF-8  *** START OF THIS PROJECT GUTENBERG EBOOK PRIDE AND PREJUDICE ***        Produced by Anonymous Volunteer
s       PRIDE AND PREJUDICE  By Jane Austen    Chapter 1   It is a truth universally acknowledged, that a single man in posses
sion of a good fortune, must be in want of a wife.  However little known the feelings or views of such a man may be on his fi
rst entering a neighbourhood, this truth is so well fixed in the minds of the surrounding families, that he is considered the
rightful property of some one or other of their daughters.  "My dear Mr. Bennet," said his lady to him one day, "have you hea
rd that Netherfield Park is let at last?"  Mr. Bennet replied that he had not.  "But it is," returned she; "for Mrs. Long has
just been here, and she told me all about it."  Mr. Bennet made no answer.  "Do you not want to know who has taken it?" cried
his wife impatiently.  "_You_ want to tell me, and I have no objection to hearing it."  This was invitation enough.  "Why, my
dear, you must know, Mrs. Long says that Netherfield is taken by a young man of large fortune from the north of England; that
he came down on Monday in a chaise and four to see the place, and was so much delighted with it, that he agreed with Mr. Morr
is immediately; that he is to take possession before Michaelmas, and some of his servants are to be in the house by the end o
f next week."  "What is his name?"  "Bingley."  "Is he married or single?"  "Oh! Single, my dear, to be sure! A single man of
large fortune; four or five thousand a year. What a fine thing for our girls!"  "How so? How can it affect them?"  "My dear M
r. Bennet," replied his wife, "how can you be so tiresome! You must know that I am thinking of his marrying one of them."  "I
s that his design in settling here?"  "Design! Nonsense, how can you talk so! But it is very likely that he _may_ fall in lov
```

Figure 7.29: Information of various books

7. Before we can train the word vectors, we need to break the books into a list of documents. Let's think about what a document is. In this case, we want to teach the **Word2Vec** algorithm about words in the context of the sentences that they are in. So, here a document is actually a sentence. Thus we need to create a list of sentences from all the 10 books. Insert a new cell and add the following code to implement this:

```
from gensim.summarization import textcleaner
from gensim.utils import import simple_preprocess

def to_sentences(book):
    sentences = textcleaner.split_sentences(book)
    sentence_tokens = [simple_preprocess(sentence) for sentence in
sentences]
    return sentence_tokens
```

8. In the preceding code, we have used the **textcleaner** class from the **gensim** package. The **split_sentences()** function of the **textcleaner** class helps to split the text and get the list of sentences from the given text. The **simple_preprocess()** function converts a document into a list of lowercase tokens. All this processing takes place inside our **to_sentences()** function, which returns **sentence_tokens**.

9. Now we loop through each book in **books** and pass each **book** as a parameter to our **to_sentences()** function. The results will be stored in the **book_sentences** variable. Also, we will split **books** into **sentences** and **sentences** into **documents**. The result will be stored in the **documents** variable. Insert a new cell and add the following code to implement this:

    ```
    books_sentences = [to_sentences(book) for book in books]
    documents = [sentence for book_sent in books_sentences for sentence in
    book_sent]
    ```

10. If we want to check the length of the documents, we make use of the **len()** function. Insert a new cell and add the following code to implement this:

    ```
    len(documents)
    ```

    The code generates the following output:

    27725

    Figure 7.30: Length of the documents

11. Now that we have our documents, we can train our **Word2Vec** model by making use of the **Word2Vec** class provided by the **gensim** package. Insert a new cell and add the following code to implement this:

    ```
    from gensim.models import Word2Vec
    # build vocabulary and train model
    model = Word2Vec(
            documents,
            size=100,
            window=10,
            min_count=2,
            workers=10)
    model.train(documents, total_examples=len(documents), epochs=50)
    ```

The code generates the following output:

```
(23740425, 32057400)
```

Figure 7.31: Output generated using the model.train() method

12. In the code, the **Word2Vec** class has parameters such as **documents**, **size**, **window**, **min_count**, and **workers**. Now, **documents** are the sentences that we have to provide to the class. **size** represents the length of the dense vector to represent each token. **min_count** represents the minimum count of words that can be taken into consideration when training a particular model. **workers** represents the number of threads that are required when training a model.

13. The **model.train()** method has arguments such as **documents**, **total_examples**, and **epochs**. Now, **documents** represents the sentences. The **total_examples** parameter represents the count of sentences. **epochs** represents the total number of iterations over the given data.

14. The trained word vectors get stored in **model.wv**, which is an instance of **KeyedVectors**. Now we will make use of the **most_similar()** function of the **model.wv** instance to find the similar words. The **most_similar()** function takes **positive** as a parameter and returns a list of strings that contribute positively. Insert a new cell and add the following code to implement this:

```
model.wv.most_similar(positive="worse")
```

The code generates the following output:

```
[('better', 0.6523939371109009),
 ('narrower', 0.6434351205825806),
 ('happier', 0.6192134618759155),
 ('kinder', 0.5986782312393188),
 ('more', 0.5791730880737305),
 ('handsomer', 0.5779246687889099)
 ('older', 0.5424486398696899),
 ('mightier', 0.5343776941299438),
 ('hoarser', 0.5322822332382202),
 ('slighter', 0.532081127166748)]
```

Figure 7.32: Most similar words

15. Now we create a **show_vector()** function, which will display the vector. We will make use of **pyplot**, which is a plotting framework in **matplotlib**. This will allow us to plot our vector. Insert a new cell and add the following code to implement this:

```
%matplotlib inline
import matplotlib.pyplot as plt

def show_vector(word):
    vector = model.wv[word]
    fig, ax = plt.subplots(1,1, figsize=(10, 2))
    ax.tick_params(axis='both',
                   which='both',
                   left=False,
                   bottom=False,
                   top=False,
                   labelleft=False,
                   labelbottom=False)
    ax.grid(False)
    print(word)
    ax.bar(range(len(vector)), vector, 0.5)

show_vector('sad')
```

The code generates the following output:

Figure 7.33: Graph of a vector when input is "sad"

In the preceding figure, we can see the vector representation when the word provided to the **show_vector()** function is "**sad**".

We have learned about training word vectors as well as representing them using **pyplot**. Now that we have seen how to train word vectors, in the next section, we will focus more on using the **pre-trained word vectors** that are required for NLP projects.

Using Pre-Trained Word Vectors

Once the word vectors have been trained on a language source and used in a project, they can also be stored and reused for other related projects. In order to be used for other related projects, certain factors such as the training source, the number of words, and the context in which they were used are taken into consideration. This application of training from one project to another is known as **transfer learning**. The following exercise will give you a better understanding of how to load a pre-trained word vector.

> **Note**
>
> **Pre-trained word vectors** can get pretty large. For example, vectors trained on the Google News contain 3 million words, and on disk, its compressed size is 1.5GB.

Exercise 61: Loading Pre-Trained Word Vectors

In this exercise, we will load and use pre-trained word embeddings. We will also show the image representation of a few word vectors using the **pyplot** framework of the **matplotlib** library. Follow these steps to implement this exercise:

1. Open a Jupyter notebook.

2. Add the following **import** statement to the import **numpy** library:

   ```
   import numpy as np
   ```

3. In order to extract data from a ZIP file, we make use of the **zipfile** Python package. Add the following code to unzip the embeddings from the ZIP file:

   ```
   GLOVE_DIR = '../data/glove/'
   GLOVE_ZIP = GLOVE_DIR + 'glove.6B.50d.zip'

   import zipfile
   ```

```
zip_ref = zipfile.ZipFile(GLOVE_ZIP, 'r')
zip_ref.extractall(GLOVE_DIR)
zip_ref.close()
```

> **Note**
>
> The preceding ZIP file can be found at the following link: https://bit.ly/2RG7VpX.

4. **glove_vector_file** is a text file containing a dictionary. Here, words act as keys and vectors act as values. So, we need to read the file line by line, split it, and then map it to a Python dictionary. The **load_glove_vectors()** function returns a **model** Python dictionary. Insert a new cell and add the following code to implement this:

```
def load_glove_vectors(fn):
    print("Loading Glove Model")
    with open( fn,'r', encoding='utf8') as glove_vector_file:
        model = {}
        for line in glove_vector_file:
            parts = line.split()
            word = parts[0]
            embedding = np.array([float(val) for val in parts[1:]])
            model[word] = embedding
        print("Loaded {} words".format(len(model)))
    return model

glove_vectors = load_glove_vectors('../data/glove/glove.6B.50d.txt')
```

The preceding code generates the following output:

```
Loading Glove Model
Loaded 400000 words
```

Figure 7.34: Total words in the glove model

If we want to view the values of **glove_vectors**, then we insert a new cell and add the following code:

```
glove_vectors
```

```
{'the': array([ 4.1800e-01,  2.4968e-01, -4.1242e-01,  1.2170e-01,  3.4527e-01,
       -4.4457e-02, -4.9688e-01, -1.7862e-01, -6.6023e-04, -6.5660e-01,
        2.7843e-01, -1.4767e-01, -5.5677e-01,  1.4658e-01, -9.5095e-03,
        1.1658e-02,  1.0204e-01, -1.2792e-01, -8.4430e-01, -1.2181e-01,
       -1.6801e-02, -3.3279e-01, -1.5520e-01, -2.3131e-01, -1.9181e-01,
       -1.8823e+00, -7.6746e-01,  9.9051e-02, -4.2125e-01, -1.9526e-01,
        4.0071e+00, -1.8594e-01, -5.2287e-01, -3.1681e-01,  5.9213e-04,
        7.4449e-03,  1.7778e-01, -1.5897e-01,  1.2041e-02, -5.4223e-02,
       -2.9871e-01, -1.5749e-01, -3.4758e-01, -4.5637e-02, -4.4251e-01,
        1.8785e-01,  2.7849e-03, -1.8411e-01, -1.1514e-01, -7.8581e-01]),
 ',': array([ 0.013441,  0.23682 , -0.16899 ,  0.40951 ,  0.63812 ,  0.47709 ,
       -0.42852 , -0.55641 , -0.364   , -0.23938 ,  0.13001 , -0.063734,
       -0.39575 , -0.48162 ,  0.23291 ,  0.090201, -0.13324 ,  0.078639,
       -0.41634 , -0.15428 ,  0.10068 ,  0.48891 ,  0.31226 , -0.1252  ,
       -0.037512, -1.5179  ,  0.12612 , -0.02442 , -0.042961, -0.28351 ,
        3.5416  , -0.11956 , -0.014533, -0.1499  ,  0.21864 , -0.33412 ,
       -0.13872 ,  0.31806 ,  0.70358 ,  0.44858 , -0.080262,  0.63003 ,
        0.32111 , -0.46765 ,  0.22786 ,  0.36034 , -0.37818 , -0.56657 ,
        0.044691,  0.30392 ]),
```

Figure 7.35: Dictionary of glove_vectors

5. The **glove_vectors** object is basically a dictionary containing the mappings of the words to the vectors, so you can access the vector for a word, which will return a 50-dimensional vector. Insert a new cell and add the code to check the vector for the word "**dog**":

```
glove_vectors["dog"]
```

```
array([ 0.11008  , -0.38781  , -0.57615  , -0.27714  ,  0.70521  ,
        0.53994  , -1.0786   , -0.40146  ,  1.1504   , -0.5678   ,
        0.0038977,  0.52878  ,  0.64561  ,  0.47262  ,  0.48549  ,
       -0.18407  ,  0.1801   ,  0.91397  , -1.1979   , -0.5778   ,
       -0.37985  ,  0.33606  ,  0.772    ,  0.75555  ,  0.45506  ,
       -1.7671   , -1.0503   ,  0.42566  ,  0.41893  , -0.68327  ,
        1.5673   ,  0.27685  , -0.61708  ,  0.64638  , -0.076996 ,
        0.37118  ,  0.1308   , -0.45137  ,  0.25398  , -0.74392  ,
       -0.086199 ,  0.24068  , -0.64819  ,  0.83549  ,  1.2502   ,
       -0.51379  ,  0.04224  , -0.88118  ,  0.7158   ,  0.38519  ])
```

Figure 7.36: Array of glove vectors with an input of dog

In order to see the vector for the word "**cat**", add the following code:

```
glove_vectors["cat"]
```

```
array([ 0.45281 , -0.50108 , -0.53714 , -0.015697,  0.22191 ,  0.54602 ,
       -0.67301 , -0.6891  ,  0.63493 , -0.19726 ,  0.33685 ,  0.7735  ,
        0.90094 ,  0.38488 ,  0.38367 ,  0.2657  , -0.08057 ,  0.61089 ,
       -1.2894  , -0.22313 , -0.61578 ,  0.21697 ,  0.35614 ,  0.44499 ,
        0.60885 , -1.1633  , -1.1579  ,  0.36118 ,  0.10466 , -0.78325 ,
        1.4352  ,  0.18629 , -0.26112 ,  0.83275 , -0.23123 ,  0.32481 ,
        0.14485 , -0.44552 ,  0.33497 , -0.95946 , -0.097479,  0.48138 ,
       -0.43352 ,  0.69455 ,  0.91043 , -0.28173 ,  0.41637 , -1.2609  ,
        0.71278 ,  0.23782 ])
```

Figure 7.37: Array of glove vectors with an input of cat

6. Now that we have got the vectors, we can represent them as an image using the **pyplot** framework of the **matplotlib** library. Insert a new cell and add the following code to implement this:

```
%matplotlib inline
import matplotlib.pyplot as plt

def to_vector(glove_vectors, word):
    vector = glove_vectors.get(word.lower())
    if vector is None:
        vector = [0] * 50
    return vector

def to_image(vector, word=''):
    fig, ax = plt.subplots(1,1)
    ax.tick_params(axis='both', which='both',
                   left=False,
                   bottom=False,
                   top=False,
                   labelleft=False,
                   labelbottom=False)
    ax.grid(False)
    ax.bar(range(len(vector)), vector, 0.5)
    ax.text(s=word, x=1, y=vector.max()+0.5)
    return vector
```

7. In the preceding code, the **to_vector()** function accepts **glove_vectors** and **word** as parameters. The **get()** function of **glove_vectors** will find the word and convert it into lowercase. The result will be stored in the **vector** variable.

8. The **to_image()** function takes **vector** and **word** as input and shows the image representation of **vector**. To find the image representation of the word "**man**", type the following code:

```
man = to_image(to_vector(glove_vectors, "man"))
```

The code generates the following output:

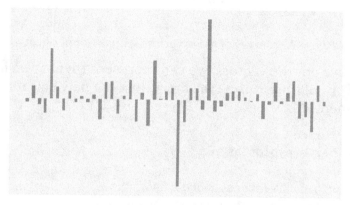

Figure 7.38: Graph generated with an input of man

9. To find the image representation of the word "**woman**", type the following code:

```
woman = to_image(to_vector(glove_vectors, "woman"))
```

This will generate the following output:

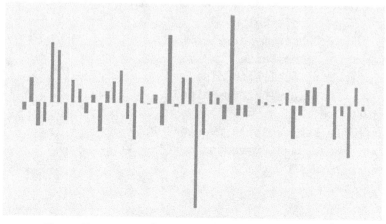

Figure 7.39: Graph generated with an input of woman

10. To find the image representation of the word "**king**", type the following code:

```
king = to_image(to_vector(glove_vectors, "king"))
```

This will generate the following output:

Figure 7.40: Graph generated with an input of king

11. To find the image representation of the word "**queen**", type the following code:

```
queen = to_image(to_vector(glove_vectors, "queen"))
```

This will generate the following output:

Figure 7.41: Graph generated with an input of queen

12. To find the image representation of "**king - man + woman - queen**", type the following code:

```
diff = to_image(king - man + woman - queen)
```

This will generate the following output:

Figure 7.42: Graph generated with (king-man+woman-queen) as input

13. To find the image representation of "**king - man + woman**", type the following code:

```
nd = to_image(king - man + woman)
```

This will generate the following output:

Figure 7.43: Graph generated with (king-man+woman) as input

We've learned how to load and use pre-trained word vectors and view their image representations. In the next section, we will focus on **document vectors** and their uses.

Document Vectors

Word vectors and word embeddings represent words. But what if we wanted to represent a whole document? Document vectors can help us do this.

Note that when we refer to a document, we are referring to a collection of words that have some meaning to a user. A document can consist of product reviews, tweets, or lines of movie dialogue, and can be a few words or thousands of words. A document can be used in a machine learning project as an instance of something that the algorithm can learn from.

Uses of Document Vectors

Some of the uses of document vectors are:

- **Similarity**: We can use document vectors to compare texts for similarity. For example, legal AI software can use document vectors to find similar legal cases.

- **Recommendations**: For example, online magazines can recommend similar articles based on those that users have already read.

- **Predictions**: Document vectors can be used as input into machine learning algorithms to build predictive models.

In the next section, we will perform an exercise based on document vectors.

Exercise 62: From Movie Dialogue to Document Vectors

In this exercise, we will convert movie dialogue into document vectors. Each line of the movie will be converted to a vector. Also, we will look at the image representation of the vector. Again, for image representation, we will be using the `pyplot` framework of the `Matplotlib` library. Follow these steps to implement this exercise:

1. Open a Jupyter notebook.

2. Import all the necessary libraries for this exercise. We will be using the `gensim` library. Insert a new cell and add the following code:

```
import pandas as pd
from gensim import utils
from gensim.models.doc2vec import TaggedDocument
from gensim.models import Doc2Vec
from gensim.parsing.preprocessing import preprocess_string, remove_
stopwords
```

```
import random
import warnings
warnings.filterwarnings("ignore")
```

3. Set the display column width to be as wide as it needs to be in order to display the movie lines. Insert a new cell and add the following code to implement this:

```
pd.set_option('display.max_colwidth', -1)
```

4. Provide the location of the **movie_lines.txt** file and assign that location to the **movie_lines_file** variable. Insert a new cell and add the following code to implement this:

```
movie_lines_file = '../data/cornell-movie-dialogs/movie_lines.txt'
```

5. The columns in the **movie_lines.txt** file are delimited by '**+++$+++**'. For loading the movie dialogue, you will need to iterate over each movie line in the file and split the columns. After that, you need to create a **DataFrame** containing the movie lines. Insert a new cell and add the following code to implement this:

```
with open(movie_lines_file) as f:
    movie_lines = [line.strip().split('+++$+++') for line in
f.readlines()];

lines_df = pd.DataFrame([{'LineNumber': d[0].strip(),
                          'Person': d[3].strip(),
                          'Line': d[4].strip(),
                          'Movie' : d[2].strip()}
                         for d in movie_lines])
lines_df = lines_df.set_index('LineNumber')
```

6. To check the basic statistics, such as the **head()**, **len()**, and **nunique()** values of the **lines_df** DataFrame, insert a new cell and add the following code:

```
lines_df.head(10)
```

The code generates the following output:

LineNumber	Line	Movie	Person
L1045	They do not!	m0	BIANCA
L1044	They do to!	m0	CAMERON
L985	I hope so.	m0	BIANCA
L984	She okay?	m0	CAMERON
L925	Let's go.	m0	BIANCA
L924	Wow	m0	CAMERON
L872	Okay - you're gonna need to learn how to lie.	m0	BIANCA
L871	No	m0	CAMERON
L870	I'm Kidding. You know how sometimes you just become this "persona"? And you don't know how to quit?	m0	BIANCA
L869	Like my fear of wearing pastels?	m0	BIANCA

Figure 7.44: Displaying the first 10 rows of the DataFrame

7. In the preceding figure, the **head(10)** function displays the first 10 rows. To check the length of the DataFrame, type the following code:

```
len(lines_df)
```

The code generates the following output:

```
304713
```

Figure 7.45: Length of the movie_lines dataframe

8. To display the count of distinct observations in a DataFrame, we need to write the following code:

```
lines_df.nunique()
```

The code generates the following output:

```
Line      265786
Movie     617
Person    5356
dtype: int64
```

Figure 7.46: The number of unique records in the movie_lines DataFrame

9. Now, as there are over 200,000 movie dialogue lines, the training might take a while. We can train on a subset of the movie lines. In order to do this, let's limit the training to **50000** rows. Insert a new cell and add the following code to implement this:

```
lines_df_small = lines_df.head(50000)
```

10. We now create a class, the object of which will create the training instances for the **Doc2Vec** model. Insert a new cell and add the following code to implement this:

```
class DocumentDataset(object):

    def __init__(self, data:pd.DataFrame, column):
        document = data[column].apply(self.preprocess)
        self.documents = [ TaggedDocument( text, [index])
                            for index, text in document.iteritems() ]

    def preprocess(self, document):
        return preprocess_string(remove_stopwords(document))

    def __iter__(self):
        for document in self.documents:
            yield documents

    def tagged_documents(self, shuffle=False):
        if shuffle:
            random.shuffle(self.documents)
        return self.documents
```

11. In the code, the **preprocess_string()** function applies the given filters to the input. The **remove_stopwords()** function is used to remove **stopwords** from the given document.

Doc2Vec requires each instance to be a **TaggedDocument** instance. So, internally, we create a list of **TaggedDocument** for each movie line in the file.

12. Now create an object of the **DocumentDataset** class. It takes two parameters. One is the **lines_df_small** DataFrame and another one the **"Line"** column name. Insert a new cell and add the following code to implement this:

```
documents_dataset = DocumentDataset(lines_df_small, 'Line')
```

13. Now we create a **Doc2Vec** model using the **Doc2Vec** class. Insert a new cell and add the following code to implement this:

```
docVecModel = Doc2Vec(min_count=1, window=5, vector_size=100, sample=1e-4,
negative=5, workers=8)
docVecModel.build_vocab(documents_dataset.tagged_documents())
```

14. In the code, the **Doc2Vec** class contains parameters such as **min_count**, **window**, **vector_size**, **sample**, **negative**, and **workers**. The **min_count** parameter ignores all the words with a frequency less than that specified. The **window** parameter sets the maximum distance between the current and predicted word in the given sentence. The **vector_size** parameter helps in setting the dimensions of each vector. **sample** is the threshold that allows us to configure the higher-frequency words that are regularly downsampled. **negative** specifies the total amount of noise words that should be drawn. **workers** specifies the total number of threads required to train the model.

15. Now we need to train the model using the **train()** function of the **Doc2Vec** class. This could take a while, depending on how many records we train. Here epochs states the total number of it required to train the document. Insert a new cell and add the following code to implement this:

```
docVecModel.train(documents_dataset.tagged_documents(shuffle=True),
                total_examples = docVecModel.corpus_count,
            epochs=10)
```

16. The model has been trained. In order to check that, we need to access one of the vectors. To do this, insert a new cell and add the following code:

```
docVecModel['L872']
```

```
array([-0.00999255,  0.01121779,  0.01635954, -0.00920819,  0.01655221,
        0.01381668, -0.01893826,  0.01890673,  0.00602449,  0.01212227,
        0.00617704,  0.00530373,  0.00438731,  0.01207815, -0.00378634,
        0.01155938, -0.01598833, -0.01621517,  0.00925925, -0.0101096 ,
       -0.00958637, -0.00076498, -0.01306241,  0.01535184, -0.00766808,
       -0.00230881,  0.00130604,  0.00711551, -0.01465199,  0.01315565,
        0.00610187,  0.02287573, -0.02039285,  0.01049415,  0.01151987,
        0.00023039,  0.01469992, -0.00128502, -0.01226405, -0.00397229,
       -0.00264685,  0.01050834, -0.0272896 , -0.00634295,  0.02935975,
        0.01914983,  0.01771204,  0.02222202, -0.01039776, -0.00694761,
       -0.00353334, -0.01116739, -0.0027794 ,  0.00787708,  0.00295052,
       -0.01273573,  0.00055382,  0.00215054,  0.0036069 , -0.00755408,
       -0.00211701, -0.02106706, -0.00284395,  0.00359178,  0.00735721,
       -0.00457718, -0.01280562,  0.01133379,  0.00290893,  0.02071206,
       -0.01011232, -0.01244753, -0.00931259, -0.00473201,  0.00364464,
        0.0218977 , -0.01144578, -0.00819259, -0.00462786, -0.02205627,
        0.00855088, -0.00608567, -0.01881625,  0.0122737 ,  0.00552338,
        0.00499275, -0.01999045, -0.00922276, -0.01314076,  0.0016761 ,
        0.01052856, -0.01436663,  0.01820513, -0.02324964,  0.00804244,
        0.01190777,  0.00248928, -0.0012316 , -0.0100961 , -0.01364813],
      dtype=float32)
```

Figure 7.47: Lines of movies represented as vectors

17. To check the image representation of any given vector, we make use of the **pyplot** framework of the **Matplotlib** library. The **show_movie_line()** function takes a line number as a parameter. Based on this line number, we find the vector and store it in the **doc_vector** variable. The **show_image()** function takes two parameters, **vector** and **line**, and displays the image representation of the vector. Insert a new cell and add the following code to implement this:

```
import matplotlib.pyplot as plt

def show_image(vector, line):
    fig, ax = plt.subplots(1,1, figsize=(10, 2))
    ax.tick_params(axis='both',
                   which='both',
                   left=False,
                   bottom=False,
                   top=False,
                   labelleft=False,
```

```
                                labelbottom=False)
        ax.grid(False)
        print(line)
        ax.bar(range(len(vector)), vector, 0.5)


    def show_movie_line(line_number):
        line = lines_df_small.ix['L872'].Line
        doc_vector = docVecModel[line_number]
        show_image(doc_vector, line)
```

18. Since we have **defined** our functions now, let's implement the **show_movie_line()** function to view the image representation of the vector. Insert a new cell and add the following code to implement this:

```
show_movie_line('L872')
```

The code generates the following output:

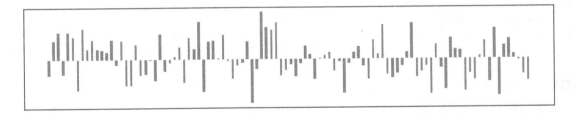

Figure 7.48: Image representation of given vector

We have learned how to represent a document as a vector. We also saw the visual representation of this. In the next section, we will solve an activity to find similar movie lines using the available document vector.

Activity 12: Finding Similar Movie Lines Using Document Vectors

In this activity, we will build a movie search engine that finds similar movie lines to the one provided by the user. We will make use of the Doc2Vec model, which we saw in an earlier exercise. Follow these steps to complete this activity:

1. Import the necessary libraries.

2. Load the movie lines file.

3. Iterate over each movie line and split the columns.

4. Create a DataFrame and load the Doc2Vec model.

5. Create a function that converts the sentences into vectors.

6. Create another function that does the similarity checks.

7. Test both the functions.

After implementing these steps, the expected output should look as follows:

```
['The Food and Drug Administration said on wednesday that deodorant sprays may cause such harmful reactions as burns and rashe
s. Although the FDA judges that the reported reactions are not sufficient to justify removal of these products from the market,
they are sufficient to warrant the proposed mandatory label warnings.',
 'She must have taken that into consideration.',
 "Beth? I can't believe it.",
 'Then do it for Peter.',
 "You brought it back to the Church. And then it made it's way back to me, again.",
 'No, man, what we were rebelling against?',
 'Yes, even in Berlin. If you will furnish me with their names and their exact whereabouts, you will have your visa in the morn
ing.',
 'No. I said "Is it a receptacle tip?"',
 "All right, we can't catch them.",
 "Put it this way.  Rolls Royces are made to last -- as least they were. But I'm afraid you're a Ferrari. A high strung racing
car -- built to win, not to last."]
```

Figure 7.49: Result of running the similar_movie_lines function on a sample line

Note

The solution for this activity can be found on page 295.

Summary

In this chapter, we learned about the motivations behind converting human language in the form of text and speech into mathematical structures such as scalars, vectors, matrices, and tensors. This helps machine learning algorithms to execute mathematical functions on them, detect patterns in language, and gain a sort of understanding of the meaning of the text. We also saw the different types of vector representation techniques, such as simple integer encoding, character-level encoding, one-hot encoding, and word encoding.

In the next chapter, we will look at the area of sentiment analysis, which is the automated understanding of tone or sentiment in text sources. Sentiment analysis uses some of the vector representation techniques that we saw in this chapter.

8

Sentiment Analysis

Learning Objectives

By the end of this chapter, you will be able to:

- Describe sentiment analysis and its applications

- Describe various tools in sentiment analysis

- Perform sentiment analysis using the TextBlob library

- Demonstrate how to load data for sentiment analysis

- Demonstrate the training of a sentiment analysis model

In this chapter, you will learn about sentiment analysis and how to use it to detect various sentiments in the data.

Introduction

In the previous chapter, we looked at how text can be represented as vectors. We also learned about the different types of encoding. This chapter deals with the area of **sentiment analysis**. Sentiment analysis is the area of NLP that involves teaching computers to identify the sentiment behind written content or parsed audio. Adding this ability to automatically detect sentiment in large volumes of text and speech opens up new possibilities for us to write useful software.

In sentiment analysis, we try to build models that detect how people feel. This starts with determining what kind of feeling we want to detect. Our application may attempt to determine the level of human emotion – most often, whether a person is sad or happy, satisfied or dissatisfied, or interested or disinterested. The common thread here is that we measure how sentiments vary in different directions. This is also called polarity.

Why is Sentiment Analysis Required?

In machine learning projects, we try to build applications that work, to a certain extent, similarly to a human being. We measure success in part by seeing how close our application is to matching human-level performance. Generally speaking, machine learning programs cannot exceed human-level performance by a significant margin, especially if our training data source is human generated.

Let's say, therefore, that we want to carry out sentiment analysis of product reviews. The sentiment analysis program should keep detect how reviewers feel. Of book, it is impractical for a person to read thousands of movie reviews. This is where automated sentiment analysis comes into picture. Artificial intelligence is useful when it is impractical for people to do some work. In this case, the work is reading thousands of reviews.

Growth of Sentiment Analysis

The field of sentiment analysis is driven by a few main factors. Firstly, it's driven by the rapid growth in online content that's used by companies to understand and respond to how people feel. Secondly, since sentiment drives human decisions, businesses that understand their customers' sentiment have a major advantage in predicting and shaping purchasing decisions. Thirdly, much of this content is available in social media and other online services, where human opinion and sentiment is a key component in business values. Finally, NLP technology has improved significantly, allowing for a much wider application of sentiment analysis.

Monetization of Emotion

The growth of the internet and internet services has enabled new business models to work with human connection, communication, and sentiment. In December 2018, Facebook had a market capitalization of approximately $400 billion and was one of the most successful companies in connecting people with features that enabled them to express their sentiments online. Twitter's market capitalization of $24 billion is somewhat smaller, but has proved to be an influential way to display sentiment online.

This means that sentiment itself has significant business value and can be monetized. There are now large amounts of information on social media about what people like or dislike. This data is of significant value not only in business but also in political campaigns.

Types of Sentiments

There are various sentiments that we can try to detect in language sources. Let's discuss few of them in detail.

Emotion

Sentiment analysis is often used to detect the emotional state of a person. It checks whether the person is happy or sad, or content or discontent. Businesses often use it to improve customer satisfaction. For example, let's look at the following statement:

"I thought I would have enjoyed the movie but it left me feeling that it could have been better."

In this statement, it seems as though the person who has just watched the movie is unhappy about it. A sentiment detector, in this case, would be able to classify the review as negative and allow the business (the movie studio, for instance) to adjust how they make movies in the future.

Action versus Passivity

This is about whether a person is prone to action or not. This is often done to determine how close a person is to making a choice. For example, in a travel reservation chatbot, you can detect whether the person is urgent about making a reservation or simply making passive queries and is therefore less likely to book a ticket right now. The level of action orientation or passivity provides additional clues to detect intention.

Tone

Speech and text are often meant to convey certain impressions that are not necessarily factual and not entirely emotional. Examples of this are sarcasm, irony, and humor. This may provide useful additional information on how the person thinks. Tone is, of book, tricky to detect, but there might be certain words or phrases that are often used in certain contexts. We can use NLP algorithms to extract statistical patterns from document sources. For example, we can use sentiment analysis to detect whether a news article is sarcastic.

Subjectivity versus Objectivity

Subjectivity is the detection of whether the given text source is subjective or objective. For example, you might want to detect whether a person has issued and expressed an opinion, or if their statement reads more like a fact and can only be true or false. Let's look at following two statements to get a better understanding:

- Statement 1: "The duck was overcooked and I could hardly taste the flavor."

- Statement 2: "Ducks are aquatic birds."

In these two statements, statement 1 should be recognized as a subjective opinion and statement 2 as an objective fact. Determining the objectivity of a statement helps in deciding the appropriate response to the statement.

Key Ideas and Terms

Let's look at some of the key ideas and terms that are used in sentiment analysis:

Classification

Classification is the NLP technique of assigning one or more classes to text documents. This helps in separating and sorting the documents. If you use classification for sentiment analysis, you assign different sentiment classes such as POSITIVE, NEGATIVE, or NEUTRAL. Sentiment analysis is a type of text classification that aims at creating a classifier that can classify the sentiment of text that has not been seen previously.

Supervised Learning

In **supervised learning**, we create a model by supplying data and labeled targets to the training algorithms. The algorithms learn using this supply. When it comes to sentiment analysis, we provide the training dataset with the labels that represent the sentiment. For example, for each text in a dataset, we would assign a value of 1 if the sentiment is positive, and a value of 0 if the statement is negative.

Polarity

Polarity is a measure of how negative or positive the sentiment is in a given language source. Polarity is used because it is simple and easy to measure and can be easily translated to a simple numeric scale. It usually ranges between 0 and 1. Values close to 1 reflect documents that have positive sentiments, whereas values close to 0 reflect documents that have negative sentiments. Values around 0.5 reflect documents that are neutral in sentiment.

It's worth noting that the polarity detected by a model depends on how it has been trained. On political Reddit threads, the opinions tend to be highly polarized. On the other hand, if you use the same model on business documents to measure sentiments, the scores tend to be neutral. So, you need to choose models that are trained in similar domains.

Intensity

Sometimes we want to measure the intensity of sentiment in a text. Most often, the level of intensity is included in the sentiment score. The intensity is measured by looking at the closeness of the score to 0 or 1.

Applications of Sentiment Analysis

There are various applications of sentiment analysis.

Financial Market Sentiment

Financial markets operate partially on economic fundamentals but are also heavily influenced by human sentiment. Stock market prices, which tend to rise and fall, are influenced by the opinions of news articles regarding the overall market or any specific securities.

Financial market sentiment is the overall attitude of investors toward securities. Market sentiment can be detected in news or social media articles. We can use NLP algorithms to build models that detect market sentiment, and use those models to predict future market prices.

Product Satisfaction

Sentiment analysis is commonly used in determining how customers are feeling about products and services. For example, Amazon makes use of its extensive product reviews dataset. This not only helps to improve its products and services, but also acts as a source of training data for its sentiment analysis services.

Social Media Sentiment

One really useful area of focus for sentiment analysis is social media monitoring. Social media has become a key communication medium with which most people around the world interact every day, and so there is a large and growing source of human language data available there. More importantly, the need for businesses and organizations to be able to process and understand what people are saying on social media has only increased. This means that the demand for sentiment analysis is growing.

Brand Monitoring

A company's brand is a significant asset and companies spend a lot of time, effort, and money to maintain the brand's value. With the growth of social media, companies are now exposed to considerable potential brand risks from negative social media conversations. On the other hand, there is also potential for positive brand growth from positive interactions and messages on social media. For this reason, businesses deploy people to monitor what is said about them and their brands on social media. Automated sentiment analysis makes this significantly easier to do.

Customer Interaction

Organizations often want to know how their customers feel during an interaction in an online chat or a phone conversation. In such cases, the objective is to detect the level of satisfaction with the service or the products. Sentiment analysis tools help companies to handle the large volumes of text and voice data that are generated during customer interaction. Customer interaction data is very valuable because so much is available, and there is a potential for revenue gain if companies can gain insights into customer satisfaction.

Tools Used for Sentiment Analysis

There are a lot of tools capable of analyzing sentiment. Each tool has its advantages and disadvantages. We will look at each of them in detail.

NLP Services from Major Cloud Providers

Online sentiment analysis is carried out by all major cloud services providers, such as Amazon, Microsoft, Google, and IBM. You can usually find sentiment analysis as a part of their text analysis services or general machine learning services. Online services offer the convenience of packaging all the necessary algorithms behind the provider's API. These algorithms are capable of performing sentiment analysis. To use such services, you need to provide the text or audio sources, and in return, the services will provide you with a measure of the sentiment. These services usually return a standard, simple score, such as positive, negative, or neutral. The score normally ranges between 0 and 1. Here are the advantages and disadvantages of NLP services from major cloud providers:

Advantages

- You require almost no knowledge of NLP algorithms or sentiment analysis. This results in fewer staffing needs.

- Sentiment analysis services provide their own computation, reducing your own computational needs.

- Online services can scale well beyond what regular companies can do on their own.

- You gain the benefits of automatic improvements and updates to sentiment analysis algorithms and data.

Disadvantages

- Online services require, at least temporarily, a reduction in privacy, since you must provide the documents to be analyzed for the service. Depending on your project's privacy needs, this may not be acceptable. There might also be laws that restrict data crossing into another national jurisdiction.

- The algorithms used in the online services are not the updated ones.

- The data on which the algorithms are trained on will more likely be large, general datasets. For example, Amazon might train their sentiment analysis service on Amazon product reviews. If you have specific sentiment analysis requirements, the results might not be as accurate, since the algorithm might have trained on some general dataset.

Online Marketplaces

Recently, there has been an emergence of AI marketplaces, which offer different algorithms from third parties. Online marketplaces differ from cloud providers. An online marketplace allows third-party developers to deploy sentiment analysis services on their platform. Here are the advantages and disadvantages of online marketplaces:

Advantages

- AI marketplaces provide the flexibility of choosing between different sentiment analysis algorithms instead of just one algorithm.

- Using algorithms from an AI marketplace reduces the need for dedicated data scientists in your project.

Disadvantages

- Algorithms from third parties are of varying quality.

- Since the algorithms are provided by smaller companies, there is no guarantee that they won't disappear.

Python NLP Libraries

There are a few NLP libraries that need to be integrated in your project instead of being called upon as services. These are called dedicated NLP libraries and they usually include many NLP algorithms coming out of academic research. Dedicated NLP libraries are usually written by really smart developers. A few examples are **spaCy**, **gensim**, and **AllenNLP**. Here are the advantages and disadvantages of Python NLP libraries:

Advantage

- It's usually state-of-the-art research that goes into these libraries, and they usually have well-chosen datasets.

Disadvantages

- Dedicated NLP libraries might not be flexible enough for complex business use cases.

- The libraries might not return the sentiment analysis output in the form that your project expects.

- Dedicated NLP libraries are not powerful enough for large-scale sentiment analysis projects. In such cases, it's better to use a general-purpose machine learning library such as TensorFlow.

Deep Learning Libraries

Deep learning libraries are meant to be used for different types of machine learning projects and not just for NLP. These libraries provide you with much more flexibility in developing your solution. They help in creating really powerful and complicated models. The advantages and disadvantages of these are explained here:

Advantages

- You have the flexibility of developing your sentiment analysis model to meet complex business needs.

- You can integrate the latest algorithms or research papers when they are available in general purpose libraries.

- You can make use of transfer learning, which takes a model trained on a large text source, to fine-tune the training as per your project's needs. This allows you to create a sentiment analysis model that is more suited for your needs.

Disadvantages

- This approach requires you to have in-depth knowledge of machine learning and possibly complicated topics such as deep learning.

- Deep learning libraries are very resource hungry, requiring lots of data to train properly. They also might require training on non-CPU hardware such as GPUs.

TextBlob

TextBlob is a Python library used for NLP. It has a simple API and is probably the easiest way to begin with sentiment analysis and other text analytic areas in Python. TextBlob is built on top of the NLTK library but is a bit easier to use. In the following sections, we will perform an exercise and an activity to get a better understanding of how TextBlob is used in sentiment analysis.

Exercise 63: Basic Sentiment Analysis Using the TextBlob Library

In this exercise, we will perform sentiment analysis on given text. For this, we will be using the **TextBlob** class of the **textblob** library. Follow these steps to implement this exercise:

1. Open a Jupyter notebook.

2. Insert a new cell and add the following code to implement to import the **TextBlob** class from the **textblob** library:

    ```
    from textblob import TextBlob
    ```

3. Create a variable named **sentence** and assign it a string. Insert a new cell and add the following code to implement this:

    ```
    sentence = "but you are Late Flight again!! Again and again! Where are the crew?"
    ```

4. Create an object of the **TextBlob** class. Add **sentence** as a parameter to the **TextBlob** container. Insert a new cell and add the following code to implement this:

```
blob = TextBlob(sentence)
```

In order to view the details of the **blob** object, insert a new cell and add the following code:

```
blob
```

The code generates the following output:

```
TextBlob("but you are Late Flight again!! Again and again! Where are the crew?")
```

Figure 8.1: Details of the blob object

5. Now we use the **sentiment** property of the **TextBlob** class, which returns a tuple. To implement this, insert a new cell and add the following code:

```
blob.sentiment
```

The code generates the following output:

```
Sentiment(polarity=-0.5859375, subjectivity=0.6)
```

Figure 8.2: Sentiment scores for polarity and subjectivity

In the code, we can see the **polarity** and **subjectivity** scores for a given text. We have completed the sentiment analysis on a given text using the **textblob** library.

In the next section, we will perform sentiment analysis on tweets about airlines.

Activity 13: Tweet Sentiment Analysis Using the TextBlob library

In this activity, we will be performing sentiment analysis on tweets related to airlines. We will also be providing conditions for determining positive, negative, and neutral tweets. The library used for sentiment analysis is TextBlob. Follow these steps to implement this activity:

1. Import the necessary libraries.

2. Load the CSV file.

3. Fetch the text column from the DataFrame.

4. Extract and remove the handles from the fetched data.

5. Perform sentiment analysis and get the new DataFrame.

6. Join both the DataFrames.

7. Apply appropriate conditions and view positive, negative, and neutral tweets.

After executing those steps, the expected output for positive tweets should be as follows:

	Tweet	At	Polarity	Subjectivity
8	Well, I didn't...but NOW I DO! :-D	@virginamerica	1.000000	1.000000
19	you know what would be amazingly awesome? BOS-FLL PLEASE!!!!!!! I want to fly with only you.	@VirginAmerica	0.600000	0.966667
22	I love the hipster innovation. You are a feel good brand.	@VirginAmerica	0.600000	0.600000
34	this is great news! America could start flights to Hawaii by end of year http://t.co/r8p2Zy3fe4 via	@VirginAmerica	1.000000	0.750000
35	Nice RT Vibe with the moodlight from takeoff to touchdown. #MoodlitMonday #ScienceBehindTheExperience http://t.co/Y7O0uNxTQP	NaN	0.600000	1.000000
36	Moodlighting is the only way to fly! Best experience EVER! Cool and calming. ♥ ✈ #MoodlitMonday	@VirginAmerica	0.587500	0.712500
42	plz help me win my bid upgrade for my flight 2/27 LAX--->SEA!!! ♥ ⚓ 🐋 🐳	@VirginAmerica	1.000000	0.400000
43	I have an unused ticket but moved to a new city where you don't fly. How can I fly with you before it expires? #travelhelp	@VirginAmerica	0.578788	0.751515
45	I'm #elevategold for a good reason: you rock!!	@VirginAmerica	1.000000	0.600000
51	Julie Andrews all the way though was very impressive! NO to	@VirginAmerica	1.000000	1.000000
57	I'm Lady Gaga!! She is amazing! 😍	@VirginAmerica	0.750000	0.900000
62	all are great , but I have to go with #CarrieUnderwood 👍 ☺	@VirginAmerica	0.800000	0.750000
68	Congrats on winning the award for Best Deals from an Airline (US) http://t.co/kj1iljaebV	@VirginAmerica	0.750000	0.525000
74	not worried, it's been a great ride in a new plane with great crew. All airlines should be like this.	@VirginAmerica	0.578788	0.651515
75	awesome. I flew yall Sat morning. Any way we can correct my bill ?	@VirginAmerica	1.000000	1.000000

Figure 8.3: Positive tweets

The expected output for negative tweets should be as follows:

	Tweet	At	Polarity	Subjectivity
33	awaiting my return phone call, just would prefer to use your online self-service option :(	@VirginAmerica	-0.750000	1.000000
84	it was a disappointing experience which will be shared with every business traveler I meet. #neverflyvirgin	@VirginAmerica	-0.600000	0.700000
114	come back to #PHL already. We need you to take us out of this horrible cold. #pleasecomeback http://t.co/gLXFwP6nQH	@VirginAmerica	-0.533333	0.666667
131	us too! Terrible airline! Just gave us a hotel hotline number and said sorry	@VirginAmerica	-0.750000	1.000000
181	too bad you say it takes 10 to 14 days via YOUR confirmation email. When I inquired after 3 weeks you claim 6 to 8 weeks!	@VirginAmerica	-0.875000	0.666667
187	for all my flight stuff wrong and did nothing about it. Had #worst #flight ever	@VirginAmerica	-0.750000	0.950000
354	I am deeply disappointed that your birthday promo was not applied to a trip I booked mere days before I received the email	@VirginAmerica	-0.625000	0.625000
367	on VX399 from JFK to LA - dirty plane - not up to your standards.	@VirginAmerica	-0.600000	0.800000
411	all crap channels which is why I pay to watch UK tv	@VirginAmerica	-0.800000	0.800000
446	Never had a bad experience before, but this one took the cake. Now extortion for carry on items as well?	@VirginAmerica	-0.700000	0.666667
533	thats weak. See ya \nHey !!	@united	-0.585938	0.625000
583	7 WEEKS Late FlightR AND I STILL HAVE NOT RECEIVED MY MILES FROM THE MileagePlus Gift Card $150 STARBUCKS CARD I HANDED OVER!!!	@united	-0.585938	0.600000
618	disappointed that u didnt honor my $100 credit given to me for ur mistakes. Taking my business elsewhere 👋 out.	@united	-0.750000	0.750000
622	does this process ever end? Still waiting for the reply since 2 months #pathetic #customerservice	@united	-1.000000	1.000000
634	This isn't a one time thing either! It's a shocking pattern of repeated neglect and disrespect.	@united	-1.000000	1.000000

Figure 8.4: Negative tweets

The expected output for neutral tweets should be as follows:

	Tweet	At	Polarity	Subjectivity
0	What said.	@VirginAmerica	0.000000e+00	0.000000
1	plus you've added commercials to the experience... tacky.	@VirginAmerica	0.000000e+00	0.000000
3	it's really aggressive to blast obnoxious "entertainment" in your guests' faces & they have little recourse	@VirginAmerica	6.250000e-03	0.350000
10	did you know that suicide is the second leading cause of death among teens 10-24	@VirginAmerica	0.000000e+00	0.000000
15	SFO-PDX schedule is still MIA.	@VirginAmerica	0.000000e+00	0.000000
17	I flew from NYC to SFO last week and couldn't fully sit in my seat due to two large gentleman on either side of me. HELP!	@VirginAmerica	4.761905e-02	0.290079
18	I ♥ flying 😊 👍	NaN	0.000000e+00	0.000000
23	will you be making BOS>LAS non stop permanently anytime soon?	@VirginAmerica	0.000000e+00	0.000000
25	status match program. I applied and it's been three weeks. Called and emailed with no response.	@VirginAmerica	0.000000e+00	0.000000
26	What happened 2 ur vegan food options?! At least say on ur site so i know I won't be able 2 eat anything for next 6 hrs #fail	@VirginAmerica	-7.500000e-02	0.331250

Figure 8.5: Neutral tweets

> **Note**
>
> The solution for this activity can be found on page 297.

We have seen how to perform sentiment analysis using the TextBlob library. In the next section, we will explore more about performing sentiment analysis using online web services.

Understanding Data for Sentiment Analysis

Sentiment analysis is a type of **text classification**. Sentiment analysis models are usually trained using **supervised datasets**. Supervised datasets are a kind of dataset that are labeled with the target variable – usually a column that specifies the sentiment value in the text. This is the value we want to predict in the unseen text.

Exercise 64: Loading Data for Sentiment Analysis

In this exercise, we will load data that could be used to train a sentiment analysis model. For this exercise, we will be using three datasets, namely Amazon, Yelp, and IMDB. Follow these steps to implement this exercise:

1. Open a Jupyter notebook.

2. Insert a new cell and add the following code to import the necessary libraries:

```
import pandas as pd
pd.set_option('display.max_colwidth', 200)
```

This imports the **pandas** library. It also sets the display width to **200** characters so that more of the review text is displayed on the screen.

3. Now we need to specify where the sentiment data is located. We will be loading three different datasets from **Yelp**, **IMDB**, and **Amazon**. Insert a new cell and add the following code to implement this:

```
DATA_DIR = '../data/sentiment_labelled_sentences/'
IMDB_DATA_FILE = DATA_DIR + 'imdb_labelled.txt'
YELP_DATA_FILE = DATA_DIR + 'yelp_labelled.txt'
AMAZON_DATA_FILE = DATA_DIR + 'amazon_cells_labelled.txt'
COLUMN_NAMES = ['Review', Sentiment']
```

Each of the data files has two columns: one for the review text and a numeric column for the sentiment.

> **Note**
>
> All three datasets can be found at this link: https://bit.ly/2VufVlb.

4. To load the IMDb reviews, insert a new cell and add the following code:

```
imdb_reviews = pd.read_table(IMDB_DATA_FILE, names=COLUMN_NAMES)
```

In this code, the **read_table()** method loads the file into a DataFrame.

5. Display the top **10** records in the DataFrame. Add the following code in the new cell:

```
imdb_reviews.head(10)
```

The code generates the following output:

	Review	Sentiment
0	A very, very, very slow-moving, aimless movie about a distressed, drifting young man.	0
1	Not sure who was more lost - the flat characters or the audience, nearly half of whom walked out.	0
2	Attempting artiness with black & white and clever camera angles, the movie disappointed - became even more ridiculous - as the acting was poor and the plot and lines almost non-existent.	0
3	Very little music or anything to speak of.	0
4	The best scene in the movie was when Gerardo is trying to find a song that keeps running through his head.	1
5	The rest of the movie lacks art, charm, meaning... If it's about emptiness, it works I guess because it's empty.	0
6	Wasted two hours.	0
7	Saw the movie today and thought it was a good effort, good messages for kids.	1
8	A bit predictable.	0
9	Loved the casting of Jimmy Buffet as the science teacher.	1

Figure 8.6: The first 10 records in the IMDb movie review file

6. In the preceding figure, you can see that the negative reviews have sentiment scores of **0** and positive reviews have sentiment scores of **1**.

7. To check the total records of the IMDB review file, we make use of the **value_counts()** function. Add the following code in a new cell to implement this:

```
imdb_reviews.Sentiment.value_counts()
```

The expected output with total reviews should be as follows:

```
1     386
0     362
Name: Sentiment, dtype: int64
```

Figure 8.7: Total positive and negative reviews in the IMDB review file

In the preceding figure, you can see that the data file contains a total of **748** reviews, out of which **362** are negative and **386** are positive.

8. We can format the data by adding the following code in a new cell:

```
imdb_counts = imdb_reviews.Sentiment.value_counts().to_frame()
imdb_counts.index = pd.Series(['Positive', 'Negative'])
imdb_counts
```

The code generates the following output:

	Sentiment
Positive	386
Negative	362

Figure 8.8: Counts of positive and negative sentiments in the IMDB review file

9. To load the Amazon reviews, insert a new cell and add the following code:

```
amazon_reviews = pd.read_table(AMAZON_DATA_FILE, name=COLUMN_NAMES)
amazon.reviews.head(10)
```

The code generates the following output:

	Review	Sentiment
0	So there is no way for me to plug it in here in the US unless I go by a converter.	0
1	Good case, Excellent value.	1
2	Great for the jawbone.	1
3	Tied to charger for conversations lasting more than 45 minutes.MAJOR PROBLEMS!!	0
4	The mic is great.	1
5	I have to jiggle the plug to get it to line up right to get decent volume.	0
6	If you have several dozen or several hundred contacts, then imagine the fun of sending each of them one by one.	0
7	If you are Razr owner...you must have this!	1
8	Needless to say, I wasted my money.	0
9	What a waste of money and time!.	0

Figure 8.9: Total positive and negative reviews in the Amazon review file

10. To load the Yelp reviews, insert a new cell and add the following code:

```
yelp_reviews = pd.read_table(YELP_DATA_FILE, names=COLUMN_NAMES)
yelp_reviews.head(10)
```

The code generates the following output:

	Review	Sentiment
0	Wow... Loved this place.	1
1	Crust is not good.	0
2	Not tasty and the texture was just nasty.	0
3	Stopped by during the late May bank holiday off Rick Steve recommendation and loved it.	1
4	The selection on the menu was great and so were the prices.	1
5	Now I am getting angry and I want my damn pho.	0
6	Honeslty it didn't taste THAT fresh.)	0
7	The potatoes were like rubber and you could tell they had been made up ahead of time being kept under a warmer.	0
8	The fries were great too.	1
9	A great touch.	1

Figure 8.10: Total positive and negative reviews in the YELP review file

We have learned how to load data that could be used to train a sentiment analysis model. The review files mentioned in this exercise are an example of data that could be used to train sentiment models. Each file contains review text plus a sentiment label for each. This is the minimum requirement of a supervised machine learning project: to build a model that is capable of predicting sentiments. However, the review text cannot be used as is. It needs to be preprocessed so that we can extract feature vectors out of it and eventually provide this as an input to the model.

Now that we have learned about loading the data, in the next section, we focus on training sentiment models.

Training Sentiment Models

The end product of any sentiment analysis project is a **sentiment model**. This is an object containing a stored representation of the data on which it was trained. Such a model has the ability to predict sentiment values for text that it has not seen before. To develop a sentiment analysis model, the following steps need to be taken:

1. Split the document dataset into two, namely train and test datasets. The test dataset is normally a fraction of the overall dataset. It is usually between 5% and 40% of the overall dataset, depending on the total number of examples available. If you have a lot of data, then you can afford to have a smaller test dataset.

2. Preprocess the text by stripping unwanted characters, removing stop words, and performing other common preprocessing steps.

3. Extract the features by converting the text to numeric vector representations. These representations are used for training machine learning models.

4. Run the model's training. This will be specific to the type of algorithm being used. During the training, our model will use the test dataset as a guide to learn about the text.

5. Use the model to predict the sentiment of documents that it has not seen before. This is the step that will be performed in production.

In the next section, we will solve an exercise to get a better understanding of training a sentiment model.

Exercise 65: Training a Sentiment Model Using TFIDF and Logistic Regression

In this exercise, we will build a simple sentiment analysis model. To extract the features from the text, we will make use of **TFIDF vectorization**. For the learning algorithm, we will make use of **logistic regression**. The library that we will be using for this exercise is scikit-learn. We will also make use of three datasets, from Yelp, Amazon, and IMDb. Follow these steps to implement this exercise:

1. Open a Jupyter notebook.

2. Insert a new cell and add the following code to import the necessary libraries:

```
import pandas as pd

pd.set_option('display.max_colwidth', 200)
```

3. To load all the three datasets, insert a new cell and add the following code:

```
DATA_DIR = '../data/sentiment_labelled_sentences/'

IMDB_DATA_FILE = DATA_DIR + 'imdb_labelled.txt'
YELP_DATA_FILE = DATA_DIR + 'yelp_labelled.txt'
AMAZON_DATA_FILE = DATA_DIR + 'amazon_cells_labelled.txt'

COLUMN_NAMES = ['Review', 'Sentiment']
yelp_reviews = pd.read_table(YELP_DATA_FILE, names=COLUMN_NAMES)
amazon_reviews = pd.read_table(AMAZON_DATA_FILE, names=COLUMN_NAMES)
imdb_reviews = pd.read_table(YELP_DATA_FILE, names=COLUMN_NAMES)
```

If we look at the code, even though the data comes from three different business domains, they are similar enough to each other. This is the reason we can combine them to train our sentiment analysis model.

4. Now we concatenate the different datasets into one dataset using the **concat()** function. Insert a new cell and add the following code to implement this:

```
review_data = pd.concat([amazon_reviews, imdb_reviews, yelp_reviews])
```

5. Since we combined the data from three separate files, let's make use of the **sample()** function, which returns a random selection from the dataset. This will allow us to see the reviews from different files. Insert a new cell and add the following code to implement this:

```
review_data.sample(10)
```

The code generates the following output:

	Review	Sentiment
290	Waited 2 hours & never got either of our pizzas as many other around us who came in later did!	0
483	You won't regret it!	1
334	very clear, quality sound and you don't have to mess with the sound on your iPod since you have the sound buttons on the headset.	1
197	I've never been more insulted or felt disrespected.	0
231	What a big waste of time.	0
254	Now the pizza itself was good the peanut sauce was very tasty.	1
897	I had strawberry tea, which was good.	1
715	Only Pros : Large seating area/ Nice bar area/ Great simple drink menu/ The BEST brick oven pizza with homemade dough!	1
760	Food was good, service was good, Prices were good.	1
930	Never got it!!!!	0

Figure 8.11: Output from calling the sample() function

6. We will create a **clean()** function and do some preprocessing. Basically, we want to remove some unnecessary characters. Insert a new cell and add the following code to implement this:

```
import re

def clean(text):
    text = re.sub(r'[\W]+', ' ', text.lower())
    text = text.replace('hadn t' , 'had not')\
               .replace('wasn t', 'was not')\
               .replace('didn t', 'did not')
    return text
```

7. Once the function is defined, we can clean and tokenize. It is a good practice to apply transformation functions on copies of our data, unless we are really constrained with memory. Insert a new cell and add the following code to implement this:

```
review_model_data = review_data.copy()
review_model_data.Review = review_data.Review.apply(clean)
```

8. Now sample the data again to see what the processed text looks like. Add the following code in a new cell to implement this:

```
review_model_data.sample(10)
```

The code generates the following output:

	Review	Sentiment
620	steer clear of this product and go with the genuine palm replacementr pens which come in a three pack	0
942	the mic there is a joke and the volume is quite low	0
406	i ll definitely be in soon again	1
393	excellent product i am very satisfied with the purchase	1
825	won t ever go here again	0
852	i have read other s reviews here but i haven t had any problem with it	1
535	an excellent new restaurant by an experienced frenchman	1
625	very dissapointing performance	0
908	we won t be returning	0
175	perhaps i caught them on an off night judging by the other reviews but i m not inspired to go back	0

Figure 8.12: Output from calling the sample() function

In the preceding figure, we can see that the text is converted to lowercase and only alphanumeric characters remain.

9. Now it is the time to develop our model. We will use **TfidfVectorizer** to convert each review into a **TFIDF** vector. TFIDF stands for **Term Frequency Inverse Document Frequency**. It will capture the relationship between the words in a review's text and their presence in the entire dataset. We will then use **LogisticRegression** to build a model. **LogisticRegression** is a machine learning algorithm that is used to train sentiment classification models. Insert a new cell and add the following code to import the necessary libraries:

```
from sklearn.feature_extraction.text import TfidfVectorizer
from sklearn.pipeline import Pipeline
from sklearn.model_selection import train_test_split
from sklearn.linear_model import LogisticRegression
```

10. Next, we will combine **TfidfVectorizer** and **LogisticRegression** in a **Pipeline** object, which is just a way to run a series of algorithms in a single pipeline. In order to do this, insert a new cell and add the following code:

```
tfidf = TfidfVectorizer(strip_accents=None,
                        preprocessor=None,
                        lowercase=False)
```

```
log_reg = LogisticRegression(random_state=0, solver='lbfgs')
log_tfidf = Pipeline([('vect', tfidf),
                      ('clf', log_reg)])
```

11. Once the data is ready, we need to split it into train and test sets. We will split into 70% for training and 30% for testing. This can be achieved with the help of the **train_test_split()** function. Insert a new cell and add the following code to implement this:

```
X_train, X_test, y_train, y_test = train_test_split(review_model_data.
Review, review_model_data.Sentiment,
test_size=0.3,
random_state=42)
```

12. Once we split the dataset, we fit the training data to the training pipeline. This can be done with the help of the **fit()** function. Insert a new cell and add the following code to implement this:

```
log_tfidf.fit(X_train.values, y_train.values)
```

The code generates the following output:

```
Pipeline(memory=None,
    steps=[('vect', TfidfVectorizer(analyzer='word', binary=False, decode_error='strict',
        dtype=<class 'numpy.int64'>, encoding='utf-8', input='content',
        lowercase=False, max_df=1.0, max_features=None, min_df=1,
        ngram_range=(1, 1), norm='12', preprocessor=None, smooth_idf=True,
    ...  penalty='12', random_state=0, solver='lbfgs', tol=0.0001,
        verbose=0, warm_start=False))])
```

Figure 8.13: Output from calling the fit() function on the training model

13. In order to check our model's **accuracy,** we make use of the **score()** function. Insert a new cell and add the following code to implement this:

```
test_accuracy = log_tfidf.score(X_test.values, y_test.values)
'The model has a test accuracy of {:.0%}'.format(test_accuracy)
```

```
'The model has a test accuracy of 89%'
```

Figure 8.14: Test accuracy of a model

As you can see from the preceding figure, our model has an accuracy of **89%**, which is pretty good for such a simple model with so little data.

14. The model is ready with an accuracy of **89%**. Now we can use it to predict the sentiment of sentences. Insert a new cell and add the following code to implement this:

```
log_tfidf.predict(['I loved this place', 'I hated this place'])
```

```
array([1, 0])
```

Figure 8.15: Model's prediction on test sentences

In the preceding figure, we can see how our model predicts sentiment. For a positive test sentence, it returns a score of **1**. For a negative test sentence, it returns a score of **0**.

Summary

During the book of this chapter, we defined sentiment analysis as a field of NLP concerned with the automated understanding of content generated by humans. We also learned about different types of sentiment analysis and the key ideas and terms used in it. We also explored various applications where sentiment analysis is being used, and also different tools that use sentiment analysis. More importantly, we came to know how to load and train data so that our model can use it to predict sentiment.

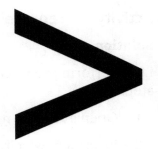

Appendix

Chapter 1: Introduction to Natural Language Processing

Activity 1: Preprocessing of Raw Text

Solution

Let's perform preprocessing on a text corpus. To implement this activity, follow these steps:

1. Open a Jupyter notebook.

2. Insert a new cell and add the following code to import the necessary libraries:

```
import nltk
nltk.download('punkt')
nltk.download('averaged_perceptron_tagger')
nltk.download('stopwords')
nltk.download('wordnet')
from nltk import word_tokenize
from nltk.stem.wordnet import WordNetLemmatizer
from nltk.corpus import stopwords
from autocorrect import spell
from nltk.wsd import lesk
from nltk.tokenize import sent_tokenize
import string
```

3. Read the content of **file.txt** and store it in a variable named "**sentence**". Insert a new cell and add the following code to implement this:

```
sentence = open("data_ch1/file.txt", 'r').read()
```

4. Apply tokenization on the given text corpus. Insert a new cell and add the following code to implement this:

```
words = word_tokenize(sentence)
```

5. To print the list of tokens, we insert a new cell and add the following code:

```
print(words[0:20])
```

The code generates the following output:

```
['In', 'this', 'book', 'authored', 'by','Sohom', 'Ghosh', 'and', 'Dwight', 'Gunning', ',', 'we', 'shall', 'learnning', 'how',
'to', 'pracess', 'Natueral', 'Language', 'and' ]
```

Figure 1.31: Tokenized words

In the preceding figure, we can see the initial 20 tokens of our text corpus.

6. To do the spelling correction in our given text corpus, we loop through each token and correct tokens that are wrongly spelled. Insert a new cell and add the following code to implement this:

```
corrected_sentence = ""
corrected_word_list = []
for wd in words:
    if wd not in string.punctuation:
        wd_c = spell(wd)
        if wd_c != wd:
            print(wd+" has been corrected to: "+wd_c)
            corrected_sentence = corrected_sentence+" "+wd_c
            corrected_word_list.append(wd_c)
        else:
            corrected_sentence = corrected_sentence+" "+wd
            corrected_word_list.append(wd)
    else:
        corrected_sentence = corrected_sentence + wd
        corrected_word_list.append(wd)
```

The code generates the following output:

```
Sohom has been corrected to: Soom
Ghosh has been corrected to: Ghost
learnning has been corrected to: learning
pracess has been corrected to: process
Natueral has been corrected to: Natural
prajects has been corrected to: projects
```

Figure 1.32: Words that have been corrected

7. To print the corrected text corpus, we add a new cell and write the following code:

```
corrected_sentence
```

The code generates the following output:

```
'In this book authored by soon Ghost and Dwight Gunning, we shall learning how to process Natural Language and extract insight
s from it. The first four chapter will introduce you to the basics of NLP. Later chapters will describe how to deal with comple
x NLP projects. If you want to get early access of it, you should book your order now.'
```

Figure 1.33: Corrected text corpus

8. To print a list of the initial 20 tokens of the corrected words, we insert a new cell and add the following code:

```
print(corrected_word_list[0:20])
```

The code generates the following output:

```
['In', 'this', 'book', 'authored', 'by', 'Soom', 'Ghost', 'and', 'Dwight', 'Gunning', ',', 'we', 'shall', 'learning', 'how', 't
o', 'process', 'Natural', 'Language', 'and']
```

Figure 1.34: List of corrected words

9. We want to add a PoS tag to all the corrected words in the list. In order to do this, we insert a new cell and add the following code:

```
print(nltk.pos_tag(corrected_word_list))
```

The code generates the following output:

```
[('In', 'In'), ('this', 'DT'), ('book', 'NN'), ('authored', 'VBN'), ('by', 'IN'), ('Soon', 'NNP'), ('Ghost', 'NNP'), ('and', 'C
C'), ('Dwight', 'NNP'), ('Gunning', 'NNP'), (',', ','), ('we', 'PRP'), ('shall', 'MD'), ('learning', 'VB'), ('how', 'WRB'), ('t
o', 'TO'), ('process', 'VB'), ('Natural', 'NNP'), ('Language', 'NNP'), ('and', 'CC'), ('extract', 'JJ'), ('insights', 'NNS'),
('from', 'IN'), ('it', 'PRP'), ('.', '.'), ('The', 'DT'), ('first', 'JJ'), ('four', 'CD'), ('chapter', 'NN'), ('will', 'MD'),
('introduce', 'VB'), ('you', 'PRP'), ('to', 'TO'), ('the', 'DT'), ('basics', 'NNS'), ('of', 'IN'), ('NLP', 'NNP'), ('.', '.'),
('Later', 'NNP'), ('chapters', 'NNS'), ('will', 'MD'), ('describe', 'VB'), ('how', 'WRB'), ('to', 'TO'), ('deal', 'VB'), ('wit
h', 'IN'), ('complex', 'JJ'), ('NLP', 'NNP'), ('projects', 'NNS'), ('.', '.'), ('If', 'IN'), ('you', 'PRP'), ('want', 'VBP'),
('to', 'TO'), ('get', 'VB'), ('early', 'JJ'), ('access', 'NN'), ('of', 'IN'), ('it', 'PRP'), ('.', '.'), ('you', 'PRP'), ('shou
ld', 'MD'), ('book', 'NN'), ('your', 'PRP$'), ('order', 'NN'), ('now', 'RB'), ('.', '.')]
```

Figure 1.35: List of corrected words tagged with appropriate PoS

10. From the list, we now want to remove the stop words. In order to do that, we insert a new cell and add the following code:

```
stop_words = stopwords.words('English')
corrected_word_list_without_stopwords = []
for wd in corrected_word_list:
    if wd not in stop_words:
        corrected_word_list_without_stopwords.append(wd)
corrected_word_list_without_stopwords[:20]
```

The code generates the following output:

```
['In',
 'book',
 'authored',
 'Soom',
 'Ghost',
 'Dwight',
 'Gunning',
 ',',
 'shall',
 'learning',
 'process',
 'Natural',
 'Language',
 'extract',
 'insights',
 '.',
 'The',
 'first',
 'four',
 'chapter']
```

Figure 1.36: List excluding the stop words

In the preceding figure, we can see that the stop words are being removed and a new list is being returned.

11. Now, with this list, if we want to apply the stemming process, then we insert a new cell and add the following code:

```
stemmer = nltk.stem.PorterStemmer()
corrected_word_list_without_stopwords_stemmed = []
for wd in corrected_word_list_without_stopwords:
    corrected_word_list_without_stopwords_stemmed.append(stemmer.stem(wd))
corrected_word_list_without_stopwords_stemmed[:20]
```

This code generates the following output:

```
['In',
 'book',
 'author',
 'soom',
 'ghost',
 'dwight',
 'gun',
 ',',
 'shall',
 'learn',
 'process',
 'natur',
 'languag',
 'extract',
 'insight',
 '.',
 'the',
 'first',
 'four',
 'chapter']
```

Figure 1.37: List of stemmed words

In the preceding code, we looped through each word in the **corrected_word_list_without_stopwords** list and applied stemming to them. The preceding figure shows the list of the initial 20 stemmed words.

12. Also, if we want to apply the lemmatization process to the corrected word list, we do so by inserting a new cell and adding the following code:

```
lemmatizer = WordNetLemmatizer()
corrected_word_list_without_stopwords_lemmatized = []
for wd in corrected_word_list_without_stopwords:
    corrected_word_list_without_stopwords_lemmatized.append(lemmatizer.
lemmatize(wd))
corrected_word_list_without_stopwords_lemmatized[:20]
```

This code generates the following output:

```
['In',
 'book',
 'authored',
 'Soom',
 'Ghost',
 'Dwight',
 'Gunning',
 ',',
 'shall',
 'learning',
 'process',
 'Natural',
 'Language',
 'extract',
 'insight',
 '.',
 'The',
 'first',
 'four',
 'chapter']
```

Figure 1.38: List of lemmatized words

In the preceding code, we looped through each word in the **corrected_word_list_without_stopwords** list and applied lemmatization to them. The preceding figure shows the list of the initial 20 lemmatized words.

13. To detect the sentence boundary in the given text corpus, we make use of the **sent_tokenize()** method. Insert a new cell and add the following code to implement this:

```
print(sent_tokenize(corrected_sentence))
```

The above code generates the following output:

```
['In this book authored by Soom and Dwight Gunning, we shall learning how to process Natural Language and extract insigh
ts from it.', 'The first four chapter will introduce you to the basics of NLP.', 'Later chapters will describe how to deal with
complex NLP projects.', 'If you want to get early access of it, you should book your order now.']
```

Figure 1.39: List of sentences

We have learned about and achieved the preprocessing of given data.

Chapter 2: Basic Feature Extraction Methods

Activity 2: Extracting General Features from Text

Solution

Let's extract general features from the given text. Follow these steps to implement this activity:

1. Open a Jupyter notebook.

2. Insert a new cell and add the following code to import the necessary libraries:

```
import pandas as pd
from string import punctuation
import nltk
nltk.download('tagsets')
from nltk.data import load
nltk.download('averaged_perceptron_tagger')
from nltk import pos_tag
from nltk import word_tokenize
from collections import Counter
```

3. Now let's see what different kinds of PoS nltk provides. Add the following code to do this:

```
tagdict = load('help/tagsets/upenn_tagset.pickle')
list(tagdict.keys())
```

The code generates the following output:

```
['LS',
 'TO',
 'VBN',
 "''",
 'WP,
 'UH',
 'VBG',
 'JJ',
 'VBZ',
 '__',
 'VBP',
 'NN',
 'DP',
 'PRP',
 ':',
 'WP$',
 'NNPS',
 'PRP$',
 'WDT',
 ',']
```

Figure 2.54: List of PoS

4. The number of occurrences of each PoS is calculated by iterating through each document and annotating each word with the corresponding **pos** tag. Add the following code to implement this:

```python
data = pd.read_csv('data_ch2/data.csv', header = 0)
pos_di = {}
for pos in list(tagdict.keys()):
        pos_di[pos] = []
for doc in data['text']:
di = Counter([j for i,j in pos_tag(word_tokenize(doc))])
    for pos in list(tagdict.keys()):
pos_di[pos].append(di[pos])
feature_df = pd.DataFrame(pos_di)

feature_df.head()
```

The code generates the following output:

	LS	TO	VBN	"	WP	UH	VBG	JJ	VBZ	--	...	MD	VB	WRB	NNP	EX	NNS	SYM	CC	CD	POS
0	0	0	0	0	1	0	0	0	0	0	...	0	0	0	0	0	1	0	0	0	0
1	0	0	0	0	0	0	0	0	0	0	...	0	0	0	0	0	1	0	0	0	0
2	0	0	0	0	0	0	0	0	0	0	...	0	0	0	0	0	0	0	0	0	0
3	0	0	0	0	1	0	0	0	1	0	...	0	0	0	0	0	0	0	0	0	0
4	0	0	0	0	0	0	0	1	1	0	...	0	0	0	0	0	0	0	0	0	0

Figure 2.55: Number of occurrences of each PoS in the sentence

5. To calculate the number of punctuation marks present in each text of the Data-Frame, add the following code:

```
feature_df['num_of_unique_punctuations'] = data['text'].apply(lambda x :
len(set(x).intersection(set(punctuation))))
feature_df['num_of_unique_punctuations'].head()
```

The code generates the following output:

```
0    0
1    0
2    1
3    1
4    0
Name: num_of_unique_punctuations, dtype: int64
```

Figure 2.56: Number of punctuation marks present in each sentence

6. To calculate the number of capitalized words, add the following code:

```
feature_df['number_of_capital_words'] =data['text'].apply(lambda x : \
                                    len([word for word in word_
tokenize(str(x)) if word[0].isupper()]))

feature_df['number_of_capital_words'].head()
```

The code generates the following output:

```
0    1
1    1
2    1
3    1
4    1
Name: number_of_capital_words, dtype: int64
```

Figure 2.57: Number of capitalized words in each sentence

7. To calculate the number of uncapitalized words, add the following code:

```
feature_df['number_of_small_words'] =data['text'].apply(lambda x : \
                                      len([word for word in word_
tokenize(str(x)) if word[0].islower()]))
feature_df['number_of_small_words'].head()
```

The code generates the following output:

```
0    4
1    3
2    7
3    3
4    2
Name: number_of_small_words, dtype: int64
```

Figure 2.58: Number of small lettered words in each sentence

8. To calculate the number of letters in the DataFrame, use the following code:

```
feature_df['number_of_alphabets'] = data['text'].apply(lambda x : len([ch
for ch in str(x) if ch.isalpha()]))
feature_df['number_of_alphabets'].head()
```

The code generates the following output:

```
0   19
1   18
2   28
3   14
4   13
Name: number_of_alphabets, dtype: int64
```

Figure 2.59: Number of letters present in each sentence

9. To calculate the number of digits in the DataFrame, add the following code:

```
feature_df['number_of_digits'] = data['text'].apply(lambda x : len([ch for
ch in str(x) if ch.isdigit()]))
feature_df['number_of_digits'].head()
```

The code generates the following output:

```
0   0
1   0
2   0
3   0
4   0
Name: number_of_digits, dtype: int64
```

Figure 2.60: Number of digits present in each sentence

10. To calculate the number of words in the DataFrame, add the following code:

```
feature_df['number_of_words'] = data['text'].apply(lambda x : len(word_
tokenize(str(x))))
feature_df['number_of_words'].head()
```

The code generates the following output:

```
0   5
1   4
2   9
3   5
4   3
Name: number_of_words, dtype: int64
```

Figure 2.61: Number of words present in each sentence

11. To calculate the number of whitespaces in the DataFrame, add the following code:

```
feature_df['number_of_white_spaces'] = data['text'].apply(lambda x :
len(str(x).split(' '))-1)
feature_df['number_of_white_spaces'].head()
```

The code generates the following output:

```
0    4
1    3
2    7
3    3
4    2
Name: number_of_white_spaces, dtype: int64
```

Figure 2.62: Number of whitespaces present in each sentence

12. Now let's view the full feature set we have just created. Add the following code to implement this:

```
feature_df.head()
```

The code generates the following output:

	LS	TO	VBN	-	WP	UH	VBG	JJ	VBZ	:	...	CC	CD	POS	num_of_unique_punctuations	number_of_capital_words	number_of_small_words
0	0	0	0	0	1	0	0	0	0	0	...	0	0	0	0	1	4
1	0	0	0	0	0	0	0	0	0	0	...	0	0	0	0	1	3
2	0	0	0	0	0	0	0	0	0	0	...	0	0	0	1	1	7
3	0	0	0	0	1	0	0	0	1	0	...	0	0	0	1	1	3
4	0	0	0	0	0	0	0	1	1	0	...	0	0	0	0	1	2

Figure 2.63: DataFrame consisting of features we have created

Activity 3: Extracting Specific Features from Texts

Solution

Let's extract the special features from the text. Follow these steps to implement this activity:

1. Open a Jupyter notebook.

2. Import the necessary packages and declare a **newsgroups_data_sample** variable with the help of the following code:

```
import nltk
nltk.download('stopwords')
from nltk.corpus import stopwords
from nltk import word_tokenize
from nltk.stem import WordNetLemmatizer
```

```
from sklearn.feature_extraction.text import TfidfVectorizer
from sklearn.feature_extraction.text import CountVectorizer
from sklearn.datasets import fetch_20newsgroups
import re
import string
import pandas as pd


newsgroups_data_sample = fetch_20newsgroups(subset='train')
lemmatizer = WordNetLemmatizer()
```

3. In order to store the text data in a DataFrame, insert a new cell and add the following code:

```
newsgroups_text_df = pd.DataFrame({'text' : newsgroups_data_
sample['data']})
newsgroups_text_df.head()
```

The code generates the following output:

	text
0	From: lerxst@wam.umd.edu (where's my thing\nS...
1	From: guykuo@carson.u.washington.edu (Guy Kuo)...
2	From: twillis@ec.ecn.purdue.edu (Thomas E Will...
3	From: jgreen@amber (Joe Green)\nSubject: Re: W...
4	From: jcm@head-cfa.harvard.edu (Jonathan McDow...

Figure 2.64: Storing the corpus in a DataFrame

4. The data present in the DataFrame is not clean. In order to clean it, insert a new cell and add the following code:

```
stop_words = stopwords.words('english')
stop_words = stop_words + list(string.printable)

newsgroups_text_df['cleaned_text'] = newsgroups_text_df['text'].apply(\
lambda x : ' '.join([lemmatizer.lemmatize(word.lower()) \
    for word in word_tokenize(re.sub(r'([^\s\w]|_)+', ' ', str(x))) if
word.lower() not in stop_words]))
```

5. Now that we have clean data, we add the following code to create a BoW model:

```
bag_of_words_model = CountVectorizer(max_features= 20)
bag_of_word_df = pd.DataFrame(bag_of_words_model.fit_transform(newsgroups_
text_df['cleaned_text']).todense())
bag_of_word_df.columns = sorted(bag_of_words_model.vocabulary_)
bag_of_word_df.head()
```

The code generates the following output:

	article	ax	com	edu	get	host	know	like	line	max	nntp	one	organization	people	posting	subject	time	university	would	writes
0	0	0	0	2	0	1	1	0	1	0	1	0	1	0	1	1	0	1	0	0
1	1	0	0	3	0	1	0	0	1	0	1	0	1	0	1	1	0	1	0	0
2	0	0	0	2	1	0	1	1	2	0	0	1	1	1	0	1	1	1	0	0
3	1	0	2	2	1	1	1	1	1	0	1	0	1	0	1	1	0	0	0	1
4	2	0	2	3	0	0	0	0	1	0	0	0	1	0	0	1	0	0	0	1

Figure 2.65: BoW representation of the 20 most frequent terms

6. To create a TF-IDF model, insert a new cell and add the following code:

```
tfidf_model = TfidfVectorizer(max_features=20)
tfidf_df = pd.DataFrame(tfidf_model.fit_transform(newsgroups_text_
df['cleaned_text']).todense())
tfidf_df.columns = sorted(tfidf_model.vocabulary_)
tfidf_df.head()
```

The code generates the following output:

	article	ax	com	edu	get	host	know	like	line	max	nntp	one	organization	people	posting	subject
0	0.000000	0.0	0.000000	0.522408	0.000000	0.338589	0.399935	0.000000	0.183761	0.0	0.341216	0.000000	0.190375	0.00000	0.327584	0.183242
1	0.282739	0.0	0.000000	0.691691	0.000000	0.298827	0.000000	0.000000	0.162181	0.0	0.301146	0.000000	0.169019	0.00000	0.289115	0.161723
2	0.000000	0.0	0.000000	0.411404	0.325661	0.000000	0.314954	0.308844	0.289428	0.0	0.000000	0.277716	0.149923	0.35893	0.000000	0.144306
3	0.234838	0.0	0.499523	0.382949	0.303137	0.248201	0.293170	0.287482	0.134706	0.0	0.250127	0.000000	0.139553	0.00000	0.240134	0.134325
4	0.493319	0.0	0.524670	0.603340	0.000000	0.000000	0.000000	0.000000	0.141486	0.0	0.000000	0.000000	0.146579	0.00000	0.000000	0.141087

Figure 2.66: TF-IDF representation of the 20 most frequent terms

7. Once both the models are created, we need to compare them. To check the most informative terms for the second document, as ascertained by the BoW model, we write the following code:

```
rw = 2
list(bag_of_word_df.columns[bag_of_word_df.iloc[rw,:] == bag_of_word_
df.iloc[rw,:].max()])
```

The code generates the following output:

$$['edu', 'line']$$

Figure 2.67: Most informative term as per the BoW model

8. To check the most informative terms for the second document, as ascertained by the TF-IDF model, we write the following code:

```
rw = 2
list(tfidf_df.columns[tfidf_df.iloc[rw,:] == tfidf_df.iloc[rw,:].max()])
```

The code generates the following output:

$$['edu']$$

Figure 2.68: Most informative term as per the TF-IDF model

9. To check the occurrence of the word "line" in the documents, we write the following code:

```
bag_of_word_df[bag_of_word_df['line']!=0].shape[0]
```

The code generates the following code:

$$11282$$

Figure 2.69: Number of times the word "line" occurred in the corpus

10. To check the occurrence of the word "edu" in the documents, we write the following code:

```
bag_of_word_df[bag_of_word_df['edu']!=0].shape[0]
```

The code generates the following output:

$$7393$$

Figure 2.70: Number of times the word "edu" occurred in the corpus

As we can see from the last two steps, the difference arises because the word "line" occurs in 11,282 documents, whereas the word "edu" occurs in 7,393 documents only. Thus, the word "edu" is rarer and is more informative than the word "line." Unlike the BoW model, the TF-IDF model is able to capture this meticulous detail. In most cases, TF-IDF is preferred over BoW.

Activity 4: Text Visualization

Solution

1. Open a Jupyter notebook.

2. Insert a new cell and add the following code to import the necessary libraries:

```
from wordcloud import WordCloud, STOPWORDS
import matplotlib.pyplot as plt
%matplotlib inline
from nltk import word_tokenize
from nltk.stem import WordNetLemmatizer
import nltk
from collections import Counter
import re
```

3. To fetch the dataset and read its content, add the following code:

```
text = open('data_ch2/text_corpus.txt', 'r').read()
text
```

The code generates the following output:

'Control role kind exist. Front security Mrs picture example season side.\nHim dog on outside home the hou
se participant. Cultural minute wait time network suddenly property.\nSkin represent long board including
generation do. Technology him hour use identify weight person. Pressure very beat site view tell wrong.\nW
all remember more thing move. Really mission you. Remain buy language safe color how common. Decade key st
reet such camera practice.\nHusband field alone no hold nothing indeed. Blue teach inside behavior program
find.\nQuestion popular couple table. Question similar decision account animal. Know power despite environ
mental. Pass almost here until nature enjoy.\nDuring job budget central. Recently energy other space. Poss
ible true wonder listen low stock.\nCouple believe way program opportunity mean about sea. Happy rather ma
in sister hundred. Also on skin method difference bank.Pretty yes garden reflect economic trouble else. Ou
tside exist future. Staff alone out heart recent class scientist.\nSpring road or college around several.
After remain social various other. Plan your long left.\nBegin truth into stage same. While voice cause ch
arge outside such company. Lead anyone able music why but energy company.\nDevelop toward off special. Tur
n generation friend west activity north red major. Stock else stock race final.\nArm good left little whet
her recently. Three girl player behavior friend expert. Fact between develop explain short building try me
thod.\nEducation light cut either. Account approach woman. Sense give mother carry.\nStandard team goal se
ek somebody drive event. Office song effect source goal. Enough success morning environment two out.\nPoin
t quality point thought significant sound. Thank very sea way.\nTonight growth professional.\nConsumer beh
avior away decide catch. Indeed know manage ever.\nClass perform consider style brother. Argue account maj
or.Appear daughter practice eye daughter lot. Strategy player marriage population also.\nPerson food inter
view. Ago turn term add.\nWould owner into official so case. Course political particularly customer.\nMe w

Figure 2.71: Text corpus

4. The text in the fetched data is not clean. In order to clean it, we make use of various pre-processing steps, such as tokenization and lemmatization. Add the following code to implement this:

```
nltk.download('wordnet')
lemmatize = WordNetLemmatizer()
cleaned_lemmatized_tokens = [lemmatizer.lemmatize(word.lower()) \
                            for word in word_tokenize(re.sub(r'([^\
s\w]|_)+', ' ', text))]
```

5. Now we need to check the set of unique words, along with their frequencies, to find the 50 most frequently occurring words. Add the following code to implement this:

```
Counter(cleaned_lemmatized_tokens).most_common(50)
```

The code generates the following output:

```
[('program', 14),
 ('effect', 14),
 ('choice', 14),
 ('account', 13),
 ('way', 13),
 ('democrat', 13),
 ('television', 13),
 ('gun', 13),
 ('outside', 12),
 ('key', 12),
 ('sea', 12),
 ('office', 12),
 ('factor', 12),
 ('business', 12),
 ('there', 12)
```

Figure 2.72: The 50 most frequent words

6. Once we get the set of unique words along with their frequencies, we will remove the stop words. After that, we generate the word cloud for the top 50 most frequent words. Add the following code to implement this:

```
stopwords = set(STOPWORDS)
cleaned_text = ' '.join(cleaned_lemmatized_tokens)
wordcloud = WordCloud(width = 800, height = 800,
                background_color ='white',
                max_words=50,
                stopwords = stopwords,
                min_font_size = 10).generate(cleaned_text)
plt.imshow(wordcloud, interpolation='bilinear')
plt.axis("off")
plt.show()
```

The code generates the following output:

Figure 2.73: Word cloud representation of the 50 most frequent words

As you can see in the figure, words that occur more frequently, such as "program," "effect," and "choice," appear in larger sizes in the word cloud. Thus, the word cloud for the given text corpus is justified.

Chapter 3: Developing a Text classifier

Activity 5: Developing End-to-End Text Classifiers

Solution

Let's build an end-to-end classifier that helps classify Wikipedia comments. Follow these steps to implement this activity:

1. Open a Jupyter notebook.

2. Insert a new cell and add the following code to import the necessary packages:

```python
import pandas as pd
import seaborn as sns
import matplotlib.pyplot as plt
%matplotlib inline
import re
import string
from nltk import word_tokenize
from nltk.corpus import stopwords
from nltk.stem import WordNetLemmatizer
from sklearn.feature_extraction.text import TfidfVectorizer
from sklearn.model_selection import train_test_split
from pylab import *
import nltk
import warnings
warnings.filterwarnings('ignore')
from sklearn.metrics import accuracy_score,roc_curve,classification_
report,confusion_matrix,precision_recall_curve,auc
```

3. In this step, we will read a data file. It has two columns: **comment_text** and **toxic**. The **comment_text** column contains various user comments and the **toxic** column contains their corresponding labels. Here, label 0 denotes that a comment is not toxic and label 1 denotes that a comment is toxic. Add the following code to do this:

```python
data = pd.read_csv('data_ch3/train_comment_small.csv')
data.head()
```

The preceding code generates the following output:

	comment_text	toxic
0	explanation\nWhy the edits made under my usern...	0
1	D'aww! He matches this background colour I'm s...	0
2	Hey man, I'm really not trying to edit war. It...	0
3	"\nMore\nI can't make any real suggestions on ...	0
4	You, sir, are my hero. Any chance you remember...	0

Figure 3.63: Text data and labels stored as a DataFrame

4. We'll now create a generic function for all classifiers, called **clf_model**. It takes four inputs: type of model, features of the training dataset, labels of the training dataset, and features of the validation dataset. It returns predicted labels, predicted probabilities, and the model it has been trained on. Add the following code to do this:

```
def clf_model(model_type, X_train, y_train, X_valid):
    model = model_type.fit(X_train,y_train)
    predicted_labels = model.predict(X_valid)
    predicted_probab = model.predict_proba(X_valid)[:,1]
    return [predicted_labels,predicted_probab, model]
```

5. Furthermore, another function is defined, called **model_evaluation**. It takes three inputs: actual values, predicted values, and predicted probabilities. It prints a confusion matrix, accuracy, f1-score, precision, recall scores, and area under the ROC curve. It also plots the ROC curve:

```
def model_evaluation(actual_values, predicted_values, predicted_
probabilities):
    cfn_mat = confusion_matrix(actual_values,predicted_values)
    print("confusion matrix: \n",cfn_mat)
    print("\naccuracy: ",accuracy_score(actual_values,predicted_values))
    print("\nclassification report: \n", classification_report(actual_
values,predicted_values))
    fpr,tpr,threshold=roc_curve(actual_values, predicted_probabilities)
    print ('\nArea under ROC curve for validation set:', auc(fpr,tpr))
    fig, ax = plt.subplots(figsize=(6,6))
    ax.plot(fpr,tpr,label='Validation set AUC')
    plt.xlabel('False Positive Rate')
    plt.ylabel('True Positive Rate')
```

```
ax.legend(loc='best')
plt.show()
```

6. In this step, we'll use a lambda function to extract tokens from each text in this DataFrame (called data), check whether any of these tokens are stop words, lemmatize them, and concatenate them side by side. We'll use the join function to concatenate a list of words into a single sentence. We'll use a regular expression (re) to replace anything other than letters, digits, and white spaces with blank space. Add the following code to implement this:

```
lemmatizer = WordNetLemmatizer()
stop_words = stopwords.words('english')
stop_words = stop_words + list(string.printable)
data['cleaned_comment_text'] = data['comment_text'].apply(\
lambda x : ' '.join([lemmatizer.lemmatize(word.lower()) \
    for word in word_tokenize(re.sub(r'([^\s\w]|_)+', ' ', str(x))) if
word.lower() not in stop_words]))
```

7. Now, we'll create a tf-idf matrix representation of these cleaned texts. Add the following code to do this:

```
tfidf_model = TfidfVectorizer(max_features=500)
tfidf_df = pd.DataFrame(tfidf_model.fit_transform(data['cleaned_comment_
text']).todense())
tfidf_df.columns = sorted(tfidf_model.vocabulary_)
tfidf_df.head()
```

The preceding code generates the following output:

	10	100	11	12	20	2005	2006	2007	2008	24	...	wp	write	writing	written	wrong	wrote	www	year	yes	yet
0	0.0	0.0	0.000000	0.0	0.0	0.0	0.0	0.0	0.0	0.0	...	0.0	0.0	0.0	0.0	0.0	0.0	0.0	0.0	0.0	0.0
1	0.0	0.0	0.537393	0.0	0.0	0.0	0.0	0.0	0.0	0.0	...	0.0	0.0	0.0	0.0	0.0	0.0	0.0	0.0	0.0	0.0
2	0.0	0.0	0.000000	0.0	0.0	0.0	0.0	0.0	0.0	0.0	...	0.0	0.0	0.0	0.0	0.0	0.0	0.0	0.0	0.0	0.0
3	0.0	0.0	0.000000	0.0	0.0	0.0	0.0	0.0	0.0	0.0	...	0.0	0.0	0.0	0.0	0.0	0.0	0.0	0.0	0.0	0.0
4	0.0	0.0	0.000000	0.0	0.0	0.0	0.0	0.0	0.0	0.0	...	0.0	0.0	0.0	0.0	0.0	0.0	0.0	0.0	0.0	0.0

5 rows x 500 columns

Figure 3.64: TF-IDF representation of the DataFrame

8. Use sklearn's **train_test_split** function to divide the dataset into training and validation sets. Add the following code to do this:

```
X_train, X_valid, y_train, y_valid = train_test_split(tfidf_df,
    data['toxic'], test_size=0.2, random_state=42,stratify = data['toxic'])
```

9. Here, we'll train a logistic regression model using sklearn's **LogisticRegression()** function and evaluate it for the validation set. Add the following code:

```
from sklearn.linear_model import LogisticRegression
logreg = LogisticRegression()
results = clf_model(logreg, X_train, y_train, X_valid)
model_evaluation(y_valid, results[0], results[1])
```

The preceding code generates the following output:

```
confusion matrix:
[[28646   210]
 [ 2088   971]]

accuracy:  0.9279962400125333

classification report:
              precision    recall  f1-score   support

           0       0.93      0.99      0.96     28856
           1       0.82      0.32      0.46      3059

   micro avg       0.93      0.93      0.93     31915
   macro avg       0.88      0.66      0.71     31915
weighted avg       0.92      0.93      0.91     31915


Area under ROC curve for validation set: 0.8845268970028765
```

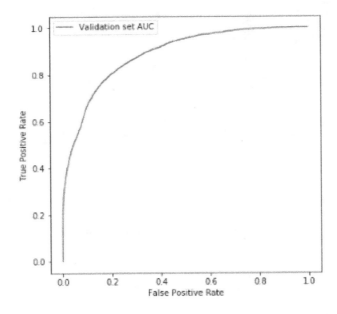

Figure 3.65: Performance of the logistic regression model

10. We'll train a random forest model using sklearn's **RandomForestClassifier()** function and evaluate it for the validation set. Add the following code:

```
from sklearn.ensemble import RandomForestClassifier
rfc = RandomForestClassifier(n_estimators=20,max_depth=4,max_
features='sqrt',random_state=1)
results = clf_model(rfc, X_train, y_train, X_valid)
model_evaluation(y_valid, results[0], results[1])
model_rfc = results[2]
```

The preceding code generates the following output:

```
confusion matrix:
 [[28856     0]
 [ 3059     0]]

accuracy:  0.904151652827824

classification report:
               precision    recall  f1-score   support

           0       0.90      1.00      0.95     28856
           1       0.00      0.00      0.00      3059

   micro avg       0.90      0.90      0.90     31915
   macro avg       0.45      0.50      0.47     31915
weighted avg       0.82      0.90      0.86     31915


Area under ROC curve for validation set: 0.8147441698078444
```

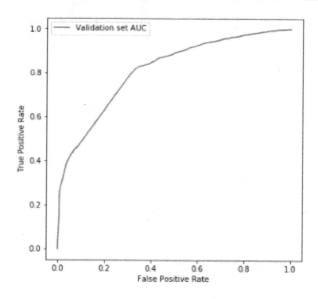

Figure 3.66: Performance of the random forest model

11. Moreover, we extract important features, which are the tokens or words that play a more vital role in determining whether a comment will be toxic. Add the following code:

```
word_importances = pd.DataFrame({'word':X_train.
columns,'importance':model_rfc.feature_importances_})
word_importances.sort_values('importance', ascending = False).head(4)
```

The preceding code generates the following output:

	word	importance
443	unpleasant	0.127846
456	waste	0.105699
186	hate	0.097928
227	life	0.075561

Figure 3.67: Words and their importance

12. We train an XGBoost model using the **XGBClassifier()** function and evaluate it for the validation set. Add the following code to do this:

```
from xgboost import XGBClassifier
xgb_clf=XGBClassifier(n_estimators=20,learning_rate=0.03,max_
depth=5,subsample=0.6,colsample_bytree= 0.6,reg_alpha= 10,seed=42)
results = clf_model(xgb_clf, X_train, y_train, X_valid)
model_evaluation(y_valid, results[0], results[1])
model_xgb = results[2]
```

The preceding code generates the following output:

```
confusion matrix:
 [[28785    71]
  [ 2323   736]]

accuracy:  0.9249882500391665

classification report:
                precision    recall  f1-score   support

           0       0.93      1.00      0.96     28856
           1       0.91      0.24      0.38      3059

   micro avg       0.92      0.92      0.92     31915
   macro avg       0.92      0.62      0.67     31915
weighted avg       0.92      0.92      0.90     31915


Area under ROC curve for validation set: 0.7742179256164664
```

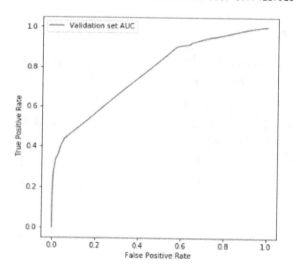

Figure 3.68: Performance of the XGBoost model

13. Moreover, we extract the importance of features, that is, tokens or words that play a more vital role in determining whether a comment is toxic. Add the following code to do this:

```
word_importances = pd.DataFrame({'word':X_train.
columns,'importance':model_xgb.feature_importances_})
word_importances.sort_values('importance', ascending = False).head(4)
```

The preceding code generates the following output:

	word	importance
443	unpleasant	0.414984
456	waste	0.096639
41	as	0.086625
64	carefree	0.033793

Figure 3.69: Words and their importance

Chapter 4: Collecting Text Data from the Web

Activity 6: Extracting Information from an Online HTML Page

Solution

Let's extract the data from an online source and analyze it. Follow these steps to implement this activity:

1. Open a Jupyter notebook.

2. Import the **requests** and **BeautifulSoup** libraries. Pass the URL to **requests** with the following command. Convert the fetched content into HTML format using BeautifulSoup's HTML parser. Add the following code to do this:

```
import requests
from bs4 import BeautifulSoup
r = requests.get('https://en.wikipedia.org/wiki/Rabindranath_Tagore')
soup = BeautifulSoup(r.text, 'html.parser')
```

3. To extract the list of headings, look for the **h3** tag. Here, we only need the first six headings. We will look for a **span** tag that has a **class** attribute with the following set of commands:

```
for ele in soup.find_all('h3')[:6]:
    tx = BeautifulSoup(str(ele),'html.parser').find('span',
attrs={'class':"mw-headline"})
    if tx is not None:
        print(tx['id'])
```

The preceding code generates the following output:

```
Drama
Short_stories
Novels
Poetry
Songs_(Rabindra_Sangeet)
Art_works
```

Figure 4.41: List of h3 tag headings

4. To extract information regarding works by Tagore, look for the **table** tag. Traverse through the rows and columns of these tables and extract the texts by entering the following code:

```
table = soup.find_all('table')[1]
for row in table.find_all('tr'):
    columns = row.find_all('td')
    if len(columns)>0:
        columns = columns[1:]
    print(BeautifulSoup(str(columns), 'html.parser').text.strip())
```

The preceding code generates the following output:

```
[]
[Bhānusiṃha Ṭhākurer Paḍāvalī, (Songs of Bhānusiṃha Ṭhākur), 1884
]
[Manasi, (The Ideal One), 1890
]
[Sonar Tari, (The Golden Boat), 1894
]
[Gitanjali, (Song Offerings), 1910
]
[Gitimalya, (Wreath of Songs), 1914
]
[Balaka, (The Flight of Cranes), 1916
]
[]
[Valmiki-Pratibha, (The Genius of Valmiki), 1881
]
[Kal-Mrigaya, (The Fatal Hunt), 1882
]
[Mayar Khela, (The Play of Illusions), 1888
]
[Visarjan, (The Sacrifice), 1890
]
[Chitrangada, (Chitrangada), 1892
]
[Raja, (The King of the Dark Chamber), 1910
]
[Dak Ghar, (The Post Office), 1912
]
[Achalayatan, (The Immovable), 1912
]
[Muktadhara, (The Waterfall), 1922
]
[Raktakarabi, (Red Oleanders), 1926
]
[Chandalika, (The Untouchable Girl), 1933
]
[]
[Nastanirh, (The Broken Nest), 1901
]
[Gora, (Fair-Faced), 1910
]
[Ghare Baire, (The Home and the World), 1916
]
[Yogayog, (Crosscurrents), 1929
]
[]
[Jivansmriti, (My Reminiscences), 1912
]
[Chhelebela, (My Boyhood Days), 1940


]
```

Figure 4.42: List of Tagore's work

5. To extract the list of universities named after Tagore, look for the **ol** tag. Add the following code to implement this:

```
[BeautifulSoup(str(i),'html.parser').text.strip() for i in soup.find('ol')
if i!='\n']
```

The preceding code generates the following output:

```
['Rabindra Bharati University, Kolkata, India.',
 'Rabindra University, Sahjadpur, Shirajganj, Bangladesh.[1]',
 'Rabindra Maitree University, Courtpara, Kustia,Bangladesh.[2]',
 'Bishwakabi Rabindranath Tagore Hall, Jahangirnagar University, Bangladesh',
 'Rabindra Nazrul Art Building, Arts Faculty, Islamic University, Bangladesh',
 'Rabindra Library (Central), Assam University, India',
 'Rabindra Srijonkala University, Keraniganj, Dhaka, Bangladesh']
```

Figure 4.43: List of universities named after Rabindranath Tagore

Activity 7: Extracting and Analyzing Data Using Regular Expressions

Solution

Let's extract the data from an online source and analyze various things. Follow these steps to implement this activity:

1. To begin, let's try to collect data using **requests** with the following code:

```
import urllib3
import requests
from bs4 import BeautifulSoup
r = requests.get('https://www.packtpub.com/books/info/packt/faq')
r.status_code
```

The preceding code generates the following output:

403

Figure 4.44: HTTP status code

To check the text data of the fetched content, type the following code:

```
r.text
```

The preceding code generates the following output:

```
'<html>\r\n<head><title>403 Forbidden</title></head>\r\n<body bgcolor"white">\r\n<center><h1>403 Forbidden</h1></cen
ter>\r\n<hr><center>nginx/1.4.5</center>\r\n</body>\r\n</html>\r\n'
```

Figure 4.45: Text content

Here, **403** means forbidden. Thus, we will be using **urllib3**.

2. Let's extract data using **urllib3** and store it in a soup with the following commands:

```
http = urllib3.PoolManager()
rr = http.request('GET', 'https://www.packtpub.com/books/info/packt/faq')
rr.status
rr.data[:1000]
```

The preceding code generates the following output:

```
b'<!DOCTYPE html>\n    <html xmlns="http://www.w3.org/1999/xhtml" lang="en" xml:lang="en">\n    <head>\n        <title>Frequent
ly Asked Questions | PACKT Books</title>\n        <script>\n        dataLayer = [];\n        </script>\n        <script typ
e="text/javascript" src="https://d1ldz4te4covpm.cloudfront.net/sites/all/themes/packt_v4/js/util/advertisement.js"></script>\n
<script type="text/javascript" src="https://dz13w8afd47il.cloudfront.net/sites/all/themes/packt_v4/js/core/packt_freelearning.j
s"></script>\n        <script type="text/javascript">\n        var data_layer_page_type = \'other\';\n        </scr
ipt>\n        <meta http-equiv="Content-Type" content="text/html; charset=utf-8" />\n<link rel="shortcut icon" href="https://d1
ldz4te4covpm.cloudfront.net/misc/favicon.ico" type="image/x-icon" />\n<meta name="description" content="How Can I Download My e
Book? How Long Does Delivery Take? View Packt Publishing&#039;s Frequently Asked Questions regarding ordering information '
```

Figure 4.46: Content of the fetched file

3. A list of questions can be obtained by looking for a **div** tag that has a **class = faq-item-question-text float-left** attribute, as shown here:

```
soup = BeautifulSoup(rr.data, 'html.parser')
questions = [question.text.strip() for question in soup.find_
all('div',attrs={"class":"faq-item-question-text float-left"})]
questions
```

The above code generates the following output:

```
['How can I download eBooks?',
 'what format are Packt eBooks?',
 'How can I download code files for eBooks and Videos?',
 'How can I download Videos?',
 'Can I send an ebook to my Kindle?',
 'what are the different types of courses available on Packt website?',
 'which courses are accessible with the subscription?',
 'what are assessments?' How can I access them?',
 'where will I get the answers to the assessments?',
 'Does the course contain any content?',
 'How can i access the text content?',
 'what is an Integrated Course?',
 'what is a Bespoke Video course?',
 'If I complete a course, will I get any certification?',
 'How do I download a Video course?',
 'Is "Readium" required to open certain blended courses?',
 'How can I gift an eBook/Video/Course/Subscription?']
```

Figure 4.47: List of questions on the FAQ page

A list of answers can be obtained by looking for a **div** tag that has a **class = faq-item-answer** attribute:

```
answers = [answer.text.strip() for answer in soup.find_
all('div',attrs={"class":"faq-item-answer"})]
answers
```

The preceding code generates the following output:

```
['Once you complete your eBook purchase, the download link for your eBook will be available in your Packt account. You can acce
ss your eBook by following the steps below:\n\nLogin to your account\nClick on "My Account"\nClick on "My owned products"\nDown
load the eBook in your desired format\nIf you own an eBook and are viewing the product page you can also download it from there
\nIf you have purchased an Early Access eBook\u202ftitle you can only download the published chapters\u202ffrom your account or
read them online with an active subscription. You can download the complete eBook, only once the eBook is published.',
 'Packt eBooks can be downloaded as a PDF, EPUB or MOBI file. They can also be read online using subscription.\nYou can upgrade
your purchased eBook to a Print copy of the same title with a 34% off by using our\u202fUpgrade to Print\u202foption available
in "My eBook" section.',
 'There are a number of simple ways to access Code Files. You can download them directly from the product page by clicking the
'Code Files' button just above the Book Description.\nYou will also be able to download Code Files from inside your account. Go
to 'My Account', click 'My eBooks', expand the product for which you wish to access the Code Files and then click on the 'Code
Files' button. The download will start immediately.\nIf you have purchased our eBook/Video from another source, please follow t
he steps below to download the code files:\n\nRegister on our website using your email address and the password\nGo to the 'Sup
port' tab in the top horizontal drop down menu\nClick on\u202f'Code Downloads & Errata'\nType the name of the book in the searc
h box\nYour eBook/Video\u202fshould appear in a drop down - select the one you want\nUse the drop down to tell us where you pur
chased the product from\nFinally, click on the 'Code Download link' to download the Code Files\nOnce the file is downloaded ple
ase make sure that you unzip or extract using the latest version of:\n\nWinrar / 7zip for Windows\nZipeg / iZip / Unrarx for Ma
c\n7-zip / Peazip for Linux\nThe above mentioned applications support all extension files.',
```

Figure 4.48: List of answers on the FAQ page

4. Next, we'll create a DataFrame consisting of these questions and answers:

```
import pandas as pd
pd.DataFrame({'questions':questions, 'answers':answers}).head()
```

The above code generates the following output:

	questions	answers
0	How can I download eBooks?	Once you complete your eBook purchase, the dow...
1	What format are Packt eBooks?	Packt eBooks can be downloaded as a PDF, EPUB ...
2	How can I download code files for eBooks and V...	There are a number of simple ways to access Co...
3	How can I download Videos?	Once you complete your Video purchase, the dow...
4	Can I send an eBook to my Kindle?	Yes, if you follow the previous instructions o...

Figure 4.49: DataFrame of the question and answers

5. To extract email addresses, we make use of a regular expression. Insert a new cell and add the following code to implement this:

```
rr_tc = http.request('GET', 'https://www.packtpub.com/books/info/packt/
terms-and-conditions')
rr_tc.status
soup2 = BeautifulSoup(rr_tc.data, 'html.parser')
import re
set(re.findall(r"[A-Za-z0-9._%+-]+@[A-Za-z0-9.-]+\.[A-Za-z]{2,4}",soup2.
text))
```

The preceding code generates the following output:

{'customercare@packtpub.com'}

Figure 4.50: Extracted email address

6. To extract phone numbers using a regular expression, insert a new cell and add the following code:

```
re.findall(r"\+\d{2}\s{1}\(0\)\s\d{3}\s\d{3}\s\d{3}",soup2.text)
```

The preceding code generates the following output:

```
['+44 (0) 121 265 648', '+44 (0) 121 212 141']
```

Figure 4.51: Extracted phone numbers

Activity 8: Dealing with Online JSON Files

Solution

1. Open a Jupyter notebook.

2. Import the necessary packages. Pass the given URL as an argument. Add the following code to implement this:

```
import json
import urllib3
from textblob import TextBlob
from pprint import pprint
import pandas as pd
http = urllib3.PoolManager()
rr = http.request('GET', 'https://jsonplaceholder.typicode.com/comments')
rr.status
```

The preceding code generates the following output:

```
200
```

Figure 4.52: HTTP status code

Here, the HTTP code **200**, indicates that the request was successful.

3. Load the **json** file and create a DataFrame from it. To implement this, insert a new cell and add the following code:

```
data = json.loads(rr.data.decode('utf-8'))
import pandas as pd
df = pd.DataFrame(data).head(15)
df.head()
```

The preceding code generates the following output:

	body	email	Id	name	postId
0	laudantium enim quasi est quidem magnam volupt...	Eliseo@gardner.biz	1	id labore ex et quam laborum	1
1	est natus enim nihil est dolore omnis voluptat...	Jayne_Kuhic@sydney.com	2	quo vero reiciendis vellt similique earum	1
2	quia molestiae reprehenderit quasi aspernatur\...	Nikita@garfield.biz	3	odio adilpisci rerum aut animi	1
3	non et atque\noccaecati deserunt quas accusant...	Lew@alysha.tv	4	alias odio sit	1
4	harum non quasi et ratione\ntempore iure ex vo...	Hayden@althea.biz	5	vero eaque aliquid doloribus et culpa	1

Figure 4.53: The DataFrame of the fetched file

4. Since we can use the language translation function of **TextBlob** a limited number of times, we will restrict this DataFrame to 15 rows. The following code snippet can be used to translate text to English:

```
df['body_english'] = df['body'].apply(lambda x: str(TextBlob('u'+str(x)).
translate(to='en')))
df[['body', 'body_english']].head()
```

The preceding code generates the following output:

	body	body_english
0	laudantium enim quasi est quidem magnam volupt...	For them, as it were, is, indeed, the very gre...
1	est natus enim nihil est dolore omnis voluptat...	uest was born, all the pain, the pleasure is n...
2	quia molestiae reprehenderit quasi aspermatur\...	Uqula discomfort criticized as dislikes\nof pr...
3	non et atque\noccaecati deserunt quas accusant...	unon and and the \nof denouncing pleasure and f...
4	harum non quasi et ratione\ntempore Iure ex vo...	not as it were, and by reason of uhari\nat the...

Figure 4.54: DataFrame showing the new body_english column

5. Now, we will use **TextBlob** to find out the sentiment score of each of these comments:

```
df['sentiment_score'] = df['body_english'].apply(lambda x:
str(TextBlob('u'+str(x)).sentiment.polarity))
df[['body_english', 'sentiment_score']]
```

The preceding code generates the following output:

	body_english	sentiment_score
0	For them, as it were, is, indeed, the very gre...	1.0
1	uest was born, all the pain, the pleasure is n...	0.0
2	Uquia discomfort criticized as dislikes\nof pr...	0.5
3	unon and and the\nof denouncing pleasure and f...	-0.4166666666666667
4	not as it were, and by reason of uhari\nat the...	0.32023809523809527
5	Udolorem at fault, but one which must be aband...	0.0
6	but in labor and in pain, and in the same, and...	0.4
7	he wishes to become corrupt in the pleasure of...	0.0
8	discomfort, and at once take usapiente\nso tha...	-0.33888888888888885
9	Uvoluptate regular very important for us to fi...	0.31777777777777777
10	our sorrows, is that because it is either uût\...	0.35555555555555557
11	uexpedita greater deserving easy\ndesires to f...	0.12666666666666668
12	Ufugit them only was this grief of things,\nfi...	-0.07500000000000001
13	the exercise of which is the pleasure of those...	0.275
14	the flattery of her, but I hated to think of p...	-0.9

Figure 4.55: Sentiment scores of tweets

Activity 9: Extracting Data from Twitter

Solution

Let's extract tweets using the Tweepy library, calculate sentiment scores, and visualize the tweets using a word cloud. Follow these steps to implement this activity:

1. Log in to your Twitter account with your credentials. Then, visit https://dev.twitter.com/apps/new, fill in the necessary details, and submit the form.

2. Once the form is submitted, go to the **Keys** and **tokens** tab; copy `consumer_key`, `consumer_secret`, `access_token`, and `access_token_secret` from there.

3. Open a Jupyter notebook.

4. Import the relevant packages and follow the authentication steps by writing the following code:

```
consumer_key = 'your consumer key here'
consumer_secret = 'your consumer secret key here'
access_token = 'your access token here'
access_token_secret = 'your access token secret here'
```

```
import pandas as pd
import numpy as np
import pickle
import json
from pprint import pprint
from textblob import TextBlob
from wordcloud import WordCloud, STOPWORDS
import matplotlib.pyplot as plt
import tweepy

auth = tweepy.OAuthHandler(consumer_key, consumer_secret)
auth.set_access_token(access_token, access_token_secret)
api = tweepy.API(auth)
```

5. Call the Twitter API with the **#WorldWaterDay** search query. Insert a new cell and add the following code to implement this:

```
tweet_list = []
cnt = 0
for tweet in tweepy.Cursor(api.search, q='#WorldWaterDay', rpp=100).
items():
    tweet_list.append(tweet)
    cnt = cnt + 1
    if cnt == 100:
        break
tweet_list[0]
```

The preceding code generates the following output:

Status(_api=<tweepy.api.API object at 0x1a21e67c18>, _json={'created_at': 'Sat Mar 23 19:11:49 +0000 2019', 'id': 11095332252
55358464, 'id_str': '1109533225255358464', 'text': 'RT @unisdr: Agriculture accounts for 70% of global water withdrawals, mos
tly for irrigation. Industry takes 20% of the total, dominated by…', 'truncated': False, 'entities': {'hashtags': [], 'symbol
s': [], 'user_mentions': [{'screen_name': 'unisdr', 'name': 'UNISDR', 'id': 62780688, 'id_str': '62780688', 'indices': [3, 1
0]}], 'urls': []}, 'metadata': {'iso_language_code': 'en', 'result_type': 'recent'}, 'source': '<a href="http://twitter.com/d
ownload/android" rel="nofollow">Twitter for Android</a>', 'in_reply_to_status_id': None, 'in_reply_to_status_id_str': None,
'in_reply_to_user_id': None, 'in_reply_to_user_id_str': None, 'in_reply_to_screen_name': None, 'user': {'id': 2837214585, 'id
_str': '2837214585', 'name': 'DRR Kenya', 'screen_name': 'DRRKenya', 'location': '', 'description': '', 'url': None, 'entitie
s': {'description': {'urls': []}}, 'protected': False, 'followers_count': 635, 'friends_count': 517, 'listed_count': 215, 'cr
eated_at': 'Sun Oct 19 14:40:23 +0000 2014', 'favourites_count': 10007, 'utc_offset': None, 'time_zone': None, 'geo_enabled':
False, 'verified': False, 'statuses_count': 18784, 'lang': 'en', 'contributors_enabled': False, 'is_translator': False, 'is_t
ranslation_enabled': False, 'profile_background_color': 'C0DEED', 'profile_background_image_url': 'http://abs.twimg.com/image
s/themes/theme1/bg.png', 'profile_background_image_url_https': 'https://abs.twimg.com/images/themes/theme1/bg.png', 'profile_
background_tile': False, 'profile_image_url': 'http://pbs.twimg.com/profile_images/524465009120657408/VezbveFz_normal.png',
'profile_image_url_https': 'https://pbs.twimg.com/profile_images/524465009120657408/VezbveFz_normal.png', 'profile_link_colo
r': '1DA1F2', 'profile_sidebar_border_color': 'C0DEED', 'profile_sidebar_fill_color': 'DDEEF6', 'profile_text_color': '33333
3', 'profile_use_background_image': True, 'has_extended_profile': False, 'default_profile': True, 'default_profile_image': Fa
lse, 'following': False, 'follow_request_sent': False, 'notifications': False, 'translator_type': 'none'}, 'geo': None, 'coor

Figure 4.56: The Twitter API called with the #WorldWaterDay search query

6. Convert the Twitter **status** objects to **json** objects. Insert a new cell and add the following code to implement this:

```
status = tweet_list[0]
json_str = json.dumps(status._json)
pprint(json.loads(json_str))
```

The preceding code generates the following output:

```
{'contributors': None,
 'coordinates': None,
 'created_at': 'Sat Mar 23 19:11:49 +0000 2019',
 'entities': {'hashtags': [],
              'symbols': [],
              'urls': [],
              'user_mentions': [{'id': 62780688,
                                 'id_str': '62780688',
                                 'indices': [3, 10],
                                 'name': 'UNISDR',
                                 'screen_name': 'unisdr'}]},
 'favorite_count': 0,
 'favorited': False,
 'geo': None,
 'id': 1109533225255358464,
 'id_str': '1109533225255358464',
 'in_reply_to_screen_name': None,
 'in_reply_to_status_id': None,
 'in_reply_to_status_id_str': None,
```

Figure 4.57: Twitter status objects converted to JSON objects

7. To check the text of the fetched JSON file, add the following code:

```
json.loads(json_str)['text']
```

The preceding code generates the following output:

```
'RT @unisdr: Agriculture accounts for 70% of global water withdrawals, mostly for irrigation. Industry takes 20% of t
he total, dominated by_'
```

Figure 4.58: Text content of the JSON file

8. Now we'll create a DataFrame consisting of the text of tweets. Add a new cell and write the following code to do this:

```
tweet_text = []
for i in range(0,len(tweet_list)):
    status = tweet_list[i]
    json_str = json.dumps(status._json)
    tweet_text.append(json.loads(json_str)['text'])
unique_tweet_text = list(set(tweet_text))
tweet_text_df = pd.DataFrame({'tweet_text' : unique_tweet_text})
tweet_text_df.head()
```

The preceding code generates the following output:

	tweet_text
0	RT @Alfreddezayas: Safe water means safely man...
1	RT @Rotary: In Ghana, #Rotary clubs and @USAID...
2	RT @France24_en: Today is UN #WorldWaterDay 💧!...
3	RT @ChinaDaily: The government aims to achieve...
4	RT @AgenciaAJN: #WorldWaterDay Israel recycle...

Figure 4.59: DataFrame with the text of tweets

9. To detect the language of all the tweets, we make use of the TextBlob library. Add the following code to do this:

```
tweet_text_df['language_detected'] = tweet_text_df['tweet_text'].
apply(lambda x : \

str(TextBlob('u'+str(x)).detect_language()))
tweet_text_df.head(20)
```

The preceding code generates the following output:

	tweet_text	language_detected
0	RT @Alfreddezayas: Safe water means safely man...	en
1	RT @Rotary: In Ghana, #Rotary clubs and @USAID...	en
2	RT @France24_en: Today is UN #WorldWaterDay 🌐!...	en
3	RT @ChinaDaily: The government aims to achieve...	en
4	RT @AgenciaAJN: #WorldWaterDay Israel recycle...	en
5	RT @JemilahMahmood: #WorldWaterDay reminds us ...	en
6	RT @OurRevolution: On #WorldWaterDay we stand ...	en
7	World Water Day takes place every year and aim...	en
8	RT @Pontifex: Let us thank God for "sister wat...	en
9	RT @AiyshwaryaM: .@MBPatil was not only instru...	en
10	RT @Pontifex_it: Ringraziamo Dio per "sorella ...	it
11	RT @YosemiteNPS: Happy #WorldWaterDay! Did you...	en
12	RT @Rotary: We solve problems by bringing peop...	en
13	RT @unisdr: Agriculture accounts for 70% of gl...	en
14	RT @EU_ENV: Today is #WorldWaterDay 💧 \nWater ...	en
15	RT @GapInc: 1/3 of the world's population curr...	en
16	RT @UNHumanRights: 📷 Health \n🌐 Food Security ...	en
17	#VirtualReality is changing how we see #Climat...	en
18	RT @UN_Women: How does drought affect access t...	en
19	RT @UNAUSA: Read this before you turn the fauc...	en

Figure 4.60: Language of tweets detected

10. To have a look at the non-English tweets, we add the following code:

```
tweet_text_df[tweet_text_df['language_detected']!='en']
```

The preceding code generates the following output:

	tweet_text	language_detected
10	RT @Pontifex_it: Ringraziamo Dio per "sorella ...	it
26	RT @TRTBelgesel: Türk sivil toplum kuruluşları...	tr
30	RT @CellerRocaBBVA: 💧 En el #DíaMundialdelAgua...	es
52	RT @domainechambord: L'eau est une ressource p...	fr
69	RT @funcagua: Hoy es un buen día para reflexio...	es
76	RT @Pontifex_pt: Agradeçamos a Deus pela "irmã...	pt

Figure 4.61: Filtered non-English tweets

11. To check the shape of the DataFrame consisting of tweets in the English language, add the following code:

```
tweet_text_df_eng = tweet_text_df[tweet_text_df['language_
detected']=='en']
tweet_text_df_eng.shape
```

The preceding code generates the following output:

$$(75, 2)$$

Figure 4.62: Shape of the DataFrame

12. Now we'll extract the sentiment scores of the English tweets using the TextBlob library. Add the following code to do this:

```
tweet_text_df_eng['sentiment_score'] = tweet_text_df_eng['tweet_text'].
apply(lambda x: str(TextBlob('u'+str(x)).sentiment.polarity))
pd.set_option('display.max_colwidth', -1)
tweet_text_df_eng[['tweet_text', 'sentiment_score']].head(20)
```

The preceding code generates the following output:

	tweet_text	sentiment_score
0	RT @Alfreddezayas: Safe water means safely managed drinking water services: water that is accessible locally and available when needed #Wor...	0.355
1	RT @Rotary: In Ghana, #Rotary clubs and @USAID are working together to implement more than 200 sustainable programs by 2020 that will bring...	0.5
2	RT @France24_en: Today is UN #WorldWaterDay ⚫! According to the UN, 2.1 billion people do not have access to drinking water at home. Every...	0.0
3	RT @ChinaDaily: The government aims to achieve a balance between usage and replenishment of underground water in the Beijing-Tianjin-Hebei...	0.0
4	RT @AgenciaAJN: #WorldWaterDay Israel recycles and decontaminates rainwater before feeding the groundwater https://t.co/P2arxHEmmP https:/...	0.0
5	RT @JemilahMahmood: #WorldWaterDay reminds us how access to H20/sanitation are basic rights. @ifrc to champion #OneWASH with partners to re...	0.0
6	RT @OurRevolution: On #WorldWaterDay we stand in solidarity with residents of Flint, Michigan and communities across the United States who...	0.0
7	World Water Day takes place every year and aims to underline the importance of water. There is a lack of clean wate... https://t.co/2rw9DguOY9	0.3666666666666667
8	RT @Pontifex: Let us thank God for "sister water", such a simple and precious element, and let us strive to make it accessible to all. #Wor...	0.21875
9	RT @AlyshwaryaM: .@MBPatil was not only instrumental in our fight for Kaveri but also implemented an unprecedented amount of development in...	0.3
11	RT @YosemiteNPS: Happy #WorldWaterDay! Did you know over 60% of California's developed water supply comes from the Sierra Nevada? Yosemite'...	0.55
12	RT @Rotary: We solve problems by bringing people together. Creating access to clean water and sanitation requires education, collaboration,...	0.3666666666666667
13	RT @unisdr: Agriculture accounts for 70% of global water withdrawals, mostly for irrigation. Industry takes 20% of the total, dominated by...	0.16666666666666666
14	RT @EU_ENV: Today is #WorldWaterDay 💧 \nWater is life. \nWater is us. \nWater is precious. \nThis is how the EU works to #ProtectWater, for...	0.5
15	RT @GapInc: 1/3 of the world's population currently lives without access to clean water. We're doing our part to change that. #WorldWaterDa...	0.18333333333333335
16	RT @UNHumanRights: 🔲 Health \n⚫ Food Security \n🔲 Livelihood \n\nSafe water is essential for these basic human rights. If people can't enjoy th...	0.18

Figure 4.63: Sentiment scores of English Tweets

13. Once we have calculated the sentiment score of each tweet, we create a word cloud. Insert a new cell and add the following code to implement this:

```
other_stopwords_to_remove = ['https', 'amp','co']
STOPWORDS = STOPWORDS.union(set(other_stopwords_to_remove))
stopwords = set(STOPWORDS)

text=tweet_text_df_eng["tweet_text"]
wordcloud = WordCloud(width = 800, height = 800,
                background_color ='white',
                max_words=100,
                stopwords = stopwords,
                min_font_size = 10).generate(str(text))
plt.imshow(wordcloud, interpolation='bilinear')
plt.axis("off")
plt.show()
```

The preceding code generates the following output:

Figure 4.64: Word cloud of the tweets

Chapter 5: Topic Modeling

Activity 10: Topic Modelling Jeopardy Questions

Solution

Let's perform topic modeling on the dataset of Jeopardy questions. Follow these steps to implement this activity:

1. Open a Jupyter notebook.

2. Insert a new cell and add the following code to import the pandas library:

    ```
    import pandas as pd
    pd.set_option('display.max_colwidth', 800)
    ```

3. To load the Jeopardy CSV file into a pandas DataFrame, insert a new cell and add the following code:

    ```
    JEOPARDY_CSV =  'data/jeopardy/Jeopardy.csv'
    questions = pd.read_csv(JEOPARDY_CSV)
    ```

4. The data in the DataFrame is not clean. In order to clean it, we remove records that have missing values in the Question column. Add the following code to do this:

```
questions = questions.dropna(subset=['Question'])
```

5. Now import the gensim preprocessing utility and use it to preprocess the questions further. Add the following code to do this:

```
from gensim.parsing.preprocessing import preprocess_string
ques_documents = questions.Question.apply(preprocess_string).tolist()
```

6. Now we'll create a gensim corpus and a dictionary, followed by an LdaModel instance from the corpus specifying the number of topics. Add the following code to do this:

```
from gensim import corpora
from gensim.models.ldamodel import LdaModel
dictionary = corpora.Dictionary(ques_documents)
corpus = [dictionary.doc2bow(text) for text in ques_documents]
NUM_TOPICS = 8
ldamodel = LdaModel(corpus, num_topics = NUM_TOPICS, id2word=dictionary,
passes=15)
```

7. Now we'll print the resulting topics. Add the following code to do this:

```
ldamodel.print_topics(num_words=6)
```

Chapter 6: Text Summarization and Text Generation

Activity 11: Summarizing a Downloaded Page Using the Gensim Text Summarizer

Solution

Let's summarize a downloaded page with the help of the Gensim text summarizer. Follow these steps to implement this activity:

1. Open a Jupyter notebook.

2. Insert a new cell and add the following code to import the necessary libraries:

```
import warnings
warnings.filterwarnings('ignore')
from gensim.summarization import summarize
import requests
```

3. The following code uses the **requests** library to get the Why Click page. After getting the page, we change the encoding to **utf-8** in order to properly decode some of the content on the page. Then, we use **BeautifulSoup** to find the text content of the div with the ID **#why-click**. This div contains the main text of the **why-click** page:

```
from bs4 import BeautifulSoup

r = requests.get('https://click.palletsprojects.com/en/7.x/why/')
r.encoding = 'utf-8'
soup = BeautifulSoup(r.text)
why_click = soup.find(id="why-click").text.replace('\n', ' ')
```

4. Here, we create a utility function to display the sentences in a given piece of text. Note that we could simply output the text to the notebook or use **print()**. But using the **show_sentences()** function allows us to see the individual sentences in the summary. The function uses **pandas** DataFrames so that it displays nicely in the Jupyter notebook:

```
import pandas as pd

pd.set_option('display.max_colwidth',500)
def show_sentences(text):
    return pd.DataFrame({'Sentence': sent_tokenize(text)})
```

5. We have defined a function that turns text into a DataFrame containing the sentences in the text. This gives us the option to see the text as it is or see its sentences. Let's look at the article first. Add the following code:

```
why_click
```

The code generates the following output:

```
` Why Click?¶ There are so many libraries out there for writing command line utilities; why does Click exist? This question is
easy to answer: because there is not a single command line utility for Python out there which ticks the following boxes:  is la
zily composable without restrictions supports implementation of Unix/POSIX command line conventions supports loading values fro
m environment variables out of the box supports for prompting of custom values is fully nestable and composable works the same
in Python 2 and 3 supports file handling out of the box comes with useful common helpers (getting terminal dimensions, ANSI col
ors, fetching direct keyboard input, screen clearing, finding config paths, launching apps and editors, etc.)  There are many a
lternatives to Click and you can have a look at them if you enjoy them better.  The obvious ones are optparse and argparse from
the standard library. Click is actually implemented as a wrapper around a mild fork of optparse and does not implement any pars
ing itself.  The reason it's not based on argparse is that argparse does not allow proper nesting of commands by design and has
some deficiencies when it comes to POSIX compliant argument handling. Click is designed to be fun to work with and at the same
time not stand in your way.  It's not overly flexible either.  Currently, for instance, it does not allow you to customize the
help pages too much. This is intentional because Click is designed to allow you to nest command line utilities.  The idea is th
at you can have a system that works together with another system by tacking two Click instances together and they will continue
working as they should. Too much customizability would break this promise. Click was written to support the Flask microframewor
k ecosystem because no tool could provide it with the functionality it needed. To get an understanding of what Click is all abo
ut, I strongly recommend looking at the Complex Applications chapter to see what it's useful for.  Why not Argparse?¶ Click is
internally based on optparse instead of argparse.  This however is an implementation detail that a user does not have to be con
cerned with.  The reason however Click is not using argparse is that it has some problematic behaviors that make handling arbit
rary command line interfaces hard:  argparse has built-in magic behavior to guess if something is an argument or an option.  Th
is becomes a problem when dealing with incomplete command lines as it's not possible to know without having a full understandin
g of the command line how the parser is going to behave.  This goes against Click's ambitions of dispatching to subparsers. arg
parse currently does not support disabling of interspersed arguments.  Without this feature it's not possible to safely impleme
nt Click's nested parsing nature.   Why not Docopt etc.?¶ Docopt and many tools like it are cool in how they work, but very fe
w of these tools deal with nesting of commands and composability in a way like Click.  To the best of the developer's knowledg
e, Click is the first Python library that aims to create a level of composability of applications that goes beyond what the sys
```

Figure 6.16: This figure shows the original Why Click article, as shown in the Jupyter notebook

Note that we have lost the formatting of the original article since we extracted the text from HTML.

6. In this code cell, we use the **show_sentences()** function to show the sentences in the original article. There are **57** sentences in the article, as shown in the following figure:

```
show_sentences(why_click)
```

The code generates the following output:

	Sentence
0	Why Click?¶ There are so many libraries out there for writing command line utilities; why does Click exist?
1	This question is easy to answer: because there is not a single command line utility for Python out there which ticks the following boxes: is lazily composable without restrictions supports implementation of Unix/POSIX command line conventions supports loading values from environment variables out of the box supports for prompting of custom values is fully nestable and composable works the same in Python 2 and 3 supports file handling out of the box comes with useful common helpers (getting ...
2	There are many alternatives to Click and you can have a look at them if you enjoy them better.
3	The obvious ones are optparse and argparse from the standard library.
4	Click actually implements its own parsing of arguments and does not use optparse or argparse following the optparse parsing behavior.
5	The reason it's not based on argparse is that argparse does not allow proper nesting of commands by design and has some deficiencies when it comes to POSIX compliant argument handling.
6	Click is designed to be fun to work with and at the same time not stand in your way.
7	It's not overly flexible either.
8	Currently, for instance, it does not allow you to customize the help pages too much.

Figure 6.17: This figure shows the sentences from the Why Click article

7. Now we create a **summary** using the **summarize()** function, and then look at the sentences. Note that we use the defaults for **summarize**:

```
summary = summarize(why_click)
summary
```

The code generates the following output:

```
'This question is easy to answer: because there is not a single command line utility for Python out t
here which ticks the following boxes:  is lazily composable without restrictions supports implementat
ion of Unix/POSIX command line conventions supports loading values from environment variables out of
the box supports for prompting of custom values is fully nestable and composable works the same in Py
thon 2 and 3 supports file handling out of the box comes with useful common helpers (getting terminal
dimensions, ANSI colors, fetching direct keyboard input, screen clearing, finding config paths, launc
hing apps and editors, etc.)  There are many alternatives to Click and you can have a look at them if
you enjoy them better.\nThe reason it's not based on argparse is that argparse does not allow proper
nesting of commands by design and has some deficiencies when it comes to POSIX compliant argument han
dling.\nThe reason however Click is not using argparse is that it has some problematic behaviors that
make handling arbitrary command line interfaces hard:  argparse has built-in magic behavior to guess
if something is an argument or an option.\nWhy not Docopt etc.?¶ Docopt and many tools like it are co
ol in how they work, but very few of these tools deal with nesting of commands and composability in a
way like Click.\nThe upside of docopt is that it gives you strong control over your help page; the do
wnside is that due to this it cannot rewrap your output for the current terminal width and it makes t
ranslations hard.\nWhile docopt does support dispatching to subcommands, it for instance does not dir
ectly support any kind of automatic subcommand enumeration based on what's available or it does not e
nforce subcommands to work in a consistent way.\nClick aims to support fully composable command line
user interfaces by doing the following:  Click does not just parse, it also dispatches to the appropr
iate code.\nClick has strong information available for all parameters and commands so that it can gen
erate unified help pages for the full CLI and to assist the user in converting the input data as nece
ssary.\nThe aim of Click is to make composable systems, whereas the aim of docopt is to build the mos
t beautiful and hand-crafted command line interfaces.\nClick actively prevents people from implementi
ng certain patterns in order to achieve unified command line interfaces.\nDue to syntactical ambiguit
ies on the command line, there is no way to implement fully variadic arguments.'
```

Figure 6.18: The summary of the Why Click article

8. The **summarize()** function can also break the text into sentences if we pass the optional **split** parameter. The following will print a list of sentences:

```
summary = summarize(why_click, split=True)
summary
```

The code generates the following output:

```
['This question is easy to answer: because there is not a single command line utility for Python out there which ticks the foll
owing boxes:  is lazily composable without restrictions supports implementation of Unix/POSIX command line conventions supports
loading values from environment variables out of the box supports for prompting of custom values is fully nestable and composab
le works the same in Python 2 and 3 supports file handling out of the box comes with useful common helpers (getting terminal di
mensions, ANSI colors, fetching direct keyboard input, screen clearing, finding config paths, launching apps and editors, etc.)
There are many alternatives to Click and you can have a look at them if you enjoy them better.',
 'The reason it's not based on argparse is that argparse does not allow proper nesting of commands by design and has some defic
iencies when it comes to POSIX compliant argument handling.',
 'The reason however Click is not using argparse is that it has some problematic behaviors that make handling arbitrary command
line interfaces hard:  argparse has built-in magic behavior to guess if something is an argument or an option.',
 'Why not Docopt etc.?¶ Docopt and many tools like it are cool in how they work, but very few of these tools deal with nesting
of commands and composability in a way like Click.',
 'The upside of docopt is that it gives you strong control over your help page; the downside is that due to this it cannot rewr
ap your output for the current terminal width and it makes translations hard.',
 'While docopt does support dispatching to subcommands, it for instance does not directly support any kind of automatic subcomm
and enumeration based on what's available or it does not enforce subcommands to work in a consistent way.',
 'Click aims to support fully composable command line user interfaces by doing the following:  Click does not just parse, it al
so dispatches to the appropriate code.',
 'Click has strong information available for all parameters and commands so that it can generate unified help pages for the ful
l CLI and to assist the user in converting the input data as necessary.',
 'The aim of Click is to make composable systems, whereas the aim of docopt is to build the most beautiful and hand-crafted com
mand line interfaces.',
 'Click actively prevents people from implementing certain patterns in order to achieve unified command line interfaces.',
 'Due to syntactical ambiguities on the command line, there is no way to implement fully variadic arguments.']
```

Figure 6.19: This figure shows the summary of the Why Click page when using summarize with split=True

9. The **summarize()** function has a parameter called **ratio**, which you use to specify the proportion of the original text to return in the summary. Here, we use **ratio=0.1** to return 10% of the original article:

```
summary = summarize(why_click, ratio=0.1)
show_sentences(summary)
```

The code generates the following output:

	Sentence
0	This question is easy to answer: because there is not a single command line utility for Python out there which ticks the following boxes: is lazily composable without restrictions supports implementation of Unix/POSIX command line conventions supports loading values from environment variables out of the box supports for prompting of custom values is fully nestable and composable works the same in Python 2 and 3 supports file handling out of the box comes with useful common helpers (getting ...
1	There are many alternatives to Click and you can have a look at them if you enjoy them better.
2	The reason it's not based on argparse is that argparse does not allow proper nesting of commands by design and has some deficiencies when it comes to POSIX compliant argument handling.
3	The reason however Click is not using argparse is that it has some problematic behaviors that make handling arbitrary command line interfaces hard: argparse has built-in magic behavior to guess if something is an argument or an option.
4	Click aims to support fully composable command line user interfaces by doing the following: Click does not just parse, it also dispatches to the appropriate code.
5	Click has strong information available for all parameters and commands so that it can generate unified help pages for the full CLI and to assist the user in converting the input data as necessary.

Figure 6.20: The summary of the Why Click page when using summarize with ratio=0.1

10. You can also pass the **word_count** parameter to limit the number of words returned:

```
summary = summarize(why_click, word_count=200)
summary
```

The code generates the following output:

'This question is easy to answer: because there is not a single command line utility for Python out there which ticks the follo wing boxes: is lazily composable without restrictions supports implementation of Unix/POSIX command line conventions supports loading values from environment variables out of the box supports for prompting of custom values is fully nestable and composab le works the same in Python 2 and 3 supports file handling out of the box comes with useful common helpers (getting terminal di mensions, ANSI colors, fetching direct keyboard input, screen clearing, finding config paths, launching apps and editors, etc.)
    There are many alternatives to Click and you can have a look at them if you enjoy them better.\nThe reason it's not based on argparse is that argparse does not allow proper nesting of commands by design and has some deficiencies when it comes to POSIX compliant argument handling.\nThe reason however Click is not using argparse is that it has some problematic behaviors that mak e handling arbitrary command line interfaces hard: argparse has built-in magic behavior to guess if something is an argument o r an option.\nClick aims to support fully composable command line user interfaces by doing the following: Click does not just parse, it also dispatches to the appropriate code.'

Figure 6.21: This figure shows the summary of the Why Click page when using summarize with word_count=200

Chapter 7: Vector Representation

Activity 12: Finding Similar Movie Lines Using Document Vectors

Solution

Let's build a movie search engine that finds similar movie lines to the one provided by the user. Follow these steps to complete this activity:

1. Open a Jupyter notebook.

2. Insert a new cell and add the following code to import all necessary libraries:

```
import warnings
warnings.filterwarnings("ignore")

from gensim.models import Doc2Vec
import pandas as pd
from gensim.parsing.preprocessing import preprocess_string, remove_stopwords
```

3. Now we load the **movie_lines1** file. After that, we need to iterate over each movie line in the file and split the columns. Also, we need to create a DataFrame containing the movie lines. Insert a new cell and add the following code to implement this:

```
movie_lines_file = '../data/cornell-movie-dialogs/movie_lines1.txt'
with open(movie_lines_file) as f:
    movie_lines = [line.strip().split('+++$+++')
```

```
                    for line in f.readlines()];

  lines_df = pd.DataFrame([{'LineNumber': d[0].strip(),
                            'Person': d[3].strip(),
                            'Line': d[4].strip(),
                            'Movie' : d[2].strip()}
                           for d in movie_lines])
  lines_df = lines_df.set_index('LineNumber')
```

4. We have a trained document model named **MovieLinesModel.d2v**. Now we can simply load and use it. Insert a new cell and add the following code to implement this:

```
docVecModel = Doc2Vec.load('../data/MovieLinesModel.d2v')
```

5. Now, since we have loaded the document model, we create two functions, namely **to_vector()** and **similar_movie_lines()**. The **to_vector()** function converts the sentences into vectors. The second function, **similar_movie_lines()**, implements the similarity check. It uses the **docVecModel.docvecs.most_similar()** function, which compares the vector against all the other lines it was built with. To implement this, insert a new cell and add the following code:

```
from gensim.parsing.preprocessing import preprocess_string, remove_
stopwords

def to_vector(sentence):
    cleaned = preprocess_string(sentence)
    docVector = docVecModel.infer_vector(cleaned)
    return docVector

def similar_movie_lines(sentence):
    vector = to_vector(sentence)
    similar_vectors = docVecModel.docvecs.most_similar(positive=[vector])
    similar_lines = [lines_df.ix[line[0]].Line for line in similar_
vectors]
    return similar_lines
```

6. Now that we have created our functions, it is time to test them. Insert a new cell and add the following code to implement this:

```
similar_movie_lines("Sure, that's easy.  You gotta insult somebody.")
```

We have learned how to find similar movie lines with the help of document vectors.

Chapter 8: Sentiment Analysis

Activity 13: Tweet Sentiment Analysis Using the TextBlob library

Solution

Let's perform sentiment analysis on tweets related to airlines. Follow these steps to implement this activity:

1. Open a Jupyter notebook.

2. Insert a new cell and add the following code to import the necessary libraries:

    ```
    import pandas as pd
    from textblob import TextBlob
    import re
    ```

3. Since we are displaying the text in the notebook, we want to increase the display width for our DataFrame. Insert a new cell and add the following code to implement this:

    ```
    pd.set_option('display.max_colwidth', 240)
    ```

4. Now we load the **Tweets.csv** dataset. From this dataset, we are only fetching the "**text**" column. Thus, we need to mention the "**text**" column name as the value for the **usecols** parameter of the **read_csv()** function. The fetched column is later being replaced to a new column named "**Tweet**". Insert a new cell and add the following code to implement this:

    ```
    TWEET_DATA_FILE = '../data/twitter-airline-sentiment/Tweets.csv'
    tweets = pd.read_csv(TWEET_DATA_FILE, usecols=['text'])
    tweets.columns = ['Tweet']
    ```

    > **Note**
    >
    > The Tweets.csv dataset is located at this link: https://bit.ly/2NwRwP9.

5. Insert a new cell and add the following code to view the first **10** records of the DataFrame:

    ```
    tweets.head(10)
    ```

The code generates the following output:

	Tweet
0	@ViginAmerica What @dhepburn said.
1	@ViginAmerica plus you've added commercials to the experience... tacky.
2	@ViginAmerica I didn't today... Must mean I need to take another trip!
3	@ViginAmerica it's really aggressive to blast obnoxious "entertainment" in your guests' faces & they have little recourse
4	@ViginAmerica and it's really big bad thing about it.
5	@ViginAmerica seriously would pay $30 a flight for seats that didn't have this playing.\nIt's really the only bad thing about flying VA
6	@ViginAmerica yes, nearly everytime I fly VX this "ear worm" won't go away :).
7	@ViginAmerica Really missed a prime opputunity for Men Without Hats parody. there. http://t.co/mWpG7grEZP
8	@ViginAmerica Well, I didn't...but NOW I DO! :-D
9	@ViginAmerica It was amazing, and arrived at hour early. You're too good to me.

Figure 8.16: Results of first 10 tweets

6. If we look at the preceding figure, we can see that the tweets contain Twitter handles, which start with the **@** symbol. It might be useful to extract those handles. The **string** column included in the DataFrame has an **extract()** function, which uses a regex to get parts of a string. Insert a new cell and add the following code to implement this:

```
tweets['At'] = tweets.Tweet.str.extract(r'^(@\S+)')
```

This code declares a new column called **At** and sets the value to what the **extract** function returns. The **extract** function uses a regex, **^(@\S+)**, to return strings that start with **@**. To view the initial 10 records of the **"tweets"** DataFrame, we insert a new cell and write the following code:

```
tweets.head(10)
```

The expected output for first ten tweets should be as follows:

	Tweet	At
0	@ViginAmerica What @dhepburn said.	@ViginAmerica
1	@ViginAmerica plus you've added commercials to the experience... tacky.	@ViginAmerica
2	@ViginAmerica I didn't today... Must mean I need to take another trip!	@ViginAmerica
3	@ViginAmerica it's really aggressive to blast obnoxious "entertainment" in your guests' faces & they have little recourse	@ViginAmerica
4	@ViginAmerica and it's really big bad thing about it.	@ViginAmerica
5	@ViginAmerica seriously would pay $30 a flight for seats that didn't have this playing.\nIt's really the only bad thing about flying VA	@ViginAmerica
6	@ViginAmerica yes, nearly everytime I fly VX this "ear worm" won't go away :).	@ViginAmerica
7	@ViginAmerica Really missed a prime opputunity for Men Without Hats parody. there. http://t.co/mWpG7grEZP	@ViginAmerica
8	@ViginAmerica Well, I didn't...but NOW I DO! :-D	@ViginAmerica
9	It was amazing, and arrived at hour early. You're too good to me.	@ViginAmerica

Figure 8.17: First 10 tweets along with Twitter handles

1. Now, we want to remove the Twitter handles since they are irrelevant for sentiment analysis. First, we create a function named **remove_handles()**, which accepts a DataFrame as a parameter. After passing the DataFrame, the **re.sub()** function will remove the handles in the DataFrame. Insert a new cell and add the following code to implement this:

```
def remove_handles(tweet):
    return re.sub(r'@\S+', '', tweet)
```

2. To remove the handles, insert a new cell and add the following code:

```
tweets.text = tweets.text.apply(remove_handles)
tweets.head(10)
```

The expected output for first ten tweets after removing the Twitter handles should be as follows:

	Tweet	At
0	What said.	@ViginAmerica
1	plus you've added commercials to the experience... tacky.	@ViginAmerica
2	I didn't today... Must mean I need to take another trip!	@ViginAmerica
3	It's really aggressive to blast obnoxious "entertainment" in your guests' faces & they have little recourse	@ViginAmerica
4	and it's really big bad thing about it.	@ViginAmerica
5	seriously would pay $30 a flight for seats that didn't have this playing.\nIt's really the only bad thing about flying VA	@ViginAmerica
6	yes, nearly everytime I fly VX this "ear worm" won't go away :).	@ViginAmerica
7	Really missed a prime opputunity for Men Without Hats parody. there. http://t.co/mWpG7grEZP	@ViginAmerica
8	Well, I didn't...but NOW I DO! :-D	@ViginAmerica
9	It was amazing, and arrived at hour early. You're too good to me.	@ViginAmerica

Figure 8.18 First 10 tweets after removing the Twitter handles

From the preceding figure, we can see that the Twitter handles have been separated from the tweets.

3. Now we can apply sentiment analysis on the tweets. First we need to create a **get_sentiment()** function, which accepts a DataFrame and a column as parameters. Using this function, we create two new columns, **Polarity** and **Subjectivity**, which will show the sentiment scores of each tweet. Insert a new cell and add the following code to implement this:

```
def get_sentiment(dataframe, column):
    text_column = dataframe[column]
    textblob_sentiment = text_column.apply(TextBlob)
    sentiment_values = [ {'Polarity': v.sentiment.polarity,
                         'Subjectivity': v.sentiment.subjectivity}
                for v in textblob_sentiment.values]
    return pd.DataFrame(sentiment_values)
```

This function takes a DataFrame and applies the **TextBlob** constructor to each value of **text_column**. Then it extracts and creates a new DataFrame with the columns for **Polarity** and **Objectivity**.

4. Since the function has been created, we test it, passing the necessary parameters. The result of this will be stored in new DataFrame, **sentiment_frame**. Insert a new cell and add the following code to implement this:

```
sentiment_frame = get_sentiment(tweets, 'text')
```

To view the initial four values of the new DataFrame, type the following code:

```
sentence_frame.head(4)
```

The code generates the following output:

Polarity	Subjectivity
0.000000	0.0000
0.000000	0.0000
-0.390625	0.6875
0.006250	0.3500

Figure 8.19 First four rows of the sentiment DataFrame

5. To join the original **tweet** DataFrame to the **sentiment_frame** DataFrame, we make use of the **concat()** function. Insert a new cell and add the following code to implement this:

```
tweets = pd.concat([tweets, sentiment_frame], axis=1)
```

To view the initial 10 rows of the new DataFrame, we add the following code:

```
tweets.head(10)
```

The expected output with sentiment scores added should be as follows:

	Tweet	At	Polarity	Subjectivity
0	What said.	@ViginAmerica	0.000000	0.000000
1	plus you've added commercials to the experience... tacky.	@ViginAmerica	0.000000	0.000000
2	I didn't today... Must mean I need to take another trip!	@ViginAmerica	-0.390625	0.687500
3	It's really aggressive to blast obnoxious "entertainment" in your guests' faces & they have little recourse	@ViginAmerica	0.006250	0.350000
4	and it's really big bad thing about it.	@ViginAmerica	-0.350000	0.383333
5	seriously would pay $30 a flight for seats that didn't have this playing.\nIt's really the only bad thing about flying VA	@ViginAmerica	-0.208333	0.633333
6	yes, nearly everytime I fly VX this "ear worm" won't go away :).	@ViginAmerica	0.466667	0.766667
7	Really missed a prime opputunity for Men Without Hats parody. there. http://t.co/mWpG7grEZP	@ViginAmerica	0.200000	0.200000
8	Well, I didn't...but NOW I DO! :-D	@ViginAmerica	1.000000	1.000000
9	It was amazing, and arrived at hour early. You're too good to me.	@ViginAmerica	0.466667	0.600000

Figure 8.20 Tweets DataFrame with sentiment scores added

From the preceding figure, we can see that for each **tweet**, **polarity**, and **subjectivity** scores have been calculated.

6. To distinguish between the positive, negative, and neutral tweets, we need to add certain conditions. We will consider tweets with polarity scores greater than **0.5** as positive, and tweets with polarity scores less than or equal to **-0.5** as negative. For neutral, we will consider only those tweets that fall in the range of **-0.1** and **0.1**. Insert a new cell and add the following code to implement this:

```
positive_tweets = tweets[tweets.Polarity > 0.5]
negative_tweets = tweets[tweets.Polarity <= - 0.5]
neutral_tweets = tweets[ (tweets.Polarity > -0.1) & (tweets.Polarity < 0.1) ]
```

To view positive, negative, and neutral tweets, we add the following code:

```
positive_tweets.head(15)
negative_tweets.head(15)
neutral_tweets
```

This displays the result of positive, negative, and neutral tweets.

Index

About

All major keywords used in this book are captured alphabetically in this section. Each one is accompanied by the page number of where they appear.

A

acronym: 166
adaptation: 194
algorithm: 20, 76-77, 84,
      87, 101, 124, 162-163,
      165, 174, 176, 193,
      198-200, 207, 217,
      222, 246, 248, 259,
      275, 284-285, 287
algorithms: 28, 30, 50,
      75-77, 88-90, 95,
      100-101, 123, 128, 132,
      136, 161-163, 165, 191,
      195, 197-199, 220-222,
      228, 238, 242, 245, 259,
      266, 272-276, 287
allennlp: 276
alphanum: 213
analyses: 21
analysis: 4, 10, 53, 76-77,
      95-96, 100, 111, 120,
      162-166, 168, 174-176,
      266, 269-278, 280,
      284-285, 289
argmax: 235, 237
arithmetic: 219
arrays: 221, 224, 226, 242
ascertain: 56
assess: 180
assessment: 24
astype: 119

B

bagging: 101
bi-grams: 33-35
bilinear: 70
branches: 149

buzzsumo: 194
byomkesh: 55, 66
bytree: 108, 110

C

campaigns: 271
chatbot: 155-156, 197, 271
chatbots: 195
cleantext: 178
cluster: 77-78, 82-83,
      85, 87, 164, 198
clustered: 82, 198
clustering: 77-78, 82-84,
      88, 123, 164, 198
clusters: 77-78, 82-84,
      86-88, 123, 164
collect: 23, 135, 139, 141,
      144, 153-154, 158, 162
collected: 23, 132
collecting: 135-136,
      139, 152
collection: 23, 58, 101,
      162-163, 166, 174,
      220-221, 259
command: 32, 138-139
commands: 139, 141, 146
complies: 245
concat: 5, 285
corpus: 10, 22, 30, 50,
      56-60, 62-64, 68-69,
      71-72, 78-80, 85, 103,
      115, 120, 128, 130-132,
      179-180, 185-186, 202,
      209, 214-216, 246, 263

D

databases: 146
dataframe: 51, 56-57,
      62, 64-65, 80-82,
      86, 91-92, 96-99,
      103-105, 113, 116-117, 119,
      121-122, 129, 144, 148,
      153-154, 176, 178, 183,
      187, 190-191, 204, 206,
      260-263, 266, 278, 281
dataframes: 203, 279
dataset: 23, 54, 58, 65, 69,
      72, 76, 78-79, 81, 84-85,
      89, 101, 112, 115-116,
      120-121, 124, 126-129,
      132, 145, 161, 163,
      168, 177-179, 184-185,
      190-191, 200, 203, 207,
      246, 263, 272-273,
      275, 280, 284-288
datasets: 58, 69,
      78, 85, 89, 115,
      120, 128, 275-276,
      280-281, 284-285
dendogram: 82
dendrogram: 77-78, 82-83
dirichlet: 162-163, 174, 176
django: 153
domains: 196, 273, 285

E

elucidated: 132
enumerate: 206, 229-231
epochs: 249-250, 263

G

gaussiannb: 93

I

imshow: 70

J

jaccard: 65-67

L

ldamodel: 167, 179-180, 185-188, 191
lemmatize: 17-18, 47, 67, 81, 86, 91, 97, 103, 116, 121
lemmatized: 17-18
lemmatizer: 17-18, 47, 66-67, 79, 81, 85-86, 91, 97, 103, 115-116, 121
linewidth: 188
linguistic: 222
linkage: 82-83
linreg: 98-99
loglog: 60
log-log: 60
logreg: 92
longer: 84
lsimodel: 167-168, 170-171

N

nelson: 165
networkx: 205
n-gram: 7
ngrams: 34-36

n-grams: 7, 33
nlargest: 209, 211
nlines: 69
non-cpu: 277
non-linear: 95

O

outliers: 198
outlined: 23
oxejwu: 143

P

params: 188, 251, 255, 264

R

regexes: 177-178
render: 71-72
row-column: 62, 145
rule-based: 2

T

tag-based: 136-137, 139
tagged: 262-263
tagger: 8-9
tagging: 8-9
tagore: 144
tagset: 54
tagsets: 54
tailor: 197
talked: 6
target: 80, 92-94, 104-108, 116, 121, 129, 183, 280
targets: 272
tastes: 89
taught: 222

tdwpri: 127
teaching: 270
textblob: 33, 35-37, 47-49, 51-54, 148, 154, 269, 277-278, 280
textract: 155-156
textrank: 193, 198-200, 207, 217
textual: 96
tf-idf: 24, 50, 62-65, 68, 73, 76, 81-82, 86, 92-94, 97-99, 104-105, 114-115, 117, 119-120, 122, 127-132
tokens: 7-11, 14, 22, 31, 33, 47, 50, 58, 60, 69, 81, 86, 91, 97, 103, 115-116, 119, 121, 154, 162, 170-171, 178, 184-185, 187-188, 214, 229, 232, 248-249
tolist: 178
trigram: 7
trigrams: 7
tri-grams: 34-36
truncate: 77-78, 82
truncated: 82-83
truncating: 82
truncation: 82
trying: 2, 12
tuples: 214
tweepy: 154
tweeted: 31, 36, 38
tweets: 23-24, 38, 154, 176-180, 259, 278-280
twitter: 38, 154, 158, 194, 271
typical: 197
typically: 199

U

unigrams: 7

W

why-click: 208
wordcloud: 69-70
word-level: 238
wordnet: 17, 47, 79,
    85, 103, 115, 121

X

xgboost: 101-102, 106,
    108-111, 127-128, 143
xlabel: 60, 82, 87,
    123, 173, 182
xticks: 181

Y

yellow: 50
yields: 169
ylabel: 60, 82, 87,
    123, 173, 182

Z

zipfile: 201, 252-253
zmripc: 144

CPSIA information can be obtained
at www.ICGtesting.com
Printed in the USA
FSHW022051090520
70040FS

9 781789 954043